World Intellectual Property
Report 2019

The Geography
of Innovation:
Local Hotspots,
Global Networks

WIPO
WORLD
INTELLECTUAL PROPERTY
ORGANIZATION

Table of contents

Geography has always played a central role in the organization of economic activity. Cities first formed as trading hubs for agricultural and manufactured goods. Many of them emerged where trading routes intersected or where goods moved from one mode of transportation to another. With the onset of the industrial revolution, cities became centers of large-scale industrial production. As industrialization advanced, some expanded into megacities, while others saw their fortunes decline.

In the innovation-driven economy of the 21st century, cities continue to play a pivotal role. However, the forces shaping the geography of economic activity have changed. Companies want to be in urban hotspots, because that is where the most skilled and talented workers live. Well-paying and rewarding jobs as well as the buzz of city life, in turn, attract yet more highly skilled individuals to those hotspots. Innovation also relies crucially on the exchange of ideas among people. Such exchanges usually happen best when people live and work in close proximity to each other.

Yet, the economic geography of the 21st century has another important dimension. Technology has facilitated new ways of collaborating and sharing knowledge, connecting skilled individuals located far apart. The emerging global innovation landscape is thus one of geographically concentrated centers of excellence around the world, which are embedded in a global network carrying knowledge in many directions.

The evolving geography of innovation matters. Governments around the world strive to promote a policy environment conducive to innovation. Doing so requires an understanding of the local dynamics of innovation ecosystems. For example, where can government-funded research best enhance nascent technological capabilities? How can smart city planning encourage opportunities for knowledge sharing and collaboration? More broadly, the spread of innovative activity within economies increasingly affects the regional distribution of incomes. Understanding the driving forces behind this trend, in turn, enables better policy responses.

Our *World Intellectual Property Report 2019* offers an empirical perspective on the global geography of innovation. It does so by following the geographical footprint that innovators have left in millions of patent and scientific publication records over the past few decades. WIPO's *Global Innovation Index* has already embraced this big data approach in identifying the world's largest science and technology clusters. This report goes further. It employs more data going back several decades, analyzes time trends and explores in some detail how innovators from around the world collaborate with each other. The emerging picture is a complex one, with a limited number of global innovation hotspots in a few countries accounting for most innovative activity. Collaboration is widespread, taking place in increasingly larger teams and – for most but not all countries – it is increasingly cross-border in nature.

In addition to this economy-wide perspective, the report includes two case studies that explore in detail the evolving geography of innovation for two fields of technology undergoing rapid change. One case study focuses on autonomous vehicles technology. It details how innovation is reshaping the car industry, with information technology (IT) companies challenging established carmakers. This transformation is broadening the innovation landscape, with several IT-focused hotspots – which traditionally were not at the center of automotive innovation – gaining prominence.

The other case study focuses on agricultural biotechnology. Scientific and inventive activity in crop biotechnology is concentrated in a few high-income economies and China, and – within those economies – mostly in large metropolitan areas. Relative to other areas of innovation, however, it is more geographically widespread, spanning many countries in Africa, Latin America and Asia. This partly reflects a need to adapt innovations to local conditions.

The evidence presented in this report highlights how globally intertwined innovation has become. Crucially, the ability of companies and researchers to collaborate across borders has relied on policies largely favoring openness and international cooperation. The report makes the case for maintaining policy openness and further strengthening international cooperation. Solving increasingly complex technological problems will require ever larger and more specialized teams of researchers. International collaboration helps form such teams and will therefore be indispensable in continuously pushing the global technology frontier.

While offering original insights, the analysis presented in this report also comes with certain caveats. Patent

The evidence presented in this report highlights how globally intertwined innovation has become.

and scientific publication data provide rich and internationally comparable information on innovative activity. However, they neither capture all such activity, nor do they fully portray the rich interactions taking place among innovators. In addition, the dynamic forces that shape the direction of global innovation networks are manifold and interact with one another in intricate ways. Further research that offers empirical guidance on these forces would be of much value.

We hope that this report contributes to a greater appreciation of the importance that geography exerts on innovative activity and, in doing so, that it helps in refining policies to promote innovation and ensuring that its benefits are widely shared.

Francis GURRY
Director General

Acknowledgements

This report was developed under the general direction of Francis Gurry (Director General) and supervised by Carsten Fink (Chief Economist). The report was prepared by a team led by Julio Raffo (Head of Innovation Economics), Intan Hamdan-Livramento (Economist), Maryam Zehtabchi (Economist) and Deyun Yin (Fellow), all from WIPO's Economics and Statistics Division (ESD).

The report draws on various background papers commissioned for this report. In particular, Chapter 1 is based on a literature review prepared by Riccardo Crescenzi (London School of Economics, LSE), Simona Iammarino (LSE), Carolin Ioramashvili (LSE), Andrés Rodríguez-Pose (LSE) and Michael Storper (LSE and University of California, Los Angeles).

Ernest Miguelez (Groupe de Recherche en Économie Théorique et Appliquée, GREThA, Bordeaux), Francesco Lissoni (GREThA Bordeaux and Bocconi University), Christian Chacua (GREThA Bordeaux), Massimiliano Coda-Zabetta (GREThA Bordeaux) and Gianluca Tarasconi contributed the background report and assisted in the data preparation for Chapter 2.

Chapter 3 relies on background research conducted by Kristin Dziczek (Center for Automotive Research, CAR group), Eric Dennis (CAR group), Qiang Hong (CAR group), Diana Douglas (CAR group), Yen Chen (CAR group), Valerie Sathe-Brugeman (CAR group) and Edwin Marples (CAR group).

Finally, Gregory D. Graff (Colorado State University) contributed to the background report for Chapter 4.

The report team benefited greatly from external reviews and comments of the draft chapters and background papers by Cristina Chaminade (Lund University), Frédérique Sachwald (Science and Technology Observatory, Hcéres), Maryann P. Feldman (University of North Carolina), Kazuyuki Motohashi (University of Tokyo), Luciana Marques Vieira (School of Business Administration of Sao Paulo, FGV EAESP), José Maria da Silveira (Universidade Estadual de Campinas, UNICAMP) and Can Huang (Zhejiang University).

Additional input, comments and data were kindly provided by Lesya Baudoin, Daniel Benoliel, Shakeel Bhatti, Maurice Blount, Lee Branstetter, Richard Corken, Alica Daly, Gaétan de Rassenfosse, Philipp Großkurth, Christopher Harrison, Irene Kitsara, Agénor Lahatte, Orion Penner, Leontino Rezende Taveira, David Sapinho, Florian Seliger and Usui Yoshiaki.

Hao Zhou and Kyle Bergquist assisted in putting together data used in this report.

Samiah Do Carmo Figueiredo, Caterina Valles Galmès and Cécile Roure provided valuable administrative support.

Finally, gratitude is due to editorial and design colleagues in the Publications Division for leading the production of the report and to Richard Waddington for his editing work. The WIPO Library provided helpful research support throughout the report's development and the Printing Plant provided high-quality printing services. All worked hard to meet tight deadlines.

The geography of innovation can seem paradoxical: the generation of scientific knowledge and innovation is both increasingly global and intensely concentrated in a few local hotspots.

New players, particularly Asian countries, are responsible for more and more scientific research and inventions, which were once the almost exclusive domain of a handful of rich economies. At the same time, this greater international spread has been accompanied – at country level – by increased concentration of innovative activity within a few densely populated areas. These urban areas are vibrant innovation ecosystems, such as Silicon Valley outside San Francisco in the U.S or China's Shenzhen–Hong Kong, a more recent hotspot.

This paradox is more apparent than real, however; the world's most innovative urban agglomerations are also the most open to the outside world. Sometimes, they are better connected internationally than they are to their national hinterlands. Together, they form what economists have come to refer to as global innovation networks. Skilled individuals and innovative companies are at the center of these networks. Highly skilled workers gravitate toward innovative urban areas because they want to interact with one another and enjoy the amenities of metropolitan life. Large cities offer companies a large local market, specialized suppliers and academic institutions that allow them to reap economies of scale and scope. Knowledge, in turn, flows more fluidly among company and university researchers when they work in close proximity, fueling the innovation engine.

This WIPO report analyses these dual trends, exploiting a rich data set of millions of patent applications and scientific publications. Its findings argue for increasing openness and support for collaboration if innovation is to continue to flourish.

Knowledge creation is spreading to more and more countries

For most of the period from 1970 to 2000 only three countries – the United States of America (U.S.), Japan and Germany – accounted for two thirds of all patenting activity worldwide. When the remaining Western European economies are included the share reached some 90 percent. But in the years since, the rest of the world has come from almost nowhere to account for almost one third of all patenting activity. Published scientific data have spread even more widely, with the rest of the world going from less than a quarter of all such publication to around half over the last 20 years.

China and the Republic of Korea are largely responsible for the rising share of new areas in knowledge production and innovation; together, they account for over 20 percent of patents registered in the years 2015–2017, compared to under 3 percent in 1990–1999. Other countries, notably Australia, Canada, India and Israel, have also contributed to the global spread of innovation. Many middle-income countries, however, and all lower-income countries, continue to have substantially lower levels of patenting activity.

The increasingly dispersed and interconnected flow of knowledge and innovation has mirrored the development of complex global networks, or value chains, for the production and delivery of goods and services. In particular, multinational companies have located knowledge-intensive production stages – most importantly research and development (R&D) – in urban agglomerations that offer specialized knowledge and skills. More generally, it is the need for greater collaboration in the face of growing technological complexity that has driven both the increasing concentration of innovation in certain urban areas and its global spread.

Innovation is increasingly local

On the basis of geocoded inventor and scientific author data, this report explores the geography of innovation within countries and identifies the world's main agglomerations of scientific and technological activity. It looks at two types: global innovation hotspots, which show the highest density of scientific publication or patent activity; and specialized niche clusters, where the density of inventors and scientific authors is high in a given field but not high enough generally to be a global hotspot.

Innovation is geographically concentrated in a limited number of areas

The emerging landscape of global hotspots and niche clusters shows that inventive and scientific activity within each country is persistently concentrated in a few large, cosmopolitan and prosperous urban areas. In the U.S., hotspots around New York, San Francisco and Boston accumulated roughly a quarter of all U.S. patents filed from 2011 to 2015. In China, those around Beijing, Shanghai and Shenzhen increased their share from 36 percent to 52 percent of all Chinese patents during the same period.

Less than 19 percent of all inventive and scientific output worldwide is generated by inventors or researchers located outside hotspots and niche clusters. Despite this big change in the global innovation picture, more than 160 countries – the vast majority – still generate little innovation activity and do not host any hotspot or niche cluster.

Big cities are not necessarily hubs of innovation

Not all large metropolitan areas are innovation dense. For example, North America hosts most hotspots in dense urban areas along the east and west coasts, while many dense inland urban areas do not have an equivalent density of innovation. Asia, Latin America and Africa host many dense urban areas with no corresponding innovation density. Despite high populations, top metropoles – for example, Bangkok, Cairo, Cape Town, Kuala Lumpur and Santiago de Chile – only have a modest degree of innovation density in some specialized fields.

And less dense urban areas can sometimes host niche clusters. Some examples are Ithaca in the U.S., Stavanger in Norway and Bern in Switzerland, which are highly innovative cities due to the strong innovation footprint of local academic institutions, industries or, sometimes, the presence of a key company.

Collaboration is increasingly the norm

Data show that teams are involved in an increasing majority of scientific papers and patents. In the early 2000s, teams already produced 64 percent of all scientific papers and 54 percent of all patents. By the second half of the 2010s, these figures had grown to almost 80 percent and 70 percent, respectively.

Most high-income economies also show rising international collaboration. The forces pushing academia and companies to cross borders seeking partners for innovation are manifold. The scientific community has a long tradition of engaging in international collaboration, while multinational companies seek efficiency gains from the international division of their R&D and through international collaboration.

The main exceptions to the trend toward internationalization are East Asia's top economies where Japan, the Republic of Korea and, more recently, China have seen falling shares of international collaboration, though not in absolute number terms.

A few countries account for most of the international ties

Most international collaboration is concentrated among a few main countries. In the period from 2011 to 2015,

the U.S. and Western Europe accounted for 68 and 62 percent, respectively, of all international inventive and scientific collaboration. Most of the collaboration happens among inventors and researchers from these countries. New entrants to these collaboration networks, from countries such as China, India, Australia and Brazil, still mostly collaborate with the aforementioned economies rather than with each other.

Hotspots and clusters drive international collaboration and global networks

Most global innovation hotspots have increased their international collaboration over the last two decades. This collaboration – whether national or international, patents or publication – forms a thick web of ties that constitutes the global innovation networks. The shape of these networks has evolved, typically with more nodes and ties being added over time.

Inventors and scientists within hotspots and niche clusters collaborate internationally more than those outside, particularly in scientific articles. Over the last two decades, the share of scientific publication involving international collaboration between scientists from inside hotspots has been more than triple that between scientists outside of them.

Collaboration is concentrated

Notwithstanding new network nodes and their ties, the hotspots in the U.S., Europe and Asia remain the core of the global networks both in terms of output and connectivity. Overall, larger hotspots collaborate both nationally and internationally, whereas niche clusters and smaller hotspots collaborate predominantly at the national level. For instance, many French and United Kingdom (U.K.) hotspots connect with the rest of the world mostly through Paris and London respectively. In China, Shanghai, Beijing and Shenzhen act as the top gatekeepers.

Yet, not all hotspots have the same relevance in terms of connections. U.S. hotspots are among the most connected nodes. Beijing, London, Paris, Seoul, Shanghai and Tokyo are also highly connected, but much less so. Interestingly, the high volume of inventive and scientific activity of the U.S. hotspots does not fully explain their higher connectivity. Many other hotspots – for example, Tokyo or Seoul – show larger or similar scientific or inventive output but are not so highly connected.

The intensity of international collaboration varies considerably across countries. For example, hotspots in India and Switzerland are highly connected internationally, while those in the Republic of Korea and Japan are weakly connected. In many hotspots, internationalization often goes hand-in-hand with an increase in the share of local-only interactions. In many Chinese hotspots the number of co-inventions within hotspots has grown remarkably, leading to a decline in share of both national and international collaboration outside these hotspots.

Multinational companies lie at the center of the web

Patent data shed light on the corporate R&D networks at the center of global innovation networks. Multinational companies from around the world increasingly list foreign inventors in their patent applications and those foreign inventors come from a widening set of countries. In the 1970s and 1980s, only 9 percent of patents filed by U.S. companies had foreign inventors; by the 2010s, this share had risen to 38 percent. Western European companies saw a similarly sharp increase, from 9 percent to 27 percent in the same period.

Such international patent sourcing still mostly happens between companies and inventors from high-income economies. In the 1970s and 1980s, 86 percent of the international patent sourcing was between multinational companies and inventors from the U.S., Japan and Western European countries. However, this share fell to 56 percent in the 2010s.

Middle-income economies are new players in MNC networks

Two main developments explain this fall. On the one hand, multinationals from these countries increasingly outsourced R&D activities to middle-income economies, particularly China, India and, to a lesser extent, Eastern Europe. For instance, in the 2010s, more than a quarter of all international patent sourcing by U.S. multinational companies had an inventor from China or India. On the other hand, multinationals from middle-income economies also actively participate in global innovation networks. Companies from Asia, Eastern Europe, Latin

America and Africa rely intensively on the ingenuity of U.S., Western European and Chinese inventors.

Innovation hubs move and can disperse over time

Multinationals can have very different needs and strategies as to where to source for talent, and these can change over time. For example, Google and Siemens have concentrated inventive activities within their top hubs. In the 2010s, San Jose–San Francisco accounted for 54 percent of Google's patents, up from 36 percent in the 2000s. Similarly, Nuremberg – the most important source of patents for German manufacturing company Siemens – accounted for 32 percent during the 2010s against 27 percent in the 2000s.

The concentration is even greater in Asian companies, though it has slightly decreased over time. Tokyo and Shenzhen–Hong Kong were the most important inventive sources for Sony and Huawei in the 2010s, accounting for 71 percent and 81 percent of patents, respectively. However, this is down from a respective 83 percent and 88 percent in the previous decade, suggesting a relative dispersion of innovation.

Innovation is reshaping the car industry

The report delves deeper into the evolving geography of innovation by studying two industries seeing profound change. One is the automotive sector, which is in the early phases of technological disruption. New entrants – from within the automotive industry and from the information technology (IT) industry – are challenging established players.

Fully autonomous vehicles (AV) have yet to reach the market. Nevertheless, artificial intelligence (AI) data analytics and the interconnectivity of devices and components are reformulating the industry's business model toward services and the so-called "platform economy." Traditional automakers fear being displaced in their core business of making and marketing cars.

Patent data suggest that traditional automakers and their suppliers are at the forefront of AV innovation. Ford, Toyota and Bosch – accounting for 357, 320 and 277 of AV patent families, respectively – are the top three AV patent applicants. However, non-automakers also feature in the list of top patent applicants. Google, and its AV subsidiary Waymo, are in eighth position with 156 patents, ahead of traditional automakers like Nissan, BMW and Hyundai. Uber and Delphi each have 62 AV patents and are ranked joint 31st.

Incumbents and new entrants collaborate among and between themselves

Neither the incumbents nor the new entrants currently have all the required competencies for producing AVs. They either need to join forces or else develop internally the respective skills they lack. AV innovation is a long-term and costly endeavor. Stakeholders have high incentives to collaborate and share risks and costs with different type of partners. Three types of collaboration are forming: between incumbent automakers; between tech firms, and between automakers and tech firms. The emerging collaboration network is an amalgam of all the above: none is mutually exclusive, and they coexist.

Automotive and IT firms stay tied to their traditional clusters

The top automakers and top IT giants still strongly favor home-based sites for their inventive activities. There is some shift in geography at the margins, so it might be too early to give a definitive answer as to whether AV technology will change the geography of innovation in the automotive industry.

Innovation is sown in biotech labs and harvested in agricultural clusters

Crop biotechnology is an industry where innovation has to be adapted to local agro-ecological conditions. While most plant biotechnology inventions may come from high-income countries – for example, the U.S., Western Europe and East Asian countries – they still need adapting to different climate and soil conditions. Most of the transgenic crops used in emerging middle-income countries during the late 1990s were locally adapted germplasms of their North American counterparts. As a result, plant biotechnology innovation clusters exist in many parts of the world. However, the data show that crop biotechnology innovation in many countries in Africa, Latin America and the Caribbean, and Asia is geographically concentrated.

The landscape of plant biotech innovation

A handful of countries accounts for the bulk of biotechnology inventive and scientific output. The U.S., Germany, China, Japan and the Republic of Korea accumulate more than 55 percent and 80 percent of all crop biotechnology articles and patents, respectively. Only Argentina, Australia, India, Israel, Mexico and Singapore join them in the list of countries hosting plant biotechnology clusters; and, except for Australia, they all have only one.

There is a geographic divide between where plant biotech innovation occurs and where transgenic crops are farmed. In most cases, crop biotechnology hotspots are located in large metropolitan areas, either in global innovation hotspots or in specialized niche clusters with strong biotech competences. This also holds for developing countries, where national crop biotechnology clusters are typically located in large urban areas, such as São Paulo in Brazil and Cape Town.

Some clusters are close to rural areas – for example, Viçosa in Brazil or Irapuato in Mexico. Wherever they are, their presence is usually associated with influential public institutions, such as universities, international agricultural research centers and/or national agriculture research systems.

Increasing private–public collaboration

Private firms, particularly the four major agrobusiness companies – Bayer and BASF from Germany, ChemChina and Corteva Agriscience from the U.S. – undertake a large part of the R&D investment in plant biotechnology. The need for access to proprietary technologies has spurred collaboration within the industry through cross-licensing, licensing-in, joint research ventures and even mergers and acquisitions.

Nevertheless, there is an increasing need for collaboration with the public sector to access, for example, pools of germplasms and cultivars – crop varieties with desirable traits – often held by public research institutions. For public institutions the high costs of commercializing crop biotechnology products almost always require collaboration with large multinational companies. Since the 2000s, co-patenting between private firms and public institutions has overtaken co-patenting among private firms to become the main type of collaboration. In fact, since the 2010s, co-patenting between private firms has slipped to third in importance behind co-patenting between public institutions.

Openness in pursuit of innovation brings mutual gains

What does the global geography of innovation, as portrayed in this report, imply for policymaking? The growth of global innovation networks has relied on policies favoring openness and international cooperation, but this should not be taken for granted – especially as public perceptions have become more skeptical of the benefits of globalization.

Economic theory offers good reasons why the free exchange of knowledge is beneficial: it promotes the specialization of different innovation clusters around the world, leading to more efficient and diverse knowledge production. The public good nature of knowledge reinforces the benefits of openness: if knowledge flows generate economic benefits abroad without diminishing those at home, there are bound to be mutual gains from openness.

Theoretically, there may well be circumstances in which strategic restrictions on trade and knowledge flows could benefit the growth paths of economies. However, the experience of high-income economies over the past decades suggests an overall positive impact from the flow of knowledge about new technologies.

Falling R&D productivity reinforces the case for openness

Continuously pushing the technological frontier is becoming exceedingly difficult. Evidence suggests that achieving the same level of technological progress as in the past requires more and more R&D effort.

Falling R&D productivity calls for constantly increasing investments in innovation. It also calls for collaboration and openness. Finding solutions to increasingly complex technological problems requires larger teams of researchers and greater specialization in research, both of which can be promoted by openness and international collaboration.

Making openness work requires international cooperation…

International cooperation in relation to innovation has many dimensions. It is needed to promote incentives for investments in innovation that reflect the demands and size of the global economy. It can also play an important role in making it easier for innovators to do business internationally. Lastly, governments can pool resources and fund large-scale scientific projects that exceed national budgets or require technical knowledge available in different countries.

…and policies that address growing regional divergence

One worrying trend of the past few decades is the increasing inter-regional polarization of incomes, innovative activity and high-skilled employment and wages within countries. Openness strengthens the gravitational pull toward champion regions. As this report demonstrates, the most vibrant innovation hotspots, which are embedded in global innovation networks, tend to be located in what are already the richest metropolitan agglomerations within countries.

Regional support and development policies can play an important role in helping regions that have fallen behind. While not reversing the gravitational pull of successful regions, they can promote innovation-driven growth that benefits economies as a whole.

Innovation is increasingly concentrated in urban "hotspots." At the same time, these hotspots are connecting and collaborating across the world.

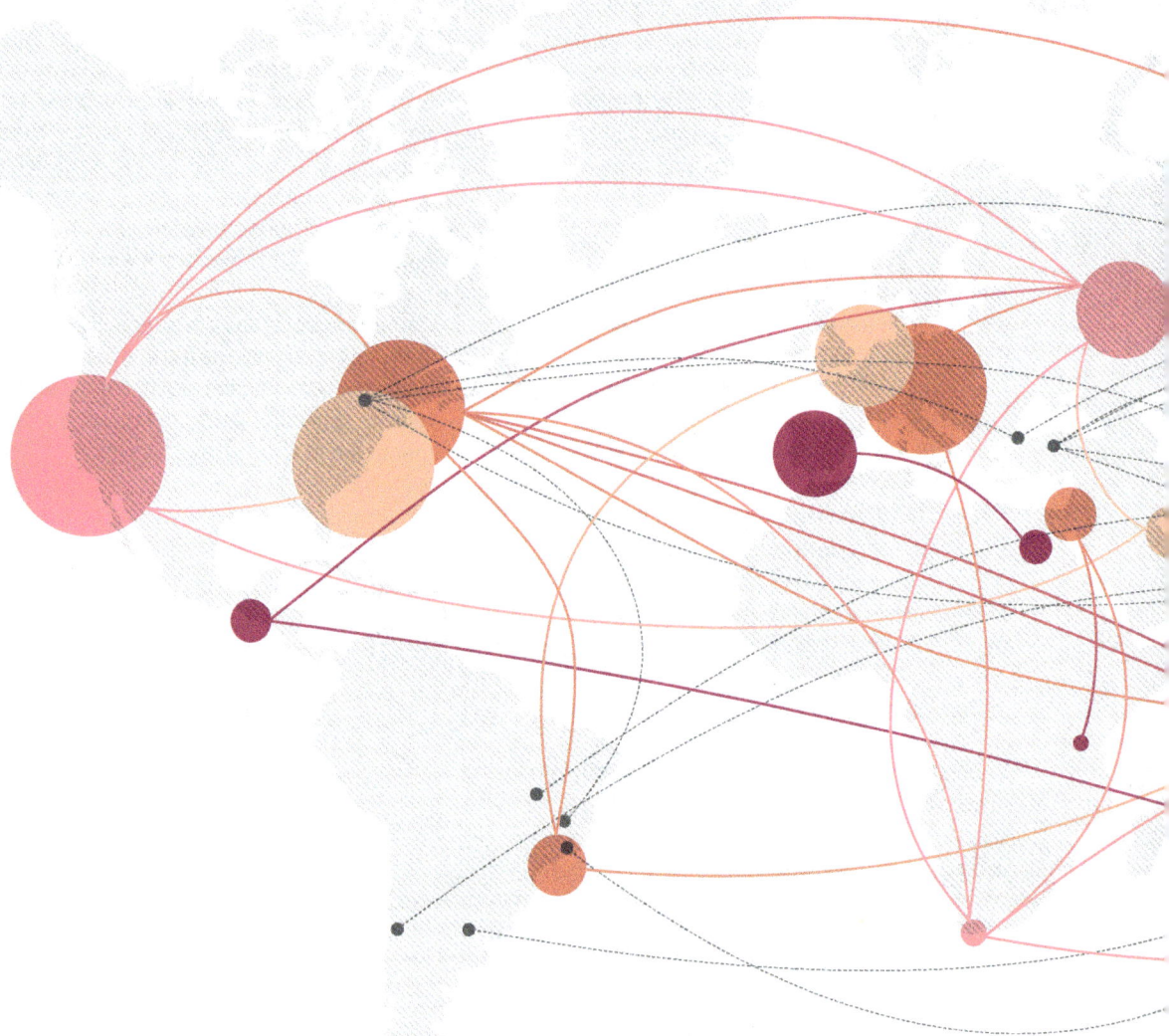

Chapter 1

The changing global geography of innovation

Technological innovation is the engine that propels economic growth and fosters higher living standards. As described in WIPO's *World Intellectual Property Report 2015*, the growth record of the past 200 years has been historically unprecedented. A series of technological breakthroughs have greatly improved the quality of life and generated widespread material prosperity. Even so, some national economies have seen faster and more sustained growth than others. The geographical distribution and the spread of innovation activities – whether technological or knowledge-generating – go a long way to explaining why some economies have developed faster than others. New technologies, in turn, have shaped where and how innovation has taken place.[1]

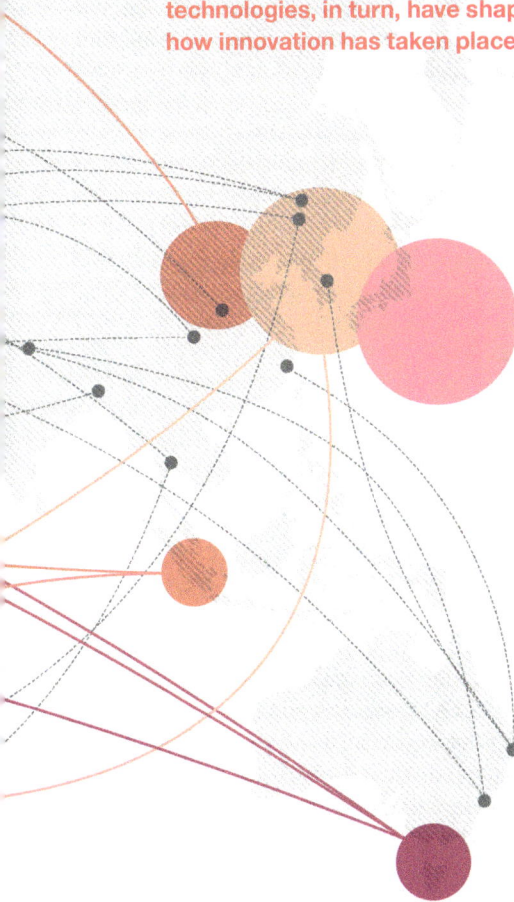

The first industrial revolution – spurred in the late 18th century by new manufacturing processes powered by steam – concentrated the world's industrial output in Western Europe, particularly, the United Kingdom (U.K.).[2] It changed the face of the world economy, generating a different global development hierarchy. Equally important, it also led to persistent regional divergences within Europe, with a select set of regions and cities – such as Manchester and London in the U.K., Normandy, Paris and Lyon in France, the Ruhrgebiet in Germany, Liège in Belgium or the Franco-German region that included Lorraine, Saarland and Luxembourg – constituting the "European core."[3]

The second industrial revolution – driven by a broad array of electro-mechanical inventions in the second half of the 19th century – witnessed the entry of North America into the high-income club of the world, while broadening the industrialized regions of Europe. There was not a perfect overlap between the countries, cities and regions at the core of the two revolutions. Some previously core regions declined while others thrived. In Europe, the waves of industrialization expanded concentrically, taking in, among others, southwest France, northeastern Spain, the Milan–Venice corridor in northern Italy, Berlin, Vienna, Krakow and Prague, as well as moving north to Oslo and Sweden's Gothenburg. In the United States of America (U.S.), northeastern cities – such as Boston, New York and Baltimore – remained industrially important, but industrialization expanded to several Midwest cities, such as Chicago, Detroit, Minneapolis and Cleveland.

Starting in the 1970s and 1980s, a third industrial revolution has occurred, broadly involving digital technologies, life-science and biological technologies, financial engineering and significant breakthroughs in transport and logistics. It has coincided with major increases in global trade and investment flows. Innovation and economic development has spread to northeast Asia, moving from Japan to the Republic of Korea and later to China. Tokyo, Seoul, Shenzhen and Beijing have grown into megacities shaping the direction of technological progress today. The "incumbent" high-income economies in Europe and North America continue to be at the forefront of innovation, but again with a new geographical landscape within them.

What forces can explain why innovation has concentrated in certain geographical areas and has spread only unevenly? Going beyond the broad patterns outlined above, how exactly is the global geography of innovation changing? How do companies in today's globalized age organize their innovation activities across the world?

This report endeavors to provide a perspective on these questions. It does so in three parts. First, it reviews economic thinking and empirical evidence explaining the geographical distribution of innovative activity – a task performed in this opening chapter. Second, it draws on patent and scientific publication data with geocoded inventors and scientific authors from around the world to show how this geography of innovation has evolved over the past decades. The discussion of the emerging trends – presented in Chapter 2 – will portray this geography in terms of global innovation networks (GINs), geographically concentrated innovation hotspots and niche innovation clusters connected to one another, which are increasingly leading the way. The report will also illustrate the operation of such GINs through two case studies – one on autonomous vehicles and the other on agricultural biotechnologies. These case studies will be presented in Chapters 3 and 4, respectively. Finally, the report concludes – in Chapter 5 – with policy perspectives on its main findings. They emphasize, in particular, the benefits of national innovation systems remaining open to the international exchange of knowledge.

This opening chapter discusses the main economic forces behind both the geographical concentration and spread of knowledge creation and diffusion. The following section reviews the main economic theories and existing evidence behind the geographical concentration of innovative activities. It shows that the processes of knowledge creation and flow, investment and appropriation are reinforcing global innovation and economic hierarchies and how they are concentrating innovation within geographical hotspots or clusters, most of them metropolitan. Section 2.2 considers how these processes are at the same time leading to an increased dispersion of hotspots at a global scale. It explores the main forces – operating principally through global networks of firms, researchers and

entrepreneurs – which are linking the main innovation-creation centers around the globe. The final section explores some of the consequences arising from today's global network of highly concentrated innovation hotspots.

1.1 Concentration of innovation in urban hotspots

Framing the geography of global innovation requires understanding both the forces driving innovation's concentration and its spread. One prominent feature of the geography of economic development is common to both established high-income economies and successful emerging middle-income ones: the geography of high incomes is increasingly metropolitan, reflecting renewed inter-regional divergence within countries. These metropolitan areas are also hotbeds for the formation of ecosystems of innovation. In the U.S., two prominent examples are the southern part of the San Francisco Bay Area in Northern California and the Greater Boston metropolitan region in Massachusetts, often dubbed *Silicon Valley* and *Route 128*, respectively.

What economic forces explain the agglomeration of innovation?

One of the toughest questions for geography, economics and development studies is to ascertain why such hotbeds, or agglomerations, of innovation arise and flourish where they do. This question goes from the general factors that lie behind the clustering of innovation to the specific geographies of those agglomerations.[4]

Several different economic theories address this question. These most commonly consider the economic forces relating to pools of skilled labor, market scale and knowledge spillover – where highly innovative firms are concentrated, knowledge can filter, or "spill," from one to another. Historical accidents or deliberate policy can affect all these, but none succeed entirely in answering the question. At the same time, there are forces pushing in the opposite direction, toward geographical dispersion, but all accounts indicate these are not as a strong.

Figure 1.1 provides a graphical summary of the main forces driving concentration, discussed below.

People, companies and ideas cluster together

Figure 1.1 Main economic forces driving geographical concentration of innovation

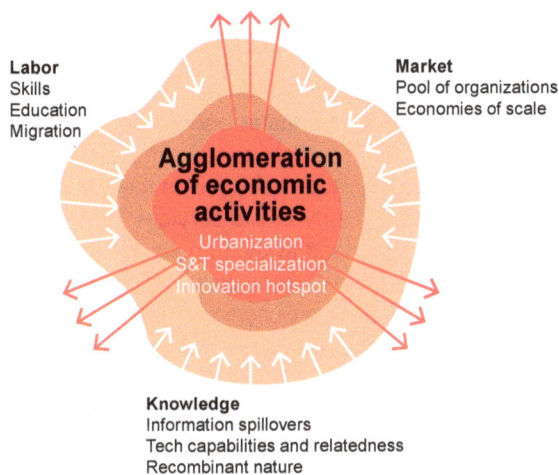

Labor
Skills
Education
Migration

Market
Pool of organizations
Economies of scale

Agglomeration of economic activities
Urbanization
S&T specialization
Innovation hotspot

Knowledge
Information spillovers
Tech capabilities and relatedness
Recombinant nature

Note: S&T = Science and technology.

Does skill supply help drive innovative agglomeration?

Mainstream economic theory offers a number of ways in which the geographical concentration of innovation can be an indirect outcome of labor supply – both quantity and quality.[5]

These theories assume that workers with different skills gravitate toward different regions. In basic terms, highly skilled workers cluster together, because they want to interact with one another, so the education and skills of the workforce in a given region can act as a force of attraction. At the same time, migration can change the skills base of the workforce of the receiving region, reinforcing the agglomeration effect.

The preferences of highly skilled workers for vibrant agglomerations and to work in innovation are part of this picture. Innovation-generating occupations offer career trajectories and life-long learning, which secure future employment opportunities at a time when automation increasingly seems to threaten many traditional white-collar occupations. Such work also offers high wages that compensate for rising costs of living and housing. Cost pressures also push less well-paid, unskilled workers to the urban periphery.

Empirical evidence shows that regions that had a higher-than-average concentration of college-educated workers in the past observe further growth in the share of college-educated workers, per capita incomes, patents and other direct and indirect proxies for innovation. The characteristics of the local labor supply seem to influence the development trajectory of innovation-generating agglomerations and impact regional innovativeness, both in the U.S. and in the European Union (EU).[6]

However, what explains the origin of a singularly skilled workforce in a given region? At some points in history, skilled workers have changed their geographical distribution, favoring spatial spread. Why has the behavior of the skilled workforce spontaneously changed in favor of geographical concentration? This was the case in the maturing phase of the second industrial revolution, when there was a massive migration of skilled workers – together with unskilled ones – from all over the world to the leading developed countries from 1940 to 1980.[7]

Historical accidents involving unusual individuals can be partial explanations for the location of innovative agglomerations, especially those involving first-mover regions in the key technologies of each industrial revolution. Thus, by some accounts, Silicon Valley is where it is, because William Shockley – the inventor of the silicon-based semiconductor – decided to relocate from New Jersey to be near his aging mother. Another anecdote concerning Shockley is that after he attracted top-quality associates to his first-mover firm, his difficult management style caused them all to quit on the same day. This event – known as "Shockley's massacre" – created a first and unexpected example of the spin-offs that have become so typical in the Silicon Valley process of development. The annals of innovation contain plenty of other such people-based stories.

Nevertheless, the randomness of such "great inventor presence" stories raises some doubts. There are so many famous individuals associated with Silicon Valley – from Shockley and Frederick Terman, one of the acknowledged "fathers" of Silicon Valley, to Apple's Steve Jobs and Google co-founders Sergey Brin and Larry Page – that it seems unlikely that all could be there by coincidence. Moreover, Saxenian (1994) powerfully argues that the mere presence of early innovators is not enough. Plenty of the early great information technologies (IT) innovators were located in Boston, but they did not stay. Facebook's Mark Zuckerberg left Boston for Silicon Valley, because Boston was not the right place to transform a breakthrough invention into a fully fledged innovation, just as had happened to New Jersey decades earlier, when William Shockley left for the Bay Area.

In addition, "skill" is not a uniform entity and different technologies may need different sets or combinations of skills that may not always overlap. A finance worker will be attracted to different locations than an IT engineer, and these locations and jobs are not interchangeable. But at the same time, different professions and skills may be complementary for the production of a given innovation.

Demand side: how market forces generate innovation hubs

Market economic forces complement labor supply ones as drivers of the geographic concentration of innovation activities. The main market economic forces are generated by the "pool" of organizations – notably private firms – within a market and the consequent economies of transport, scale and scope.

This pool is at the heart of productivity differences across regions. As with the "unusual individual cases," historical accidents involving innovation breakthroughs by a key firm within a local economy, a so-called "anchor" firm, can be equally important in starting an innovation ecosystem that then organically grows as both skilled labor and related activities relocate. At such moments, key firms can have an idiosyncratic influence on agglomeration. But this is not always the case. Motorola located the largest early semiconductor facility in the world in Phoenix, Arizona, in the 1950s, for example, but this did not establish that U.S. city as a subsequent center for IT industries.[8] Motorola had believed that it could be a geographically isolated first-mover in a technologically innovative industry. It turned out that only those first-movers that did not isolate themselves from the open source networks of the emerging Silicon Valley – such as semiconductor firm Fairchild and computer company Hewlett-Packard – were able to keep up with the rapidly rising technology curve.

Regions with industrial concentration benefit from more complete local labor markets. Firms can find specialized skills more easily, reducing costs related to employees' skill conversion or relocation. Similarly, a higher concentration of firms is more likely to generate new firms. These spin-offs are more likely to be more productive the higher the productivity of the original pool of firms. The agglomeration and innovativeness of the car industry in Detroit in the first quarter of the last century was due to a great extent to spin-offs carrying on the technological and organizational practices of their parents.

Academic institutions – such as universities – are also important factors in concentration. The concentration of university graduates and science, engineering and technology workers mirrors the spatial concentration of innovation activities. In the U.S., skilled workers, particularly in the services sector, relocate to larger cities and away from small and medium-sized ones. Academic research is also more productive and creative – i.e. more unconventional – in larger and more diverse agglomerations.[9]

New theories of economic geography have extended and perfected the argument of the pool of organizations. Unlike most traditional spatial analysis, they identify geographical concentration as a snowball process whereby regions progressively draw in supplier firms and human talent. In its simplest version, regional differences in productivity or economies of scale alone can explain the divergence in geographical concentration between two equivalent regions, or explain the reinforcement of the concentration in core regions vis-à-vis the periphery. The basic mechanism is that any confirmed difference in productivity or innovation levels in a given region accrues to generate or confirm the leading position of the more innovative or productive region.[10]

According to these theories, agglomerative market forces are at work when both firms and consumers can take advantage of clustering in one location. Agglomerations with large local markets are preferred sites for the production of consumer goods due to the economies of transportation, scale and variety. Transport economies are in place when local firms can serve a large local market faster and cheaper than distant ones. Similarly, firms supplying large markets benefit from economies of scale by splitting the sunk investment costs over more units sold and optimizing production processes through several iterations. Consumers in larger markets enjoy a higher variety of goods. Not only can consumers find the exact variety of product they are looking for in a larger market, firms can specialize in delivering it. These three mechanisms – transport, scale and scope – also affect firms producing intermediate goods locally, which reinforces economies downstream in the local supply chain.[11]

Do knowledge spillovers and technological conditions attract concentration?

But market scale and the availability of a skilled workforce do not lead straightforwardly to a region mastering the next wave of innovation. Advantages obtained from previous successful innovation processes do not assure future technological advantages.

As with large markets and complete labor markets, so-called information and knowledge spillovers are also positive externalities favoring co-location of innovative firms, academic centers and talented human resources.[12] Knowledge is not restricted to the technological and organizational practices of an existing organization or individual; it may spill from one to the other. Firms more successfully exploit economies of scale and scope if they learn from the experience of other firms. Skilled workers disseminate tacit knowledge when they interact with other skilled workers, change organizations or migrate.

Most empirical evidence points to knowledge spillovers being extremely geographically concentrated. This is mainly due to the high costs associated with codifying, exchanging and absorbing knowledge. While information, such as data, flows increasingly freely across organizations and regions, spillovers of knowledge – what is needed, for example, to interpret data – are "stickier." Firms, academic organizations and individuals have to actively interact, collaborate and, sometimes, move to make knowledge flow. The concentration of knowledge spillovers can, therefore, be both a consequence and a trigger of the agglomeration of innovation. Innovative firms will move to where knowledge spillovers are higher, reinforcing spillovers in that region and crowding out non-innovative firms to the periphery.[13] This joint innovation and spatial co-evolution can determine a regional development path, which can be largely irreversible.

While previous regional technological endowments are likely to shape subsequent creation of innovation, not all innovative regions follow the same trajectory. In the 1930s, both Princeton, New Jersey – site of RCA Laboratories – and Silicon Valley were home to close technological antecedents of the IT industry; but they developed very different innovative paths. Silicon Valley's remarkable IT innovation trajectory grew out of the pre-existing and mutually supporting manufacturing industries of power grid tubes, microwave tubes and silicon components. These industries enriched the northern Californian IT innovation ecosystem with related technological capabilities and new management approaches easily transposable to the nascent IT industry. Princeton and other East Coast hubs had a much narrower technological IT ecosystem based on few large companies.[14]

In this sense, more diversified agglomerations have a greater probability of successfully transitioning to a new technological capability than narrowly specialized ones.[15] The literature abounds with stories of how narrowly specialized economies are locked into their technologies and do not transition after negative demand shocks or technology shifts. It seems that technological innovation is more likely to occur in regions with a broader portfolio of technical competences, especially when it is easy to recombine these. Dominant industries tend to monopolize talent, supplies of economic factors of production, such as capital or entrepreneurship, and attention. Such resource concentration potentially crowds out other activities and can channel the evolution of regional economies down different pathways. For instance, Detroit – the "Motor City" – is held up as a case of over-specialization. And yet there are highly specialized centers of mechanical engineering and automotive technology that have mastered subsequent waves of technology, such as Stuttgart in Germany. Boston was once narrowly specialized in mill-based industries, but is now a high-tech center. The capacity for regional economic evolution is governed by possibilities for moving into related varieties of technologies and technological capacity.[16]

However, technological relatedness and complementarity are not the entire story. There are many examples of regions that capture major new sectors with little technological relation to their previous activities. Los Angeles was not a major mechanical engineering region in the 1920s and 1930s when it became the aircraft-engineering center of the U.S. and, by the 1940s, the world's biggest aerospace cluster. Los Angeles also had no background in the entertainment industry when the movie studios were established there around 1915. Detroit had fewer antecedents in mechanical equipment than Illinois in the 1890s, but rapidly became the center of U.S. car technology and manufacture.

In these, and many other examples, there were technological windows of opportunity. These ruptures in technological relatedness largely obviate the advantages of pre-existing agglomeration and create a relatively flat playing field for a short time in the early days of a technology's existence.

To sum up, the interaction between innovation and geography reflects the juxtaposition of individual, organizational and technological antecedents. Saxenian's (1994) seminal comparison of Boston's Route 128 and Silicon Valley shows that the types of entrepreneurship, production organization and system coordination experienced by existing firms and actors in a region will shape how that region evolves economically and what kinds of new activities it can generate and capture.

Can policy mold the forces of innovation agglomeration?

There is little systematic, large-scale evidence for the success of policies trying to create new local clusters. The last several decades are littered with failed "technopolis" or "the next Silicon Valley" policy initiatives. Government subsidies might actually attract the "wrong" kind of firms that have low productivity and depend on subsidies for survival or which are not in fact open to creating networks among local firms for fear of leaking intellectual property (IP). Because of the path dependency of industry growth and cluster creation, it is questionable how much policy can achieve. As in nature, firms form innovation ecosystems that are not easily transplantable or reproducible, as they develop embedded in territorially-specific institutional settings and social fabrics.[17]

Nevertheless, the above does not mean that all policy has failed in influencing cluster formation. Indeed, a common feature of any national innovation system is that market forces of agglomeration are not the only factor shaping the geography of innovation. The public sector, as well as the higher-education sector and academic institutions are also key actors that shape the innovativeness of countries and regions. This is particularly true in developing economies where public investment is the main driver of research and development (R&D) expenditures.[18] A variety of circumstances motivates public sector support for innovation. In some countries and regions, stagnating productivity has stimulated a revival of industrial policy. In many of the most successful former middle-income economies, industrial policy with a strong innovation component was in evidence during their economic ascent.

In the U.S., a notable successful policy story is the Research Triangle Park in North Carolina. While perhaps not equivalent to Boston or Silicon Valley, the Research Triangle Park is known as a leader in a wide variety of high-tech fields and as a model of one of the first and most successful research parks.[19] Public policy can also affect the geography of innovation more indirectly through the R&D system and, in particular, the role of universities and public research laboratories and organizations. In the U.S., from 1875 to 1975, the federal Land Grant Colleges system extended the geographical spread of research universities, while federal funding for universities reinforced the proliferation of universities. The California system is perhaps the most successful of all, with the public University of California system having six of the world's top universities. The same applies to the geographical distribution of public sector laboratories, such as the national laboratories in the U.S. or the *Conseil National de Recherche Scientifique* (CNRS) labs in France.

Analogously, most of the former middle-income economies that are now high-income and highly innovative regions of the world – such as the Republic of Korea, Singapore or Israel – made a successful effort to build top-ranked research universities.[20] In China, it seems likely that the appearance of top world innovation clusters is related to the investments in top world research universities.

There are also selective examples of successful government intervention to generate clusters in middle-income economies. For example, in 2008, the municipal government of Chongqing, China, successfully helped to transplant several smaller coastal notebook computer manufacturing clusters into the city. Their policies targeting investments in infrastructure, labor market organization and other business-friendly actions incentivized new businesses, initiatives and entrepreneurship. However, the policy moved existing clusters rather than growing new ones organically. Other initiatives in China have taken different approaches, depending on the capabilities and powers of the local administration. India's investment in a space program located in Bangalore incubated an IT cluster in the same area. Then, with the policy support provided by investment in infrastructure and human capital, the new cluster grew organically. All of these clusters started as manufacturing hubs and became innovative to varying degrees as the manufacturing phase matured. But the process also involved a significant contribution from multinational companies, whose role in global innovation networks will be examined below.[21]

All the public investments required to carry out such strategies are large and must be long-term and appropriately institutionally organized. However, there is an inherent tension between inter-regional equity and the excellence that is present in virtually every large country with a public higher education system today. As it is not practical to have equally well-endowed research universities in every locality, any successful innovation policy eventually leads to some internal concentration.

In addition, in today's agglomerated innovation environment, certain public sector institutions – especially universities – are strongly reinforced by market forces that make some more attractive to students, faculty and funders. This reduces the efficiency of public sector policies for spreading innovation around different regions and creates the risk that public entrepreneurship will follow the geographical patterns of the private sector and largely benefit those regions with strong institutions and favorable conditions. Unfortunately, innovation or industrial policy frameworks have only rarely been able to both raise the national level of innovation and distribute it relatively evenly within the national territory.

Other policies – or a lack of these – can also indirectly affect the forces behind the agglomeration of innovation. The preferences of highly skilled workers, entrepreneurs and innovative companies for certain agglomerations may reflect deliberate cluster policies, but they are also not unconnected to tax, social security and education policies, among others.[22] For instance, successful innovative regions with highly unregulated real-estate markets will likely observe a housing price uptick, which will exclude low-skilled workers and drive them to regions with lower-cost housing, as noted above.

Why do geographical concentration and spread coexist?

Threaded throughout the discussion above there is considerable reference to regional concentration within a process of global dispersion. This is the other major defining characteristic of the contemporary geography of innovation. While innovation activity is increasingly concentrated in metropolitan areas, it is also gradually spreading to hubs outside the traditional centers in the U.S. and Western Europe.

The empirical evidence simultaneously points both to the importance of the increasing global nature of innovation and to the growing forces driving the agglomeration and concentration of innovation in specific – often metropolitan – areas. Rather than being antagonists, these trends are complementary, reinforcing each other. If there is any single image that can capture this emerging geography it is that of a globalized hub-to-hub system. The world system of innovation links national systems of innovation and global firms through a spiky geography of knowledge creation. The result is a global network of these spikes or hubs, many of which are better connected to one another than they are to their national hinterlands in terms of knowledge creation and diffusion.

International openness is a distinctive trait of leading agglomerations of geographically concentrated innovation today. But long-distance exchanges of knowledge are not a new feature of the economic system. In the first and second industrial revolutions, knowledge and hardware travelled, international imitation and rivalry were active parts of the landscape, and there were always networks of people who helped along such knowledge exchange. In the past, however, such exchanges often involved the display and then possible imitation of what was created in a rival agglomeration.

Contemporary knowledge clusters have long-distance ties which have become more organized and extensive over time, and which often involve the co-development of technologies across agglomerations, both within firms and between competing firms.

Thus, knowledge-generating agglomerations today are not self-contained local systems, but rather consist of key nodes in dispersed and global networks of innovation.[23] Indeed, highly productive localized innovation systems are also those that are most tied into long-distance relationships of various sorts. New knowledge may be brought into a region through the establishment of these linkages. Innovators rely on collaborations both inside and outside the organizations and the regions where they work.

These networks of geographical spread of innovation will be discussed in the following section.

1.2   Networks and the global spread of innovation

In recent decades, global networks for the production and delivery of goods and services have expanded greatly. In comparison to previous globalization waves, the current globalization has a much higher proportion of intra-industry exchange of both components and final goods within global value chains. Prior to 2000, most of such intra-industry trade took place among a few countries, most notably in the northern hemisphere. But since then, it has more and more concerned the relationships between developing economies and the rest of the world. Global production networks often involve multiple or circular trade flows, with exports wrapped into subsequent outputs and ending up as imports, blurring the line between foreign and domestic production.[24]

The current globalization, in other words, involves intricate forms of interdependency, not just between economies as a whole, but inside the most delicate plumbing of the economic system, within and between firms and industries. This is also true of the underlying innovation networks and ecosystems, which are both a consequence of global productive integration and, increasingly, a cause of it.

Mirroring the growing globalization and complexity of production systems is an increasingly dispersed and complex plumbing system for knowledge production. The globalization of innovation is a result of an increased international integration of economic activities and the rising importance of knowledge in economic processes.[25]

From the mid-20th century until the Great Recession, beginning around 2008, technological activity was also steadily internationalizing, with new countries emerging in the international system of innovation. More recently, there is some evidence of the selective reshoring of some key R&D and innovation activities back to home countries. At the same time, however, the post-recession period has seen a growing articulation of value chains beyond national borders, involving an increasing share of intra-firm trade flows, with the knowledge flows they entail.[26]

What economic forces explain the spread of innovation?

The economic forces driving the spread of innovation are very similar to those stimulating its concentration in specific clusters. Economic agents in a given innovation hotspot spread innovation to other regions of the world and vice-versa, which is why the spread of global innovation can be thought of as a bidirectional network of knowledge and technological flows.

It is worth recapitulating that the geographical spread of innovation to peripheral areas of a region or country is often limited, because the forces pushing for concentration are too strong. Nevertheless, the same strong concentration forces operating in one urban cluster are at work in others. This can lead to reciprocal relationships that generate a further spread of innovation and knowledge. Regions spreading and receiving innovation are likely to remain connected, but these knowledge and technological flows often skip the peripheral regions of the world and link directly to the main economic agglomerations.

Figure 1.2 sums up the three main bidirectional economic forces forging the links of an international or inter-regional network – market, skilled labor and knowledge.

People, companies and ideas link beyond geographical borders

Figure 1.2 Main bidirectional economic forces spreading innovation

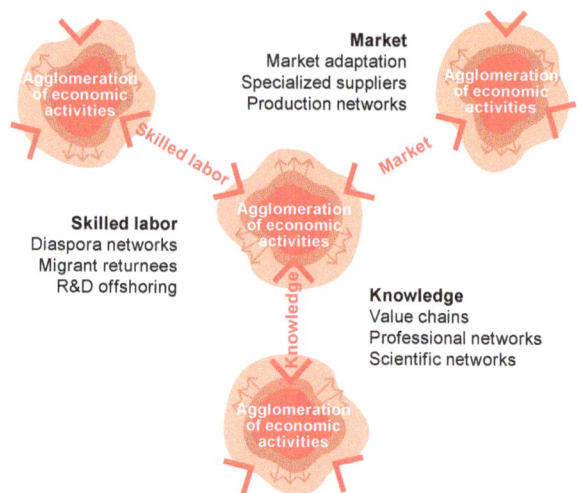

The international and inter-regional mobility of skilled innovators is a key feature of the contemporary innovation environment, creating an interpersonal link between hubs. This mobility may positively stimulate the international dispersion of innovation by strengthening these innovation networks.[27]

The global diffusion of knowledge does not take place through random mobility of people, of course, but by their moving between places in which they are likely to find the right conditions and the right people to unleash their innovativeness. As noted, these networks serve not just as a means of dispersion and mobility, but as key points of attraction for the skilled. This talented workforce can reap learning and experience premiums by being in geographical hotspots with key network nodes and whose networks are deep. The ability to acquire more experience and improve skills is considered one of the main reasons why the skilled continue to move into the most expensive cities, in spite of high costs of living, contributing to the rapid growth in geographical differences in the wages of the skilled. Evidence that both international and inter-regional "brain drain" is at a very high level today complements this picture.

Labor mobility can take various directions. After concentrating in a region, skilled migrants often generate a diaspora network linking the origin and destination regions. Moreover, many highly trained migrants return to their original region to apply their higher skills there as entrepreneurs.

Saxenian (1999) explores the interaction of people and investment networks through the mobility of skilled Asian entrepreneurs from and to Silicon Valley. She explains how skilled workers come to Silicon Valley and acquire human capital and experience; they become integrated into local networks while continuing to maintain links back home. For example, Chinese and Indian U.S.-trained engineers coordinate activities between Silicon Valley technology producers and the manufacturing and design expertise in their home country regions. As skilled Asian entrepreneurs move around, they engage in knowledge-sharing, leading to what is termed "brain circulation." By drawing on their networks, they also seem to be able to facilitate investments in new business ventures, highlighting the parallel movement of networks and foreign direct investment (FDI) channels.

Equally, multinational companies (MNCs) relocating R&D sites offshore in order to benefit from an extraordinary – or cheaper – research labor supply also generate bidirectional knowledge flows, at least with the headquarters' region. Access to talent and R&D cost are among the main known MNC motivations to internationalize R&D. Global patenting is increasingly the result of the collaboration of large teams operating within the organizational boundaries of MNCs. For instance, a significant share of Chinese and Indian patents at the U.S. Patent and Trademark Office (USPTO) are the result of collaborations of this type.[28]

Market forces and role of MNCs in internationalization of networks

The forces at work in market agglomeration and spread create links within a firm, among different firms or across different organization types. For example, market size can make a firm relocate production to reduce transport costs and benefit from economies of scale. Technology transfers will necessarily be involved in putting in place the new production site, while inverse knowledge flows will also happen when adapting the product to local taste or regulations.

A key agent in all of these long-distance technological interactions is the multinational. In addition to access to lower costs and foreign talent, MNCs opt to internationalize their R&D activities to benefit from other market externalities, such as shorter times to bring products to market and to tap into localized areas of technological excellence. Reversed flows of FDI can also benefit established innovation centers. MNCs from middle-income economies are increasingly using outward FDI to expand market reach and to capture strategic assets, such as technologies, skills, commercial knowledge and brands. Clearly, local technological competence is only important for attracting FDI of this kind if the prospective subsidiary is going to engage in technology-intensive activities.

Intra- and inter-firm offshoring of R&D increase corporate innovation performance.[29] Key knowledge-generating territories around the world are usually both home to key firms that construct and participate in these international networks and hosts to foreign firms wishing to get access to their knowledge-generating ecosystems, talent pool and researchers.

The existence of a pool of specialized suppliers is also a motivation to connect to another region. A given region may specialize in a certain technology that can benefit complementary industries, even if located in other regions. Bidirectional knowledge flows will be established between the buyer and specialized supplier in the form of technical specifications and goods with embedded technology. In industries with a complex supply chain, these links can involve several hubs, building complex and often international production networks.

Arguably, the forces driving agglomeration successfully attract MNCs and other firms – especially high value-added ones – to particular locations in both developed and developing economies. The resultant clustering makes these destinations progressively less dependent on purely cost-based and relative technological endowment considerations. Intangible location advantages, such as knowledge spillovers, are highly concentrated within specific regions, cities and local systems. The advantages arising from newly vibrant local innovation ecosystems may benefit the MNCs at this location, their headquarters and their entire value chain. The resulting knowledge flows are, therefore, eminently bi- or multidirectional between so-called home and host locations.[30]

Knowledge spread: organization and person-based interactions

Geographical proximity is not the only source of knowledge spillovers today.[31] Knowledge externalities become forces promoting the spread of innovation through organization-level interactions and inter-person or professional-level networks. These organizational and professional connections may be made stronger by geographical proximity, but the latter is not necessary for them to exist.

Long-distance organization-level interactions – for example, interactions within global value chains or across international scientific networks – lower transaction costs within firms and research organizations. These organized structures can facilitate deep knowledge interactions without the requisite of co-location. The effect is enhanced if actors operate within standardized rules or routines set by their organization or pool of organizations. In 1981, Microsoft opened a campus in Silicon Valley just to connect their Seattle operations in Bellevue (and later Redmond) with the effervescence of the Bay Area.

Likewise, more people-based and less institutionalized relations – for example, professional and scientific communities – can also effectively exchange knowledge with a commonly agreed set of rules and routines. This establishes a social proximity – ranging from inter-personal to being part of the same culture or group – among innovators, which lowers interaction costs, eases verification and increases trust to exchange and produce new knowledge.

These economic forces overlap and intertwine to the extreme point of being inseparable. Similar to the forces driving knowledge agglomeration, knowledge-spreading forces are an intrinsic part of the underlying

reasoning behind the previously discussed skilled labor- and market-spreading forces.

As seen, the internationalization of corporate R&D plays a key role in all of these long-distance technological interactions, making MNCs one of the most important types of organization and network node in the international spillover of new knowledge. MNCs' international affiliates are gaining more autonomy and becoming – where the right incentives are in place – more embedded in regional and local innovation systems. Increasing autonomy for international affiliates also means that the choice of the specific subnational location becomes more important and driven by a wider range of factors other than costs.[32] Characteristics of the regional innovation ecosystem – including its institutions – are particularly important for attracting foreign investment in innovation and technological operations and become relevant factors in attracting investments at more advanced and knowledge-intensive stages of global value chains.

The rise of global innovation networks

Knowledge and innovation production have been international phenomena for a long time, but only recently have they become really global.[33] Nowadays, actors located in different countries can carry out innovation activities in a truly integrated form. Innovation has become increasingly the outcome of global networks connecting dispersed knowledge centers.[34]

It is against this general backdrop of globalization of knowledge and innovation – where their production is done with a higher degree of functional integration – that the concept of global innovation networks has emerged. A global innovation network is a globally organized web of collaboration between organizations – firms and others – engaged in knowledge production that results in innovation. The networks are characterized by (1) their really global spread – and not confined to networks based in high-income countries; (2) their networked nature; and (3) the outcome, i.e., innovation.[35]

Their formation is the result of a knowledge-seeking strategy by the organizations involved, which makes global innovation networks different from global production networks that follow more efficiency- and market-seeking strategies. The focus of global innovation networks is, therefore, knowledge exchange and integration, and subsequent innovation, but not in production or simple manufacturing.[36] Global innovation networks happen largely through the internationalization of corporate R&D.

From this perspective, the MNCs can exert a strong influence on the geographical concentration and global spread – the shape – of global innovation networks by deciding where to locate investment, production and knowledge sourcing.[37] Geographical conditions and the existing sectoral innovation system are particularly important as drivers for the most sophisticated and high value-added stages of supply chains, such as R&D, design or advanced business services.[38] The offshoring of R&D activities has created new interconnected architectures of innovation and research as well as new co-location patterns with production activities. This has offered new opportunities for regions and cities to link up to different parts or functions of global supply chains in ways that promote economic upgrading and innovation.

At the same time, global participation is a challenge for weaker regions, given the risk of being locked into low value-added and low-innovation activities. The geographic unevenness in participation and embeddedness in global production networks and value chains generates new core–periphery patterns in the global geography of innovation.

Most of the related literature in the field of international business indicates that organization-based linkages – both intra and inter firms – are behind the formation of global innovation networks.[39] International co-inventions – the archetypical indicator for global innovation networks – have expanded greatly to India and China since the 2000s, but a large proportion remains under the control of firms in the U.S., Japan and a few Western European countries. This suggests that companies can and do slice the R&D process in multiple stages/segments – as they do for goods – allowing new countries to participate in the different segments according to their comparative advantage.[40] This facilitates the transformation of existing global value chains or production networks into global innovation networks.

Furthermore, an increasing number of studies suggest personal relationships, aside from organization-based ones, are also critical drivers of the formation of global innovation networks.[41] These relationships range from direct person-to-person innovation-related international collaborations, to the international mobility of scientists, innovators and entrepreneurs.[42] However,

organization-based interaction is often the framework where this people-based collaboration can take place. Traditionally, multinationals' internal networks have been a suitable means to partially overcome barriers related to both geographical distance and differing national cultures. But the more recent decline in the costs of travel and communication has certainly favored the rise of person-based international linkages without necessarily an accompanying organizational structure.[43]

1.3   Conclusions

Innovation has always had geographical concentrations or hotspots: Manchester was to the first industrial revolution what San Francisco is to the third. However, for a long period between these two revolutions, it appeared that within the advanced economies the spread of the capacity for innovation was incremental. The strong concentration of innovation since the end of the 20th century thus requires additional consideration.

Firms used to cluster along supply chains. In the first and second industrial revolutions, innovation activity clustered together with leading production activities, making for large industrial cities, some of which also concentrated R&D and product development. Over the last century, these patterns of agglomeration have slowly changed. Location choices have become more determined by shared skill requirements – especially in the services sector – such as labor market pooling across different but related innovation sectors.[44] In the third industrial revolution, many industries are not heavily capital-intensive in their production activities, and global supply and value chains are far longer and more complex. As a result, leading urban agglomerations of innovation today specialize in the abstract, cognitive and conceptual tasks of R&D and innovation. These highly specialized sectors and complementary broad service sectors have displaced the traditionally co-located routine production tasks observed in the past.[45]

The consequences of this new concentration of innovative activity are far reaching. Ultimately, the geographical distribution of innovation shapes the economic development path of cities and broader regions. One prominent feature of the geography of economic development in recent times is the inter-regional divergence of incomes within countries (see Chapter 5). Generally speaking, large metropolitan areas – the hotbeds of agglomerated ecosystems of innovation – are increasingly outpacing other regions in terms of income growth.

Yet, there is also divergence within these large metropolitan areas. Jobs in innovation-related activities tend to pay higher wages than others. Rapid growth in a concentrated geographical area and within a particular sector may have further effects on the local economy. While high-skilled jobs create a larger number of low-skilled jobs, inflows of high-earners, combined with limited housing supply, often result in growing inequality and falling disposable income for low-earning households.[46] Ultimately, this may lead to increased sorting by skill groups into innovative, high-earning areas and non-innovative, low-earning areas, excluding the low-skilled from the opportunities and amenities of living and working in an innovative environment.[47]

These patterns seem to prevail in the largest global innovation hotspots around the world. They are the primary homes and hosts of major knowledge-based multinational corporations and the true beneficiaries of globalization, being centers of corporate decision-making and control, knowledge generation and exchange, skills and jobs. But their prosperity is accompanied by high levels of income inequality and spatial segregation, leading some to speak of a new "urban crisis."[48]

There is still limited evidence on which to draw firm conclusions as to the causes and consequences of the concentration and spread of innovative activity. This may partially reflect the complex nature of innovation processes and their uncertain impact. However, the long-term consequences deserve careful consideration, even with partial knowledge.

Notes

1   This chapter draws on Crescenzi *et al*. (2019b).

2   Acemoglu *et al*. (2005), Mokyr (2005) and WIPO (2015).

3   Crafts and Venables (2003).

4   Storper (2018).

5   Glaeser and Maré (2001).

6   Crescenzi *et al*. (2007).

7   Kemeny and Storper (2019).

8   Scott and Storper (1987).

9   Crescenzi *et al*. (2019b).

10   Krugman (1991).

11   Boschma and Frenken (2006).

12   These three externalities are referred to as Marshallian externalities (Krugman, 1991).

13   Boschma and Frenken (2006).

14   Lécuyer (2006).

15   These are known as Jacobsian externalities (Jacobs, 1961).

16   Frenken *et al*. (2007).

17   Chatterji *et al*. (2013).

18   Mazzucato (2015).

19   Hardin (2008).

20   See, e.g., Hershberg *et al*. (2007).

21   Crescenzi *et al*. (2019b).

22   Davis and Dingel (2019) and Feldman *et al*. (2005).

23   Bathelt *et al*. (2004), Boschma (2005) and Frenken *et al*. (2007).

24   WIPO (2017).

25   Archibugi and Iammarino (2002).

26   Crescenzi *et al*. (2019b).

27   Breschi *et al*. (2017)

28   Branstetter *et al*. (2014). See also Chapter 2.

29   Nieto and Rodríguez (2011).

30   Iammarino and McCann (2018).

31   Boschma (2005).

32   Cantwell (1995).

33   Chaminade *et al*. (2016).

34   Cano-Kollmann *et al*. (2016).

35   Barnard and Chaminade (2011).

36   Chaminade *et al*. (2016)

37   Crescenzi *et al*. (2019a).

38   Alcácer and Chung (2007) and Chidlow *et al*. (2009).

39   Bathelt *et al*. (2004).

40   Branstetter *et al*. (2014).

41   Lorenzen and Mudambi (2013).

42   Breschi *et al*. (2017) and Saxenian (1994, 1999).

43   Cano-Kollman *et al*. (2016).

44   Diodato *et al*. (2018).

45   Crescenzi and Iammarino (2017) and Duranton and Puga (2005).

46   Moretti (2012).

47   Diamond (2016).

48   Florida (2017) and Rodriguez-Pose (2018).

References

Acemoglu, D., S. Johnson and J.A. Robinson (2005). Institutions as a fundamental cause of long-run growth. In Aghion, P. and S.N. Durlauf (eds), *Handbook of Economic Growth*, Vol. 1. Amsterdam: Elsevier, 385–472.

Alcácer, J. and W. Chung (2007). Location strategies and knowledge spillovers. *Management Science*, 53(5), 760–776.

Archibugi, D. and S. Iammarino (2002). The globalization of technological innovation: definition and evidence. *Review of International Political Economy*, 9(1), 98–122.

Barnard, H. and C. Chaminade (2011). Global Innovation Networks: Towards a Taxonomy. *Paper No. 2011/04*. Lund, Sweden: University of Lund, CIRCLE laboratory.

Bathelt, H., A. Malmberg and P. Maskell (2004). Clusters and knowledge: local buzz, global pipelines and the process of knowledge creation. *Progress in Human Geography*, 28(1), 31–56.

Boschma, R. (2005). Proximity and innovation: a critical assessment. *Regional Studies*, 39(1), 61–74.

Boschma, R. and K. Frenken (2006). Why is economic geography not an evolutionary science? Towards an evolutionary economic geography. *Journal of Economic Geography*, 6, 273–302. doi.org/10.1093/jeg/lbi022.

Branstetter, L., G. Li and F. Veloso (2014). The rise of international co-invention. In Jaffe, A.B. and B.F. Jones (eds), *The Changing Frontier: Rethinking Science and Innovation Policy*. Chicago, IL: University of Chicago Press, 35–168.

Breschi, S., F. Lissoni and E. Miguelez (2017). Foreign-origin inventors in the USA: testing for diaspora and brain gain effects. *Journal of Economic Geography*, 17, 1009–1038.

Cano-Kollmann, M., J. Cantwell, T.J. Hannigan, R. Mudambi and J. Song (2016). Knowledge connectivity: An agenda for innovation research in international business. *Journal of International Business Studies*, 47(3), 255–262. doi.org/10.1057/jibs.2016.8

Cantwell, J. (1995). The globalisation of technology: what remains of the product cycle model? *Cambridge Journal of Economics*, 19(1), 155–174.

Chaminade, C., C. De Fuentes, G. Harirchi and M. Plechero (2016). The geography and structure of global innovation networks: global scope and regional embeddedness. In Shearmur R., C. Carrincazeaux and D. Doloreux (eds), *Handbook on the Geographies of Innovation*. Cheltenham: Edward Elgar.

Chatterji, A., E. Glaeser and W. Kerr (2013). Clusters of Entrepreneurship and Innovation. *NBER Working Paper 19013*. Cambridge, MA: National Bureau of Economic Research.

Chidlow, A., L. Salciuviene and S. Young (2009). Regional determinants of inward FDI distribution in Poland. *International Business Review*, 18(2), 119–133.

Crafts, N. and T. Venables (2003). Globalization in history: A geographical perspective. In Bordo, M.D., A.M. Taylor and J.G. Williamson (eds), *Globalization in Historical Perspective*. Chicago, IL: University of Chicago Press, 323–370.

Crescenzi, R. and S. Iammarino (2017). Global investments and regional development trajectories: the missing links. *Regional Studies*, 51(1), 97–115.

Crescenzi, R., O. Harman and D. Arnold (2019a). Move On Up! Building, Embedding and Reshaping Global Value Chains Through Investment Flows. Insights for Regional Innovation Policies. *Working Paper*. Paris: OECD.

Crescenzi, R., S. Iammarino, C. Ioramashvili, A. Rodríguez-Pose and M. Storper (2019b). The Geography of Innovation: Local Hotspots and Global Innovation Networks. WIPO *Economic Research Working Paper No. 57*. Geneva: WIPO.

Crescenzi, R., A. Rodríguez-Pose and M. Storper (2007). On the geographical determinants of innovation in Europe and the United States. *Journal of Economic Geography*, 7(6), 673–709.

Davis, D.R. and J.I. Dingel (2019). A spatial knowledge economy. *American Economic Review*, 109(1), 153–170.

Diamond, R. (2016). The determinants and welfare implications of US workers' diverging location choices by skill: 1980–2000. *American Economic Review*, 106(3), 479–524.

Diodato, D., F. Neffke and N. O'Clery (2018). Why do industries coagglomerate? How Marshallian externalities differ by industry and have evolved over time. *Journal of Urban Economics*, 106, 1–26.

Duranton, G. and D. Puga (2005). From sectoral to functional urban specialisation. *Journal of Urban Economics*, 57(2), 343–370.

Feldman, M., J. Francis and J. Bercovitz (2005). Creating a cluster while building a firm: entrepreneurs and the formation of industrial clusters. *Regional Studies*, 39(1), 129–141.

Florida, R. (2017). *The New Urban Crisis*. New York: Basic Books.

Frenken, K., F. Van Oort and T. Verburg (2007). Related variety, unrelated variety and regional economic growth. *Regional Studies*, 41(5), 685–697.

Glaeser, E.L. and D.C. Maré (2001). Cities and skills. *Journal of Labor Economics*, 19(2), 316–342.

Hardin, J.W. (2008). North Carolina's Research Triangle Park. Overview, history, success factors and lessons learned. In Hulsink, W. and H. Dons (eds), *Pathways to High-Tech Valleys and Research Triangles*. Wageningen UR Frontis Series, 24. Dordrecht: Springer, 27–51.

Hershberg, E., K. Nabeshima and S. Yusuf (2007). Opening the ivory tower to business: university–industry linkages and the development of knowledge-intensive clusters in Asian cities. *World Development*, 35(6), 931–940.

Iammarino, S. and P. McCann (2018). Network geographies and geographical networks: co-dependence and co-evolution of multinational enterprises and space. In Clark, G.L., M.P. Feldman, M.S. Gertler and D. Wójcik (eds), *The New Oxford Handbook of Economic Geography*. Oxford: Oxford University Press.

Jacobs, J. (1961). *The Death and Life of Great American Cities*. New York: Random House.

Kemeny, T. and M. Storper (2019). Superstar Cities and Left Behind Places: Disruptive Innovation, Labor Demand and Interregional Inequality. Paper presented at the 40th Annual Meeting of the Italian Regional Science Association, L'Aquila, Italy, September.

Krugman, P. (1991). Increasing returns and economic geography. *Journal of Political Economy*, 99(3), 483–499.

Lécuyer, C. (2006). *Making Silicon Valley: Innovation and the Growth of High Tech*, 1930–1970. Cambridge, MA: MIT Press.

Lorenzen, M. and R. Mudambi (2013). Clusters, connectivity and catch-up: Bollywood and Bangalore in the global economy. *Journal of Economic Geography*, 13, 501–534. doi.org/10.1093/jeg/lbs017

Mazzucato, M. (2015). *The Entrepreneurial State: Debunking Public vs. Private Sector Myths*. London: Anthem Press.

Mokyr, J. (2005). The intellectual origins of modern economic growth. *The Journal of Economic History*, 65(2), 285–351.

Moretti, E. (2012). *The New Geography of Jobs*. Boston, MA: Houghton Mifflin Harcourt.

Nieto, M.J. and A. Rodríguez (2011). Offshoring of R&D: looking abroad to improve innovation performance. *Journal of International Business Studies*, 42, 345–361.

Rodriguez-Pose, A. (2018). The revenge of the places that don't matter (and what to do about it). *Cambridge Journal of Regions, Economy and Society* 11(1), 189–209.

Saxenian, A. (1994). Regional networks: industrial adaptation in Silicon Valley and route 128. *Cityscape*, 2(2), 41–60.

Saxenian, A. (1999). *Silicon Valley's New Immigrant Entrepreneurs*. San Francisco, CA: Public Policy Institute of California.

Scott, A.J. and M. Storper (1987). High technology industry and regional development: a theoretical critique and reconstruction. *International Social Science Journal*, 112, 215–232.

Storper, M. (2018). Regional innovation transitions. In Glückler, J., R. Suddaby and R. Lenz (eds), *Knowledge and Institutions*. Frankfurt: Springer, 197–225.

WIPO (2015). *World Intellectual Property Report 2015. Breakthrough Innovation and Economic Growth*. Geneva: WIPO.

WIPO (2017). *World Intellectual Property Report 2017. Intangible Capital in Global Value Chains*. Geneva: WIPO.

The top 10
collaborative
hotspots of the
world account
for 26% of
all international
co-inventions.

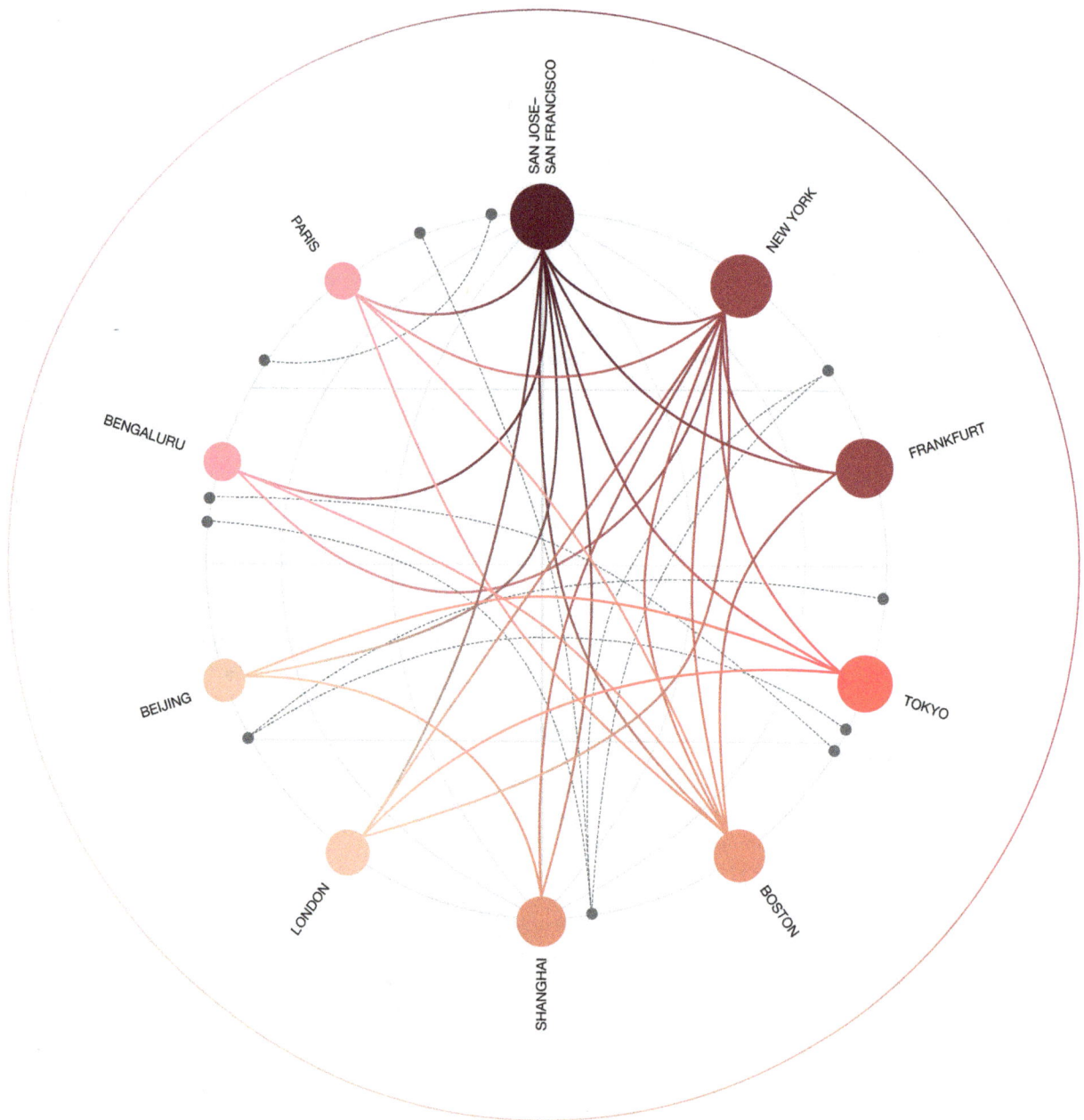

Chapter 2

Global networks of innovation hotspots

For much of the 20th century, multinational companies (MNCs) from high-income countries restricted their foreign-based research and development (R&D) operations to other rich economies, notably the U.S., Western European countries and, later, Japan. This was in marked contrast to the trend in manufacturing activities, which saw increasing outsourcing from richer to middle-income and developing economies.[1]

Starting in the 1980s and 1990s, the situation changed. The creation of new scientific and technological knowledge increasingly required interaction between institutions and organizations, whether public or private, national or multinational, irrespective of their location. Gradually, China, India, Eastern Europe and other middle-income economies gained in importance both as targets for R&D-oriented foreign direct investment (FDI) by multinational firms and as sources of new knowledge.

The rising need for complex and specialized knowledge and technological interaction at both national and international level has resulted – paradoxically – in both geographical concentration and dispersion of innovation creation, as highlighted in Chapter 1. On the one hand, organizations have sought to locate innovation activities and interactions wherever high quality and lower costs are available. On the other, market forces, economies of scale and the need for more face-to-face communication and multidisciplinary interaction, because of the complexity of the interactions, have pulled in the direction of geographical proximity.

Global innovation networks have been a key centrifugal force in the geographical distribution of knowledge-creation activities. Knowledge-seeking FDI does not target whole countries, but specific locations within them. Most international collaborations, investments or movements of skilled workers occur between specific knowledge-production centers. But global innovation networks do not merely span frontiers, they link specific locations within countries and reinforce the national prominence of these locations; within national borders, inter-regional innovation subnetworks coexist with global ones.

In view of these considerations, it is crucial to understand empirically the geographical concentration and spread of the world's scientific and technical knowledge production and interactions. This requires fine-grained mapping of innovation activities within national borders and how these contribute to the worldwide dispersion of knowledge exchanges. In particular, it is important to examine whether the growth of national knowledge-production centers or hubs results in an overall increase in international collaboration and investment or whether they simply suck-in innovative activities to the detriment of other areas in the country or beyond in a zero-sum game. This may be especially relevant for developing economies, whose national innovation systems may become less dependent on the R&D operations of foreign MNCs, thanks both to the strengthening of local firms and the implementation of specific public policies to promote local innovation, either substituting or leveraging their national and international collaborations.

Moreover, the globalization of knowledge produces imbalances in the distribution of innovative activities within countries. As knowledge-production centers worldwide gain in importance and intensify their exchanges, cities and regions that do not participate in such exchanges risk being marginalized (see Chapter 5).

This chapter documents the evolution of global knowledge-creating interactions and how the centrifugal and centripetal forces described in Chapter 1 generate global networks of extremely concentrated innovation hotspots and specialized niche clusters. It uses a novel database of geocoded scientific publication – scientific articles and conference proceedings – and patent data to track developments (see Box 2.1) and emphasize a series of long-term trends, starting from the mid-1970s.

The chapter is organized in four sections. The first section examines how internationalized the production of scientific and technological knowledge has become, with a focus on the rise in the participation of middle-income countries, notably China. It also provides complementary evidence on how knowledge production is becoming increasingly concentrated geographically by identifying the main innovation agglomerations – hotspots and clusters – within each country. The second section analyzes the scientific and technological interactions between countries, providing further evidence for the globalization of innovation. It highlights the role of international knowledge outsourcing by companies as a driving force behind the development of global innovation networks. The third section explores to what extent the two types of agglomerations concur to form an innovation network that is properly global. The final section spells out the chapter's main findings.

Box 2.1 Patent and scientific publication geocoded data

Patent data

The patent data used in this report cover all patent documents – granted or not – filed from 1970 to 2017 in all patent offices worldwide and available in the European Patent Office's (EPO) PATSTAT database and WIPO's Patent Cooperation Treaty (PCT) collections. The unit of analysis is the first filing for a set of patent documents filed in one or more countries and claiming the same invention. Each set containing one first and, potentially, several subsequent filings is defined as a patent family. In the analysis, patent families are split into those oriented internationally and those oriented only domestically. Internationally-oriented patent families refer to applicants seeking patent protection in at least one jurisdiction other than their country of residence. These include patent families containing only patent documents filed at the EPO or through the PCT. Conversely, domestic patent families refer only to filings in a home country, for instance, a Japan-based applicant filing only at the Japan Patent Office.

As far as possible, the geocoding – attributing the geographical coordinates to a given location – relates to the inventor's address based on the best available data source within a patent family.[2] Many addresses are geocoded at a very precise level – i.e., street or block – but others only at the postal code or other sub-city level. To remain internationally comparable, but also due to the limited coverage of inventors' addresses in some national collections, the clustering analysis relies only on internationally-oriented patents.

Scientific publication data

The scientific publication data used in this report comes from records from 1998 to 2017 in the Science Citation Index Expanded (SCIE) of the Web of Science, the citation database operated by the Clarivate Analytics company. The analysis focuses on observations referring to scientific articles and conference proceedings, which are the bulk of these data.

2.1   The two sides of global knowledge production

The accelerating international spread of knowledge creation

Where does knowledge production take place? Is the geographical spread of such output different to that of other economic activities? Empirical evidence indicates that activities related to knowledge production – such as R&D expenditure, patent generation or scientific publication – are typically more geographically concentrated within countries than is the case for other key economic activities, the overall population, trade or FDI. Despite this higher concentration, the global tendency is for the degree of international geographic dispersal of innovation over time.[3]

For most of the period from 1970 to 2000 only three countries – namely, the U.S., Japan and Germany – accounted for two-thirds of all patenting activity worldwide (Figure 2.1). Adding the remaining Western European economies – particularly, the U.K., France, Switzerland and Italy – takes the figure to around 90 percent.

Still, the rest of the world's share in the production of new technologies, as reflected in the number of patents, slowly rose over the three decades, mostly at the expense of several Western European economies. The rest of the world passed from less than 6 percent at the beginning of the 1970s to more than 13 percent in the early 2000s. And only a fraction of this spread was due to the Republic of Korea and China.

In the last two decades, the trend has accelerated remarkably for both technological (patents) and scientific outcomes. The rest of the world accounts for almost one-third of all patenting activity in the decade starting in 2010. Published scientific data has spread

Two decades of accelerated spread of knowledge production

Figure 2.1 Evolution of patenting (top) and publication share (bottom) by top economies

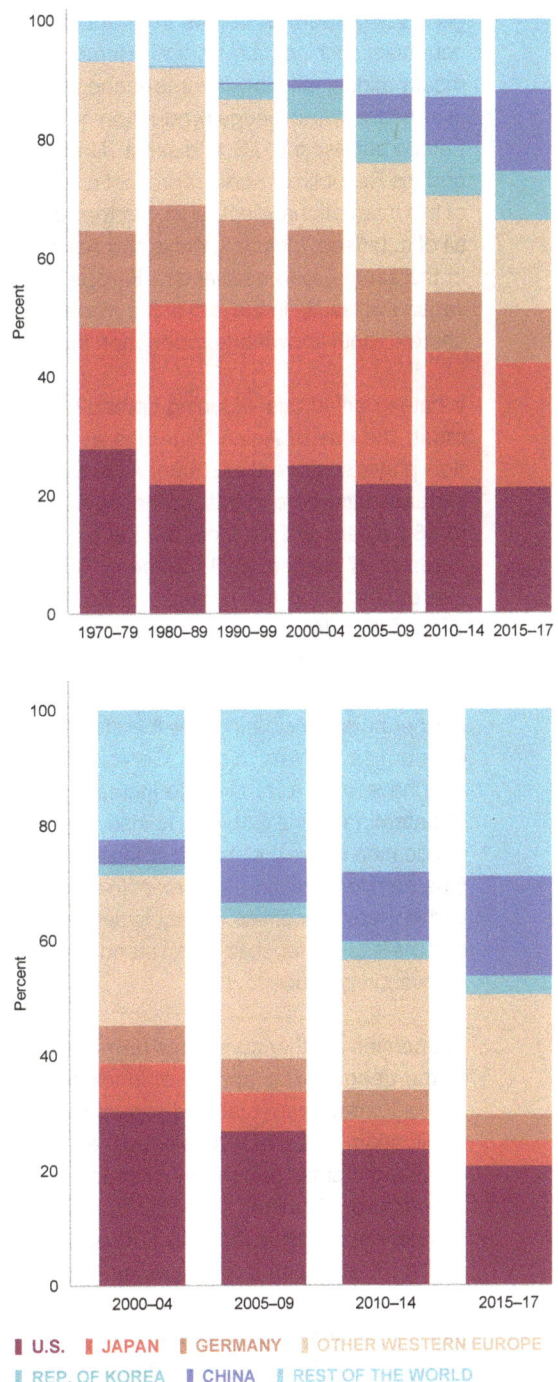

Legend: U.S. | JAPAN | GERMANY | OTHER WESTERN EUROPE | REP. OF KOREA | CHINA | REST OF THE WORLD

Source: WIPO based on PATSTAT, PCT and Web of Science data (see Technical Notes).
Notes: Other Western Europe excludes Germany. Patent figures based on international patent families.

even more widely, with the rest of the world going from less than a quarter of all scientific publication to around half in roughly the same period.

During this period, the rest of the world – a heterogeneous group that ranges from some high-income countries, such as Canada or the Republic of Korea, to mostly middle- and low-income economies – outpaced in its share of knowledge production not only Western Europe but also the U.S. and Japan. Undeniably, China and the Republic of Korea represent a substantial part of this international dispersion, but they do not explain all of it. Indeed, including these two Asian economies in the same group as Western Europe, the U.S. and Japan still results in the rest of the world increasing its share of both knowledge production indicators.

What is behind this widening spread? First and foremost, the rise of Asian countries as global innovation players: since the 2000s, Asia as a whole has increased its share of total patenting from 32 percent to 48 percent and its share of total scientific publishing from 17 percent to 36 percent. This reflects the rise of China and the Republic of Korea and comes despite the relative decline in Japan's share of patents and publications.

Furthermore, considering their low starting point, many economies in West, South, Central and Southeast Asia have seen a remarkable increase in their share of patenting (Table 2.1). This is also true for scientific publication where the share increased from more than 5 percent to more than 10 percent in only two decades. Within these economies, Turkey, Israel, India, Singapore and the Islamic Republic of Iran stand out as the largest innovation producers.

Economies in other continents have also contributed to the geographical spread of innovation in the last two decades, especially with respect to scientific publication. Oceania – mostly pushed by Australia – has seen a small but steady increase in its share of scientific publication, although its share of patents has decreased since the early 2000s. Latin American and the Caribbean economies have experienced a 36 percent increase in their share of scientific publication in the last two decades and doubled their share of patents since the 1970s, although from a very low starting point. African countries had a high relative increase in share of scientific publication, but their already very small patent share fell. At the outset of this period, Central and Eastern European countries – led by the

Russian Federation – held the largest shares of both innovation outcomes after North America, Western Europe and East Asia. However, these economies subsequently suffered a sharp drop in their share of patents and a small one in scientific publishing.

Each of these regions also reveals high concentration within a few countries, especially for patents. This is the case of India and the Islamic Republic of Iran in South and Central Asia; Singapore in Southeast Asia; the Russian Federation and Poland in Central and Eastern Europe; Brazil and Mexico in Latin America; Israel and Turkey in the Middle East; Australia in Oceania; and Egypt and South Africa in Africa. These regional leaders account for much of the little patenting activity happening in their subcontinents. They also concentrate much of the scientific publishing, particularly Brazil in Latin America and India and the Islamic Republic of Iran in South and Central Asia.

Innovations can differ in their scientific and technological value. Seminal and disruptive scientific and technological outputs influence subsequent ones and, as a result, are more cited. High-income economies spend more on producing such seminal innovative outputs. Even if an imperfect indicator of economic value, citations of patents and scientific publication also reflect how visible and appreciated the research is to other innovators and therefore how valuable.

Both patent and scientific publication data indicate that innovation is more concentrated when it is more valuable (more cited) (Figure 2.2). In particular, the U.S. holds a disproportionate share of top-cited patents and scientific publication, dwarfing the shares of other economies. Still, even here there is a trend toward dispersion. In the last two decades, the U.S., Japan and Western Europe have seen less overall concentration of more valuable innovation outcomes. Again, China and the Republic of Korea stand out. But other economies also contributed to the spread of top-cited innovation, even if the spread has not been as fast as for less cited scientific publication and patents.

In sum, China seems to largely explain the worldwide spread of scientific and technological innovation activities in the last two decades, although many other countries have contributed to this trend. But many lower-income countries are systematically excluded from international innovation.[4] Curiously, the recent rapid rise of China and, to a lesser extent, that of the Republic of Korea, also signifies a global reconcentration of

Asia's share in innovation rises strongly

Table 2.1 Evolution of patenting and scientific publishing, by regions and selected countries

Region (country)	Patents							Publications			
	1970–79	1980–89	1990–99	2000–04	2005–09	2010–14	2015–17	2000–04	2005–09	2010–14	2015–17
SCSE Asia	0.1%	0.1%	0.6%	1.0%	1.6%	2.1%	2.0%	3.2%	4.8%	6.7%	7.5%
India	0.0%	0.0%	0.1%	0.5%	1.0%	1.4%	1.3%	2.0%	2.6%	3.2%	3.5%
Singapore	0.0%	0.0%	0.1%	0.3%	0.4%	0.4%	0.3%	0.4%	0.5%	0.5%	0.5%
CEE	3.2%	3.8%	4.9%	1.1%	1.3%	1.4%	1.3%	5.8%	5.9%	5.8%	5.6%
Russian Federation	0.7%	1.4%	2.7%	0.4%	0.5%	0.5%	0.4%	2.4%	1.9%	1.7%	1.8%
Poland	0.2%	0.1%	0.1%	0.1%	0.1%	0.2%	0.2%	1.1%	1.3%	1.3%	1.3%
LAC	0.3%	0.3%	0.3%	0.4%	0.5%	0.6%	0.6%	3.0%	3.5%	4.0%	4.0%
Brazil	0.1%	0.1%	0.1%	0.2%	0.2%	0.3%	0.3%	1.5%	2.0%	2.3%	2.3%
Western Asia	0.3%	0.3%	0.7%	1.1%	1.4%	1.6%	1.7%	2.3%	2.8%	3.0%	3.1%
Turkey	0.0%	0.0%	0.0%	0.1%	0.2%	0.3%	0.4%	1.0%	1.5%	1.7%	1.7%
Israel	0.2%	0.3%	0.6%	0.9%	1.2%	1.1%	1.1%	0.9%	0.8%	0.6%	0.6%
Oceania	0.8%	1.1%	1.1%	1.4%	1.3%	0.9%	0.9%	2.4%	2.4%	2.6%	2.8%
Australia	0.7%	1.0%	1.0%	1.2%	1.1%	0.8%	0.8%	2.0%	2.1%	2.3%	2.5%
Africa	0.3%	0.2%	0.2%	0.3%	0.2%	0.2%	0.2%	1.1%	1.3%	1.6%	1.8%
Egypt	0.0%	0.0%	0.0%	0.0%	0.0%	0.0%	0.0%	0.3%	0.3%	0.4%	0.5%
South Africa	0.2%	0.2%	0.2%	0.2%	0.2%	0.1%	0.1%	0.3%	0.4%	0.4%	0.4%
Total	4.8%	5.8%	7.8%	5.3%	6.4%	6.8%	6.7%	17.8%	20.7%	23.6%	24.9%

Source: WIPO based on PATSTAT, PCT and Web of Science data (see Technical Notes).
Notes: CEE = Central and Eastern Europe; LAC = Latin America and the Caribbean; SCSE Asia = South, Central and Southeast Asia. Patent figures based on international patent families.

innovation production shares, but in different locations. This reconcentration coincides with a similar trend observed for R&D expenditure shares after 2008 at the onset of the Great Recession, with both China and the Republic of Korea increasing their share of global R&D expenditure. All in all, innovation production has increased in volume and spread more globally, but there is still a limited set of countries that produces the bulk of it.

Increasing concentration: a local affair

The geographical distribution of inventive and scientific activities within each country is uneven. In the context of the increase of innovation production and its international spread, an interesting phenomenon occurs – there is no clear evidence that knowledge production has spread within countries.

A few administrative areas in each economy often accumulate the lion's share of scientific and technological production (Table 2.2). In the U.S., three out of

50 states concentrate almost 40 percent of inventive production (patents) and almost 30 percent of scientific production (publication). And the U.S. is the least geographically concentrated among the largest economies. In Japan, three out of 47 prefectures concentrate 56 percent of patents and 35 percent of scientific publication. In China, three out of 33 provinces gather 60 percent of patents and almost 40 percent of scientific publication. In Europe, concentration is higher, but the number of regions is smaller. In Germany, three out of 16 states concentrate two-thirds of the patents and half the scientific publication. Similarly, three out of 18 French regions accumulate about 60 percent of knowledge production.

Regional concentration of patents within these economies has increased over the last decade. In all cases but France, the top three regions (Table 2.2) accumulate more patents in the latter 2011–2015 period, evidencing within-country concentration, not dispersion. Interestingly, the top three regions are not necessarily the same in the two periods, but the changes are small. For scientific publication, however, the

More the value, more the concentration

Figure 2.2 Evolution of top-cited patents (left) and scientific publications (right) by top economies and regions

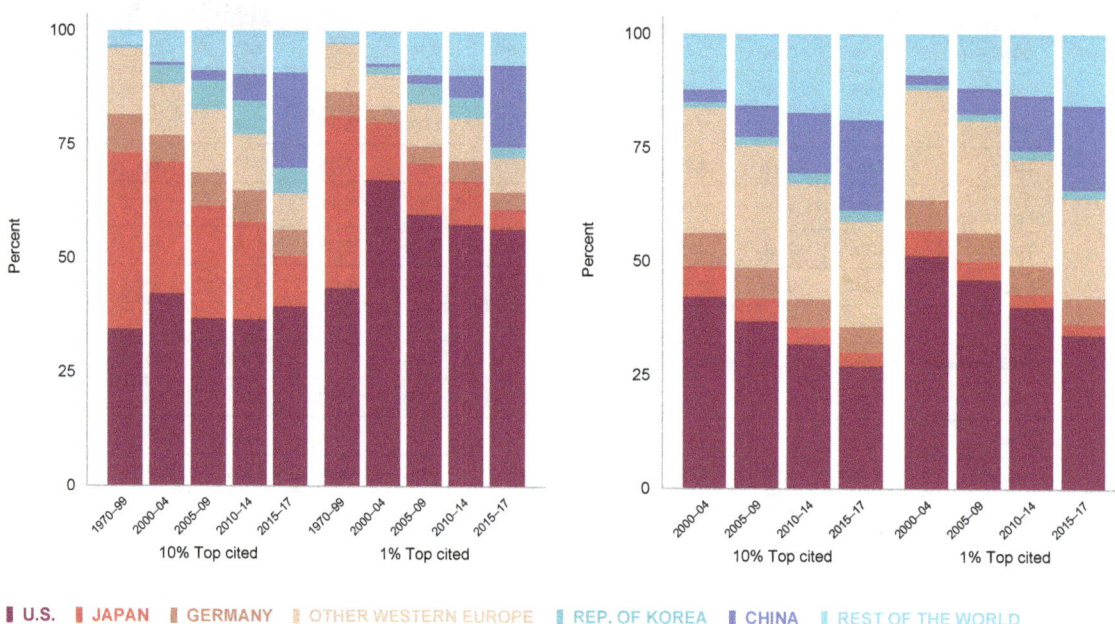

U.S. | JAPAN | GERMANY | OTHER WESTERN EUROPE | REP. OF KOREA | CHINA | REST OF THE WORLD

Source: WIPO based on PATSTAT, PCT and Web of Science data (see Technical Notes).
Notes: Patent figures based on international patent families.

Shares of top innovation subnational regions within countries

Table 2.2 Top three large administrative areas in patent and scientific publication concentration by period, selected countries

Country (level)	Patents 1991–95	%	2011–15	%	Publications 2001–05	%	2011–15	%
China (provinces)	Beijing Guangdong Shanghai	42.3	Guangdong Beijing Jiangsu	60.3	Beijing Shanghai Jiangsu	45.5	Beijing Shanghai Jiangsu	39.4
Germany (states)	Baden-Württemberg Bayern Nordrhein-Westfalen	63.8	Bayern Baden-Württemberg Nordrhein-Westfalen	65.0	Bayern Nordrhein-Westfalen Baden-Württemberg	49.4	Nordrhein-Westfalen Baden-Württemberg Bayern	50.0
France (regions)	Île-de-France Auvergne-Rhône-Alpes Grand Est	64.1	Île-de-France Auvergne-Rhône-Alpes Occitanie	59.9	Île-de-France Auvergne-Rhône-Alpes Occitanie	63.1	Île-de-France Auvergne-Rhône-Alpes Occitanie	62.7
U.K. (counties)	Greater London Hertfordshire Cambridgeshire	17.9	Greater London Cambridgeshire Oxfordshire	23.9	Greater London Cambridgeshire Oxfordshire	35.8	Greater London Oxfordshire Cambridgeshire	38.7
India (states)	Maharashtra Karnataka Telangana	51.6	Karnataka Maharashtra Telangana	60.1	Maharashtra Tamil Nadu NCT of Delhi	36.4	Tamil Nadu Maharashtra NCT of Delhi	36.1
Japan (prefecture)	Tokyo Kanagawa Osaka	51.5	Tokyo Kanagawa Osaka	56.3	Tokyo Osaka Ibaraki	35.8	Tokyo Osaka Aichi	35.4
U.S. (states)	California New York Texas	30.8	California New York Texas	36.5	California New York Massachusetts	28.2	California Massachusetts New York	28.7

Source: WIPO based on PATSTAT, PCT and Web of Science data.
Notes: Patents and scientific publications were attributed to regions according to the geocoded addresses of inventors and affiliations of authors. See Box 2.1 and the Technical Notes. Patent figures based on international patent families.

top three regions show little change during the two periods shown in the figure. China's top three provinces are the only ones to evidence some noticeable geographical spread of scientific production. The fact that the location and budget of academic institutions are the result of complex and long decision-making processes can partially explain these stable scientific publication trends.

These trends apply not only to the main innovative economies described in the previous section. In most countries, a few areas have become truly innovation hotspots, way ahead of the rest of the country. This is the case in India, Australia and several countries in Southeast Asia, the Middle East, Latin America and Africa.

However, there are substantial difficulties – common to all questions of economic geography – in making comparisons across countries based on existing subnational administrative areas. Administrative areas can differ markedly in size, population and density of innovative activity, all of which complicate comparison. In addition, the administrative borders may not coincide with the limits of the innovation agglomeration or hub.[5] A given administrative area may even encompass two or more agglomerations, or the agglomeration or agglomerations may span several administrative areas, even crossing country borders.

A vast literature in spatial analysis documents this well-known issue, which goes under the name of the modifiable areal unit problem (MAUP) and its resulting statistical distortions.[6] The solution requires creating ad hoc comparable areas that can be used in place of administrative ones. Box 2.2 provides a detailed explanation of the solution.

Box 2.2
How to measure local agglomerations of innovation

The report aims to provide an internationally comparable measure of agglomeration of scientific and technological activities. It makes use of all internationally-oriented patents from 1976 to 2015 and all scientific publications from 1998 to 2017 to identify the main geographical concentration of innovation.

The agglomerations are organically defined using a cluster identification approach based on density-based algorithms from the economic geography literature.[7] In a nutshell, the report uses the DBSCAN – *Density-based spatial clustering of applications with noise* – clustering algorithm to identify "clusters" separately from the geocoded patent and scientific publication data. The borders of each scientific publication and patent agglomeration are determined using a concave polygon approach. The overlapping polygons are merged keeping only the outer borders of all concerned agglomerations. The resulting outer areas are referred to as **global innovation hotspots (GIHs)** or, more plainly, **hotspots**. To allow for scientific and technological specialization, the above method is repeated for 25 subsamples of the same publication and patent data, which refer to 12 scientific fields and 13 technological ones, respectively.[8] Only the resulting polygons of these 25 iterations not contained within a hotspot are kept. From these, the overlapping polygons are merged in the same way as for hotspots. The final outer areas are referred to as **specialized niche clusters (SNCs)** or, more plainly, **niche clusters**.

By definition, the resulting areas: (1) are **internationally comparable**, i.e., the same scientific publication or patent (specialized) density would have determined the same hotspot (cluster) anywhere in the world; (2) can have **different scientific and technological density**, i.e., hotspots and niche clusters need only scientific publication or patent high concentration, but not necessarily both; (3) have **different specialization density**, i.e., niche clusters are defined with lower density thresholds than hotspots; (4) are **distinct geographical areas**, i.e., the polygons are non-overlapping within and across hotspots and niche clusters; and (5) have **non-predefined boundaries**, i.e., hotspots and niche clusters can have different sizes and include more than one city, state/province or country.

Based on this methodology, there are 174 global innovation hotspots and 313 specialized niche clusters worldwide, which together concentrate 85 percent of all patents and 81 percent of all scientific articles and conference proceedings published worldwide. The contribution of niche clusters is relatively small. Of course, these also include collaborations – i.e., co-inventions and co-publication – with partners outside of these innovation-dense areas.

Population density does not ensure high innovation density

Figure 2.3 Patents and scientific articles in the top 35 largest cities

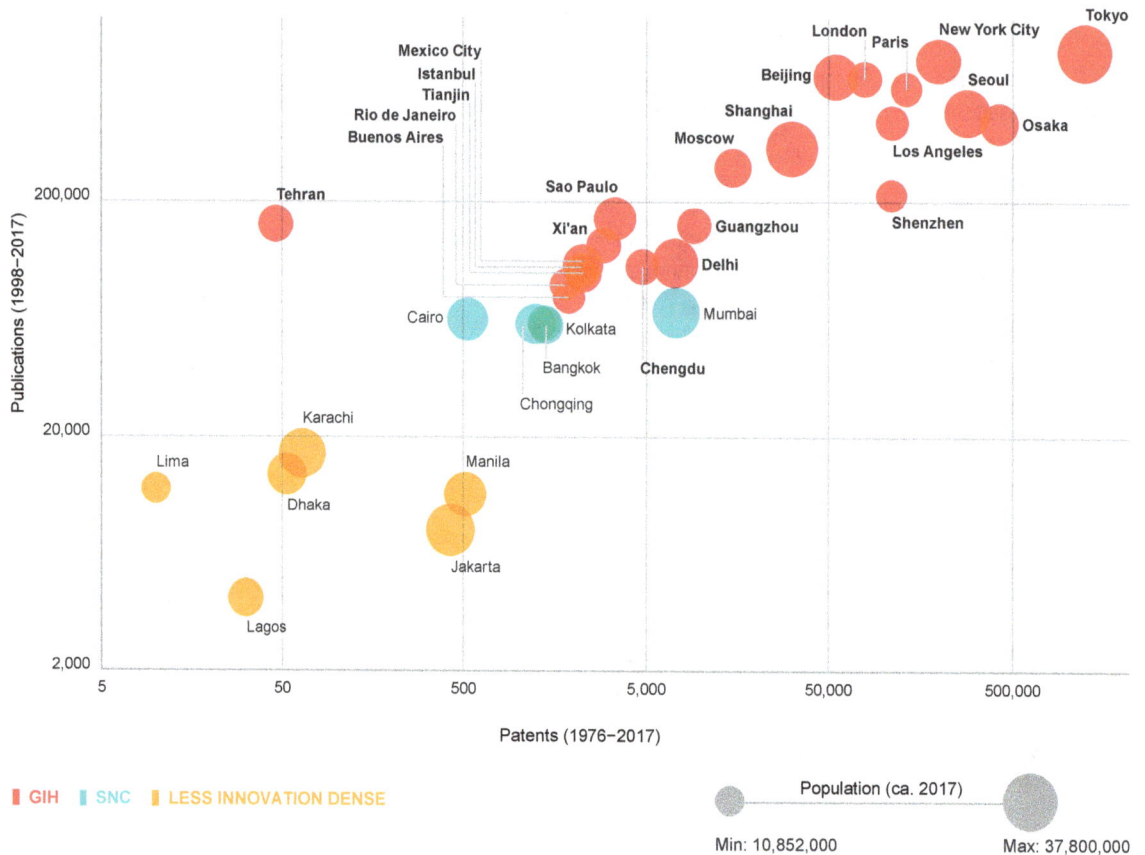

Source: WIPO based on PATSTAT, PCT and Web of Science data (see Boxes 2.1 and 2.2), and top cities from The City Mayors Foundation. Based on the 35 largest metropolitan populations in the list of largest cities in the world retrieved from The City Mayors Foundation, www.citymayors.com/statistics/largest-cities-population-125.html, September 2019.
Notes: Size of bubble refers to the metropolitan area population (circa 2017). Axis in logarithmic scale. Due to low scientific publication or patent values, Kinshasa and Shijiazhuang are omitted from the chart area. Patent figures based on international patent families.

To a great extent, these innovation-dense areas coincide with the large, urban, cosmopolitan and prosperous areas of the world. As noted, innovation is even more concentrated than general economic activity and population. For instance, only 22 out of the 35 most-populated metropolitan areas in the world are part of a global innovation hotspot (Figure 2.3). A huge disparity exists among those that are: Beijing, London, Los Angeles, New York, Seoul and Tokyo concentrate a large amount of both patents and scientific publishing, while Buenos Aires, Delhi, Istanbul, Mexico City, Moscow, São Paulo and Tehran, for example, are part of hotspots concentrating a fair, but appreciably lower, output of scientific articles and very few patents. Other highly populated urban centers have only enough innovation density in some specialized scientific or

technological fields. This is the case of the niche clusters found in Bangkok, Cairo, Chongqing and Kolkata, among others. Despite concentrating much of their national innovation output, several highly populated metropolitan areas – such as Jakarta, Karachi or Manila – do not generate sufficient innovation to classify as hosts of a hotspot or niche cluster.

On the other hand, less dense urban areas in many high-income and innovative countries can host high innovation density, especially in some specialized fields. These niche clusters – such as Ithaca in the U.S., Stavanger in Norway or Bern in Switzerland – are highly innovative due to the strong innovation footprint of local academic institutions, industries or, sometimes, a key company. In their specialized fields, these niche

Innovation density and urban density largely coincide

Figure 2.4 Worldwide distribution of innovation (GIHs and SNCs) and DMSP nightlight

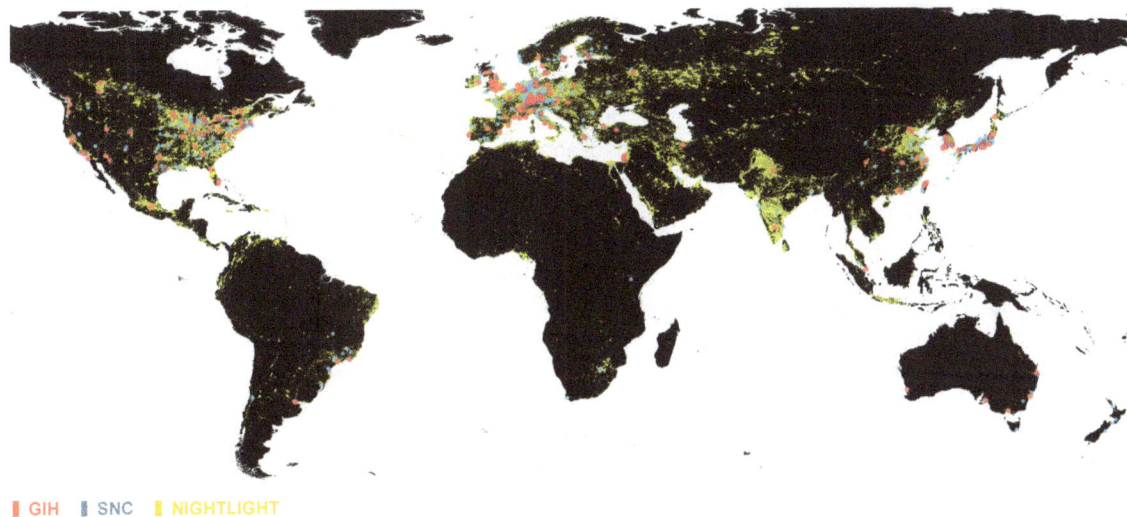

GIH   SNC   NIGHTLIGHT

North America, Western Europe and East Asia host most hubs

Figure 2.5 Global Innovation hotspots and specialized niche clusters, by region

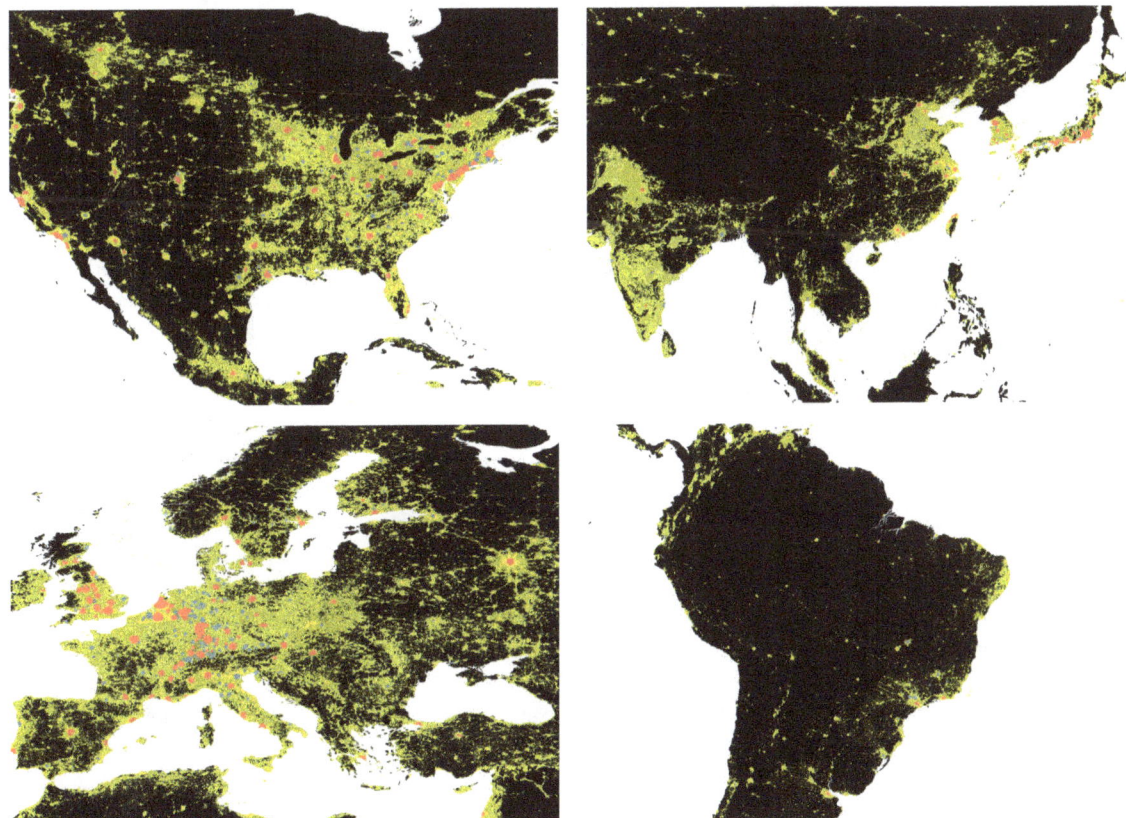

Source: WIPO based on PATSTAT, PCT and Web of Science data (see Boxes 2.1 and 2.2). Nightlight data from the U.S. National Oceanic and Atmospheric Administration's (NOAA) National Geophysical Data Center.
Note: DMSP = Defense Meteorological Satellite Program.

clusters outperform metropoles with much higher urban and overall innovation densities.

Figures 2.4 and 2.5 expand this comparison globally, based on the world distribution of nightlight as a proxy for urban-dense areas.[9] As shown in Figure 2.4, the nightlight is not well distributed across the world or within borders. Innovation follows a similar pattern of agglomeration, but it is even more geographically skewed. These agglomerations or hotspots – which are by definition denser in scientific knowledge or patent generation – typically coincide with the brightest – in terms of nightlight – areas in the world. Niche clusters also coincide with bright locations, although their specialist nature means the urban areas can be less dense.

Europe – particularly the west – has the most homogenous territorial distribution of nightlight and, not surprisingly, concentrates more than one-third of all global innovation hotspots and specialized niche clusters in the world. Despite this, there are still several illuminated areas without a corresponding innovation agglomeration. In Europe, Germany, the U.K. and France lead in quantity of innovation agglomerations, but even they have several dense urban areas without any corresponding scientific publication or patent density.

North America hosts more than a quarter of hotspots and niche clusters, mostly in dense urban areas along the east and west coasts. Most of the main cities in the center and south of the country also host innovation agglomerations; but many dense urban areas – particularly in the Midwest and southern U.S. states – do not have sufficient innovation to host a global innovation hotspot or niche cluster.

Asia hosts slightly more than a quarter of the total hotspots and niche clusters. Japan, China, the Republic of Korea and India account for the bulk of Asia's innovation agglomerations. In Japan, and to some degree the Republic of Korea, there is a high correspondence between nightlight and innovation agglomeration. Despite their numerous innovation agglomerations, China and India still have many dense urban areas with no corresponding innovation density.

The large continental territories of Oceania, Latin America and Africa host vast areas without dense urban locations. Within the former, Australia has a high co-location of urban and innovation-dense areas, with virtually no bright locations without a corresponding global innovation hotspot or niche cluster. On the

A few locations concentrate most inventive and scientific activities

Table 2.3 Concentration of patenting and publishing among GIHs and among less innovation-dense countries, 1998–2017

Top 30 hotspots (as share of all GIHs in the world)		
Hotspots (%)	30	**(17.2%)**
Countries (%)	16	**(47.1%)**
Patents (%)	3,234,850	**(69.2%)**
Scientific articles (%)	10,987,971	**(47.8%)**
Top 30 agglomerations in non-innovation dense countries		
Agglomerations (%)	30	**(5.0%)**
Countries (%)	24	**(14.4%)**
Patents (%)	11,491	**(64.1%)**
Scientific articles (%)	484,689	**(61.0%)**

Source: WIPO based on PATSTAT, PCT and Web of Science data (see Boxes 2.1 and 2.2).
Notes: Only data from 1998 to 2017 reported. Top 30 are calculated separately for patent and publication data. Top 30 agglomerations in non-innovation-dense countries are based on the same methodology described for GIHs in Box 2.2. Patent figures based on international patent families.

contrary, Africa and Latin America have mostly dense urban areas with no corresponding innovation density.

As shown in Table 2.3, the inventive and scientific activities across locations are highly skewed at all levels of innovation density. The 174 hotspots represent the most innovative-dense areas in the world; nonetheless, a limited number – mostly in high-income and middle-income countries – consistently produce most of the scientific and technological knowledge created within global innovation hotspots.

Only 30 hotspots in 16 different countries are responsible for the creation of almost 70 percent of the patents and around 50 percent of the scientific articles produced.

Very little inventive and scientific activity is produced outside the hotspots and niche clusters, and even less is produced outside the few countries hosting these. Indeed, there are more than 160 countries not hosting any hotspot or niche cluster. Even in these less innovation-dense areas, most of the knowledge produced

Persistent concentration of innovation in a few hotspots

Table 2.4 Top three GIH concentration, patents and publications, selected countries

Country	Patents					Publications				
	1991–95	%	2011–15	%		2001–05	%	2011–15	%	
China	Beijing Shanghai Shenzhen–Hong Kong	36.5	Shenzhen–Hong Kong Beijing Shanghai	52.2		Beijing Shanghai Nanjing	43.9	Beijing Shanghai Nanjing	35.8	
Germany	Frankfurt Cologne–Dusseldorf Stuttgart	37.4	Frankfurt Stuttgart Cologne–Dusseldorf	29.4		Frankfurt Cologne Berlin	34.4	Frankfurt Cologne Berlin	34.2	
France	Paris Lyon Grenoble	47.1	Paris Grenoble Lyon	42.8		Paris Lyon Grenoble	51.0	Paris Lyon Toulouse	49.4	
U.K.	London Manchester Cambridge	30.0	London Cambridge Oxford	35.0		London Cambridge Oxford	39.8	London Oxford Cambridge	41.8	
India	Bengaluru Mumbai Delhi	41.9	Bengaluru Hyderabad Delhi	46.2		Delhi Mumbai Bengaluru	27.7	Delhi Mumbai Kolkata	24.6	
Japan	Tokyo Osaka Nagoya	80.5	Tokyo Osaka Nagoya	83.4		Tokyo Osaka Nagoya	64.3	Tokyo Osaka Nagoya	64.8	
U.S.	New York City San Jose–San Francisco Boston	19.4	San Jose–San Francisco New York City Boston	23.4		New York Washington DC–Baltimore Boston	21.2	Boston New York Washington DC–Baltimore	21.4	

Source: WIPO based on PATSTAT, PCT and Web of Science data (see Boxes 2.1 and 2.2).
Notes: Patent figures based on international patent families.

is generated in just a few dense urban areas. Just 30 agglomerations located in only 24 different countries produce roughly 64 percent of patents and 61 percent of scientific articles within these non-innovation-dense countries (Table 2.3). Despite this concentration in a few agglomerations, the gap with the world's top hotspots is huge. The volume of patents and scientific publication of the top 30 agglomerations in less innovation-dense countries is only 0.4 percent and 4 percent, respectively, of that of the world's leading 30 hotspots.

But even within innovation-dense areas strong national differences emerge. Table 2.4 looks at the top three hotspots and niche clusters for selected countries in two different periods and the share of patenting and scientific publication they accumulate in their respective countries. First, the list of top three innovation-dense areas barely differs in time and between patents and scientific publication, showing the stability of the concentration phenomenon. Second, in all countries shown, the share the top three accumulates is quite high, ranging from around 20 percent up to more than 80 percent. Next, in the majority of countries the share of the top three patenting hotspots either remains quite stable or increases, showing that, within countries, inventive activities do not spread much geographically and in some cases even reconcentrate. Germany and, to a lesser extent, France are exceptions where the top

three patenting hotspots concentrate less inventive activity than two decades earlier.

Overall, concentration of scientific publication has also remained relatively stable at high rates. Within these selected economies, only China and, to a lesser extent, India show some tendency to dispersion, but their top three hotspots still hold at least a quarter and a third of all national scientific publication, respectively. Comparing publication and patents, it is interesting to observe (Table 2.4) how in certain countries, scientific publication is more concentrated than patents (which is not the general rule). This is the case of the U.K. and, to a lesser extent, France. Both countries host capital cities that are worldwide centers of scientific production and which lead the way in their respective countries.

2.2   Global networks of collaboration and sourcing

Just how globalized is collaboration?

The production of scientific and technological knowledge is increasingly collaborative. Already in 1998, teams produced the majority of scientific papers. By 2017, *lone wolf* scientists had become half as important

Increased collaborative innovation

Figure 2.6 Inventor (left) and scientific (right) team size, by period

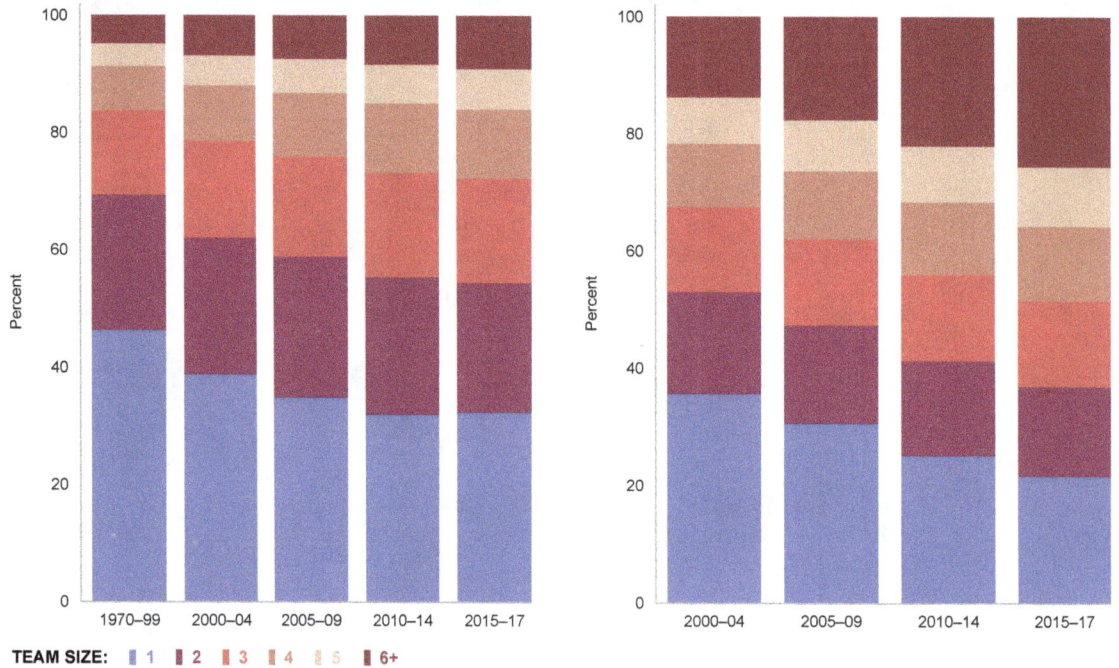

TEAM SIZE: 1 2 3 4 5 6+

Source: WIPO based on PATSTAT, PCT and Web of Science data (see Box 2.1).
Notes: Patent figures based on international patent families.

as they were 20 years before. The size of the teams is also increasing. In 2017, the average scientific paper required almost two more researchers – on average – than 20 years previously (see Figure 2.6). Moreover, the average team size has shifted upward across the board, making teams of six or more scientists the most common in the production of scientific knowledge.

Teams collaborating to achieve technological innovations (patents) are smaller but follow a similar increasing trend, with the average team number doubling since the early 1970s. By the mid-2010s, two thirds of inventions were collaborative efforts. All team sizes of inventors are increasing at the expense of single-inventor patents.

Teams are also increasingly international. As seen in Chapter 1, the forces pushing academia and companies to cross borders seeking partners for innovation are manifold. The scientific community has a long tradition of engaging in international collaboration. MNCs also seek efficiency gains from the international division of their R&D and through international collaboration. For instance, they may collaborate with R&D teams in other countries to: (i) adapt technologies to different market

needs; (ii) access a special talent pool; or (iii) simply lower the researcher costs.[10]

Increasingly, collaboration in scientific production (publication), as opposed to technological production, involves teams from organizations in at least two different countries (Figure 2.7). In only two decades, the share of international scientific collaboration practically increased by half, growing from 17 percent to 25 percent of scientific articles published. International co-inventorship is a much less frequent phenomenon. Despite the lower shares, however, collaborative international patent production showed an impressive growth trend until the second half of the 2000s, more than doubling from less than 5 percent to almost 11 percent. Since 2010, the share has fallen slightly.[11]

The fact that international teams account for a higher percentage of published scientific articles than of patents indicates once again that science production is more internationalized than technology production. Figure 2.8 breaks down data for international inventive and scientific teams by country, for the top innovative countries worldwide. With the exception of Japan and,

Collaboration for innovation is increasingly international

Figure 2.7 International co-inventorship and co-publishing, percent

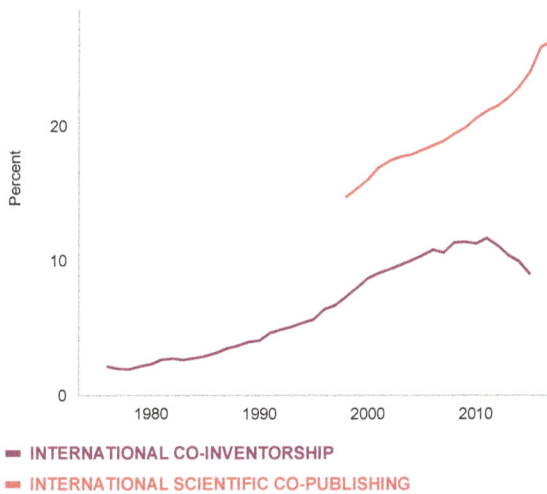

■ **INTERNATIONAL CO-INVENTORSHIP**
■ **INTERNATIONAL SCIENTIFIC CO-PUBLISHING**

Source: WIPO based on PATSTAT, PCT and Web of Science data (see Box 2.1).
Notes: Int. co-inventorship = share of patents with more than one inventor located in at least two countries; int. co-publications = share of scientific articles with more than one affiliation located in at least two countries. Patent figures based on international patent families.

to a lesser extent, the Republic of Korea, most top-filing countries show a large international co-inventorship share. The U.S. and Western European countries show mostly a rising trend. Smaller economies with internationally linked and dense urban and innovation areas – such as Switzerland – are very prone to engaging in international collaborations. India also shows a high rate of international co-inventorship. In East Asia's top economies things are different. Before the 2000s, the share of international co-inventorship in China was extraordinarily large, but the volume was small. Thereafter, when the volume of Chinese patenting picked up, the share of international co-inventorship dropped dramatically, becoming comparable to the very low shares of Japan and the Republic of Korea.

Trends for international co-publication reveal a very different picture. All main scientific publishing countries have larger shares of international co-publication than co-inventorship, with the exception of India. Moreover, these shares increased steadily over the period. However, the figures show East Asian countries being less internationally open than the U.S. and Western Europe when it comes to scientific publishing too.

Large economies are highly internationalized

Figure 2.8 International co-inventorship (left) and co-publication (right), by country

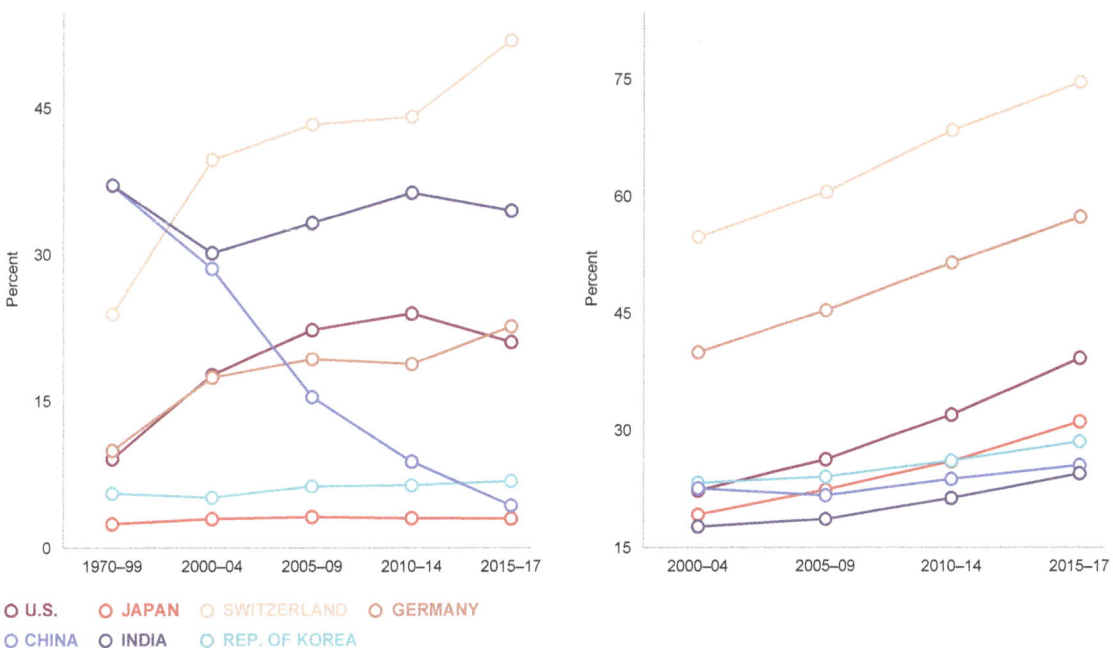

○ **U.S.**   ○ **JAPAN**   ○ SWITZERLAND   ○ **GERMANY**
○ **CHINA**   ○ **INDIA**   ○ REP. OF KOREA

Source: WIPO based on PATSTAT, PCT and Web of Science data (see Box 2.1).
Notes: Int. co-inventorship = share of patents with more than one inventor located in at least two countries; int. co-publication = share of scientific articles with more than one affiliation located in at least two countries. Patent figures based on international patent families.

Concentration and spread of international collaborations

Figure 2.9 International co-inventorship (left) and international co-publication (right) by country pairs, 1998–2002 and 2011–2015

International co-inventorship by country pairs, 1998–2002

International co-inventorship by country pairs, 2011–2015

— 2,000 ■ 5,000

Source: WIPO based on PATSTAT, PCT and Web of Science data (see Box 2.1).
Notes: Int. co-inventorship = share of patents with more than one inventor located in at least two countries; int. co-publication = share of scientific articles with more than one affiliation located in at least two countries. Only top 10 percent international links of each period reported. Bubbles report the share of links only for selected countries and regions. Patent figures based on international patent families.

International co-publication by country pairs, 1998–2002

International co-publication by country pairs, 2011–2015

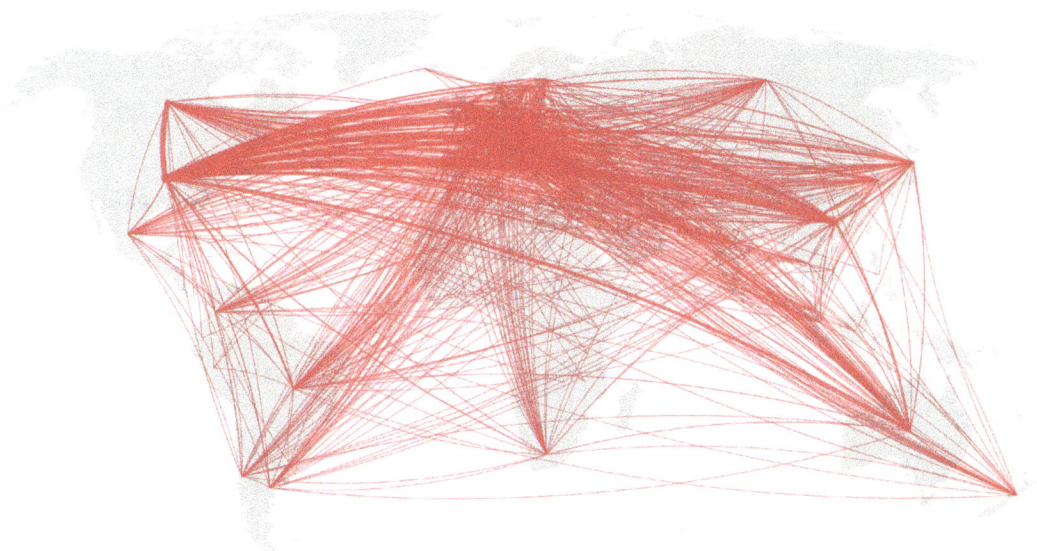

— 10,000   ■ 40,000

A select club of innovation outsourcing recipients

Figure 2.10 Companies' patenting with inventors in a different country (%), selected regions

1970–1989

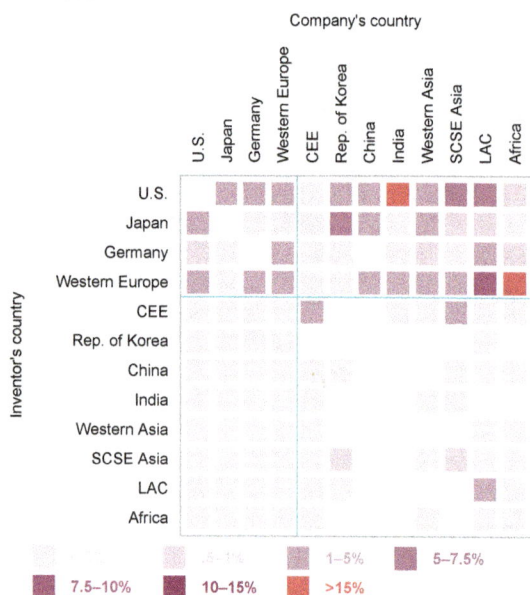

1990–1999

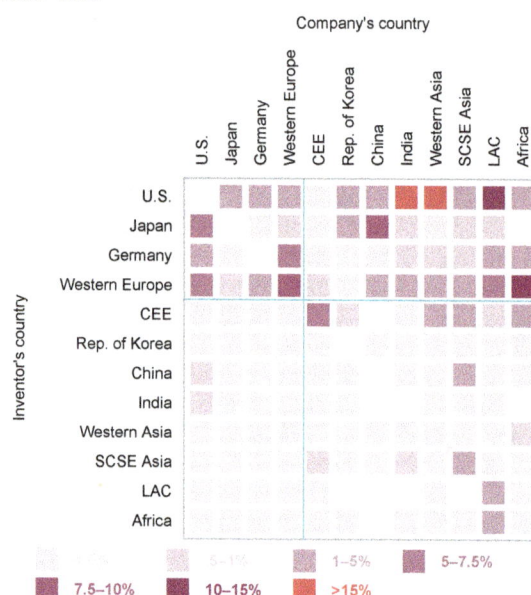

2000–2009

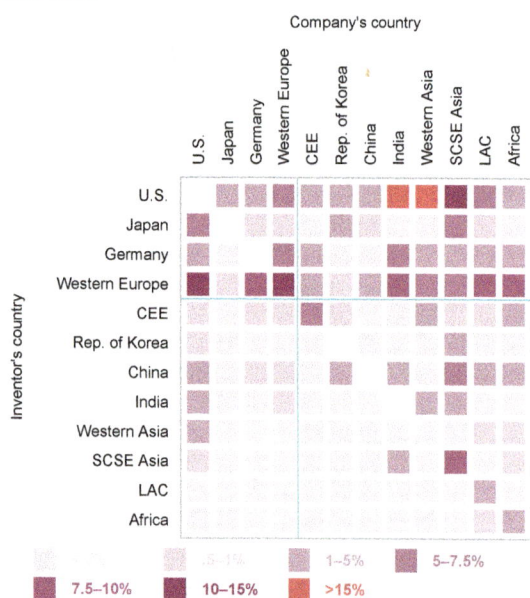

2010–2017

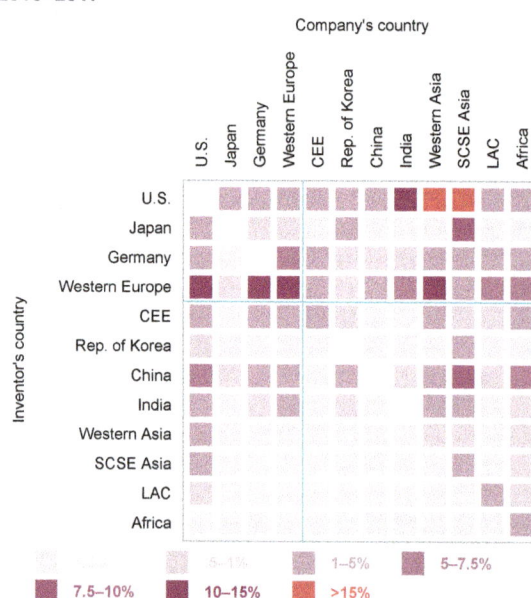

Source: WIPO based on PATSTAT and PCT data (see Technical Notes).
Notes: CEE = Central and Eastern Europe; LAC = Latin America and the Caribbean; SCSE Asia = Southern (excluding India), Central and Southeast Asia; These regions are closely based on the geographic regions from the U.N. Statistics Division's (UNSD) methodology (unstats.un.org, accessed March 2019). The only differences are that CEE includes all countries in the UNSD's Northern and Southern Europe categories not included in Western Europe and that SCSE includes Mongolia. Other Western Europe excludes Germany. Western Europe includes the 15 economies that were members of the EU prior to May 1, 2004, along with Andorra, Iceland, Liechtenstein, Malta, Monaco, Norway, San Marino and Switzerland. Patent figures based on international patent families.

Innovation within hotspots is more likely to be international

Figure 2.11 Percentage of international patent (left) and publication teams (right), inside vs. outside GIHs and SNCs

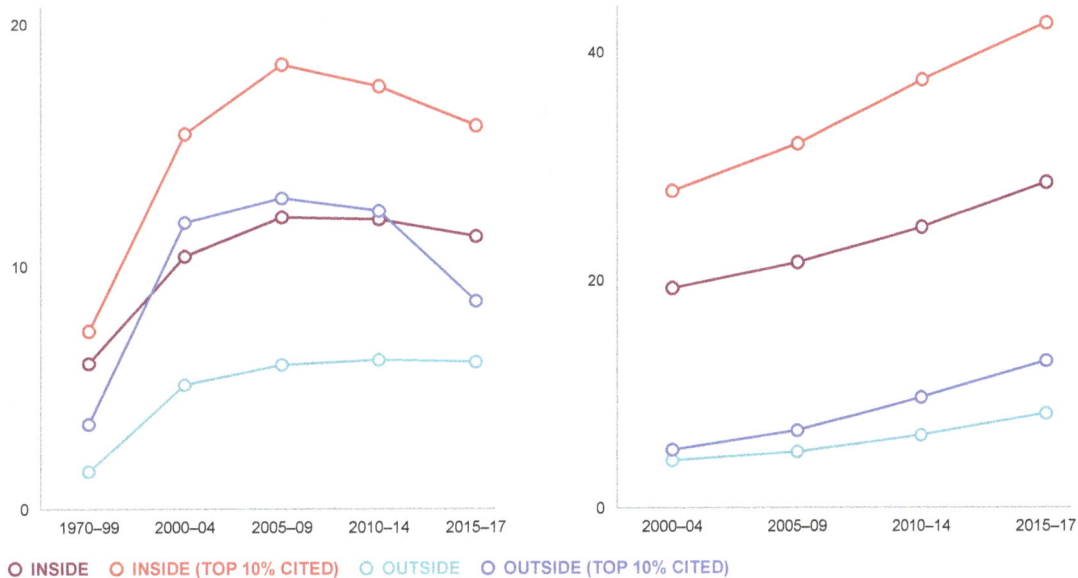

O **INSIDE**   O **INSIDE (TOP 10% CITED)**   O OUTSIDE   O **OUTSIDE (TOP 10% CITED)**

Source: WIPO based on PATSTAT, PCT and Web of Science data (see Boxes 2.1 and 2.2).
Notes: Patent figures based on international patent families.

International collaboration is also concentrated among a few main countries, although concentration is decreasing as new stakeholders enter the network (Figure 2.9). Scientific co-publishing only between the U.S., Western Europe and Japan accounted for 54 percent of all international co-authorships in 1998–2002 and 42 percent in 2011–2015. Co-inventorship among these three regions was 69 percent of overall international co-inventorship in 1998–2002 and 49 percent in 2011–2015.

The three are also involved in most of the collaboration undertaken with other economies (Figure 2.9). While collaboration within Europe is increasingly important, the U.S. is the main partner for most European countries. Canada and the U.S. – certainly due to geographic and cultural proximity – represent one of the strongest linkages in international collaboration networks at all times. Most of the remaining Canadian ties are with Western Europe, with few connections elsewhere. New entrants to these networks – such as China, India, Australia or Brazil – also mostly link with these three economies, typically with the U.S. and a few Western European countries, such as the U.K. and Germany.

Collaboration between countries and economies outside the U.S.–Western Europe–Japan triangle is much sparser. International co-inventions not involving

these central economies made up only 2 percent of all international co-inventions in 1998–2002 and 7 percent in 2011–2015. The subnetwork for scientific co-publication is slightly greater, starting from 5 percent in 1998–2002 and reaching 13 percent of all international ties in 2011–2015. Some larger economies outside the big three – such as China, India, Singapore and, to a lesser extent, Argentina, Australia, Brazil, Mexico and South Africa – have increased their participation in the subnetwork, although mostly for scientific co-publication. But their connections still mostly involve one of the big three – particularly the U.S. and Europe – rather another non-core location.

Overall, the collaboration trends suggest that the globalization of inventive activities mostly concern the U.S. and Western Europe along with China and India.

MNCs seek innovation further afield

From the late 1990s, as discussed in Chapter 1, MNCs increasingly started to outsource R&D activities to middle-income, developing economies, such as China, India and countries in Eastern Europe.[12] While initially they were adapting their technologies to local market needs, they slowly moved toward cutting-edge

Dispersion of scientific publication, reconcentration of patenting

Figure 2.12 GIHs' and SNCs' share of co-inventorship (left) and co-publication (right) interactions, by partner location

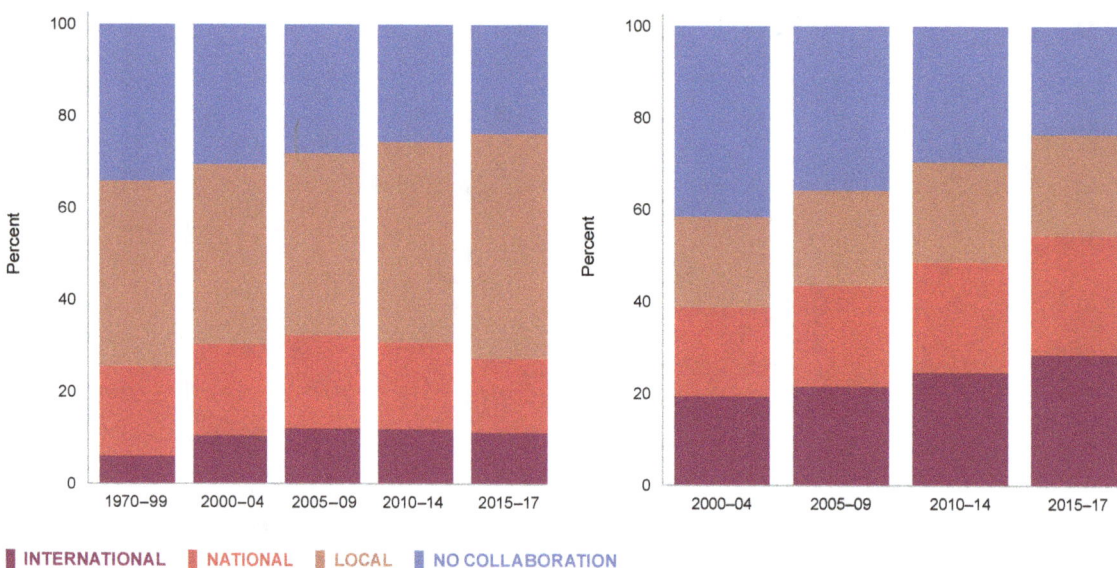

INTERNATIONAL   NATIONAL   LOCAL   NO COLLABORATION

Source: WIPO based on PATSTAT, PCT and Web of Science data (see Boxes 2.1 and 2.2).
Notes: Patent figures based on international patent families.

R&D – comparable to that undertaken in high-income economies – and developing new products for the worldwide market.[13] The dynamism of certain middle-income countries was a great attractor of R&D-related FDI, especially in India and China.

Outward R&D from the U.S. has increased more than fivefold in the last 25 years, with most of this innovation-related investment going to Germany, the U.K., Japan, Canada or France.[14] The trend for U.S. companies patenting with foreign inventors has followed a very similar pattern (Figure 2.10). In the 1970s and 1980s, only 9 percent of patents filed by U.S. companies had foreign inventors; by the 2010s, this share had risen to 38 percent. The outsourcing of technology from Canada, Japan and Western Europe kept growing until the early 2000s, before flattening. Since then, most of the increase in innovation outsourcing by U.S. companies has taken place elsewhere, mainly in China, India and, to a lesser extent, Israel. So, a large part of the U.S. knowledge-diversification strategy has involved expansion to non-high-income countries.

Internationalization of R&D has not been limited to U.S. companies, although no other large economy has been so open to such collaboration (Figure 2.10). Large

Western European economies – such as Germany, France and the U.K. – come the closest, while companies from the main East-Asian countries – i.e. Japan, the Republic of Korea and China – are far less internationalized.

There is a clear pattern of companies from all around the world increasing and widening their patenting with foreign inventors. However, as noted, most international patent sourcing still happens between companies and inventors from high-income economies, particularly from the U.S., Japan and Western Europe. Within these, Japanese companies are the least foreign-oriented, while U.S. companies rely considerably on Japanese inventors.

In the last two decades, China and the Republic of Korea have made a case to be added to this select group. They certainly have the volume of companies' patenting and of inventors participating in patenting by foreign companies. Companies from the Republic of Korea rely more intensively on Japanese and U.S. inventors than the latter do on Korean companies. Chinese companies used to rely intensively on Japanese inventors during the 1990s, but since the 2000s they have shifted to an increasingly nationally-oriented profile.

Differences in country trends, particularly for patents

Figure 2.13 GIHs' and SNCs' share of co-inventorship (top) and co-publication (bottom) interactions, by partner location, selected countries

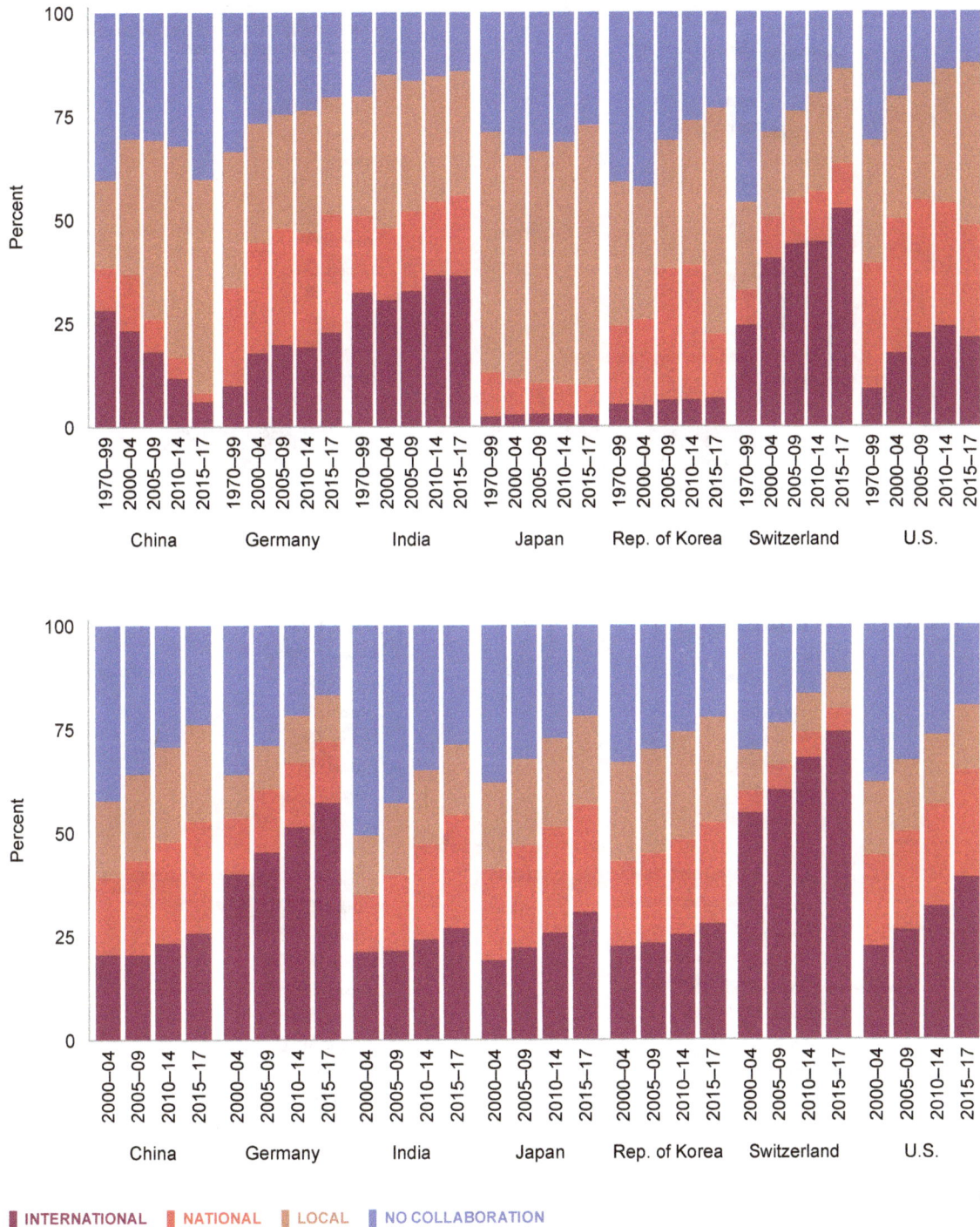

INTERNATIONAL   NATIONAL   LOCAL   NO COLLABORATION

Source: WIPO based on PATSTAT, PCT and Web of Science data (see Boxes 2.1 and 2.2).
Notes: Patent figures based on international patent families.

Different MNCs have different connectivity strategies

Figure 2.14 Global co-inventor network of selected companies

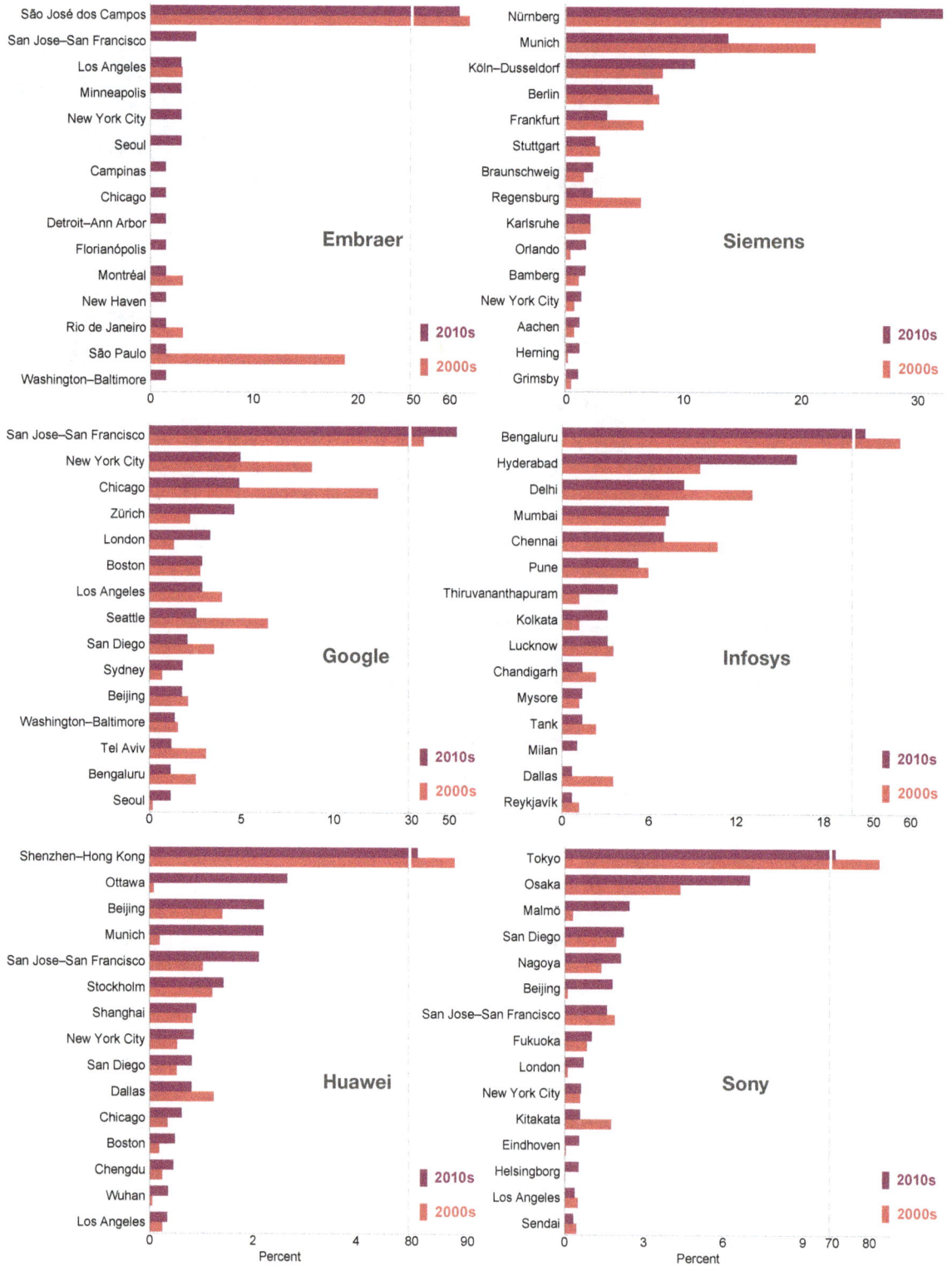

Embraer

São José dos Campos
San Jose–San Francisco
Los Angeles
Minneapolis
New York City
Seoul
Campinas
Chicago
Detroit–Ann Arbor
Florianópolis
Montréal
New Haven
Rio de Janeiro
São Paulo
Washington–Baltimore

2010s
2000s

Siemens

Nürmberg
Munich
Köln–Dusseldorf
Berlin
Frankfurt
Stuttgart
Braunschweig
Regensburg
Karlsruhe
Orlando
Bamberg
New York City
Aachen
Herning
Grimsby

2010s
2000s

Google

San Jose–San Francisco
New York City
Chicago
Zürich
London
Boston
Los Angeles
Seattle
San Diego
Sydney
Beijing
Washington–Baltimore
Tel Aviv
Bengaluru
Seoul

2010s
2000s

Infosys

Bengaluru
Hyderabad
Delhi
Mumbai
Chennai
Pune
Thiruvananthapuram
Kolkata
Lucknow
Chandigarh
Mysore
Tank
Milan
Dallas
Reykjavík

2010s
2000s

Huawei

Shenzhen–Hong Kong
Ottawa
Beijing
Munich
San Jose–San Francisco
Stockholm
Shanghai
New York City
San Diego
Dallas
Chicago
Boston
Chengdu
Wuhan
Los Angeles

2010s
2000s

Sony

Tokyo
Osaka
Malmö
San Diego
Nagoya
Beijing
San Jose–San Francisco
Fukuoka
London
New York City
Kitakata
Eindhoven
Helsingborg
Los Angeles
Sendai

2010s
2000s

Percent

Source: WIPO based on PATSTAT, PCT and Web of Science data (see Boxes 2.1 and 2.2).
Notes: Top 15 GIHs by inventor locations of patents having the company as applicant. Patent figures based on international patent families.

50

Chinese companies are currently only slightly more open to international inventors than are Japanese ones.

Nevertheless, despite the increase seen in recent decades in outsourcing by MNCs involving middle-income developing countries, companies from the latter are still more likely to draw on the innovation of high-income economies than the other way around. Companies from India, Asia, Central Eastern Europe, Latin America and Africa rely intensively on the ingenuity of inventors in the U.S., Western Europe, China and, to a lesser extent, Japan and the Republic of Korea to create for them patentable technologies. It is worth recalling, however, that companies in these economies have low patenting volumes in comparison to those in the U.S., Western Europe, Japan, China and Republic of Korea. Last and not least, there is much less direct patenting activity between companies and inventors from non-high-income countries.

There is some degree of regional collaboration. However, this follows the same pattern described above. Mexican companies source more intensively from inventors in the U.S. and Canada than the other way around. The same applies to Germany, France and the U.K. in Europe, particularly with Central Eastern Europe. Companies from all Asia reach out more intensively to inventors in Japan, the Republic of Korea, China and, to some degree, India than vice versa. Less markedly, inventors in Brazil and South Africa appear as regional sources for Latin American and African companies. However, companies in Asian, Latin American or African non-high-income economies interact mostly with inventors outside their respective continents, typically in the U.S. and Western Europe.

2.3   Local innovation and global networks of innovative hubs

The globalization of agglomerations

Not only do hotspots and niche clusters concentrate more scientific publication and patent output, they also collaborate more internationally (Figure 2.11). The difference is even greater for highly cited patents and scientific articles. During the last two decades, international scientific collaboration went from 19 percent to 29 percent of all scientific articles produced inside innovation-dense areas and the most-cited within this international collaboration went from 28 percent to 43 percent.

The same gap applies to co-inventions inside and outside hotpots and niche clusters. In the second half of the 2010s, 11 percent of inventions from hotspots and niche clusters had international partners – and almost 16 percent in the case of top-cited patents – while only 6 percent of patents originating outside of these had an international co-inventor. However, there is no evidence of the gap increasing. In fact, international co-invention inside and outside agglomerations shows a similar stagnating and to some extent declining trend, starting in the second half of the 2000s and probably linked to a wider slowdown in globalization (see below).

Figure 2.12 shows several noteworthy patterns. As discussed in Section 2.2, the percentage of scientific and inventive output in these innovation-dense agglomerations that does not involve any local, national or international collaboration has decreased. Inventions with a single inventor went from one-third in the 1970s and 1980s to less than a quarter by 2017. Scientific publication by a sole author went from more than 40 percent in the early 2000s to less than 25 percent in the second half of the 2010s. The more the hotspots and niche clusters collaborate, the denser the network of knowledge they create.

In other respects, the picture differs depending on whether it is inventive or scientific output. For patents, the share of local-only teams is larger than that of national and international ones, while this is not the case for scientific publications. Nevertheless, for scientific publication, international co-publication has continuously grown faster than national and local collaborations. The same trend is observed for patents from the early 1980s until the second half of the 2000s.[15]

Since around 2005, however, there has been a fresh rise in the share of local-only patents. This change coincides with a slowdown in the pace of globalization and internationalization generally, as reflected in slower growth of trade, FDI flows and financial integration. It also coincides with a decrease in the share of patents generated by teams that are national but not just local. The explanation for the latter could be that part of the slowdown in the globalization of knowledge creation and innovation has to do with the rise of local hotspots rather than with the development of new national innovation systems. As will be shown, this pattern is stronger in some specific Asian countries.

Global network of innovative agglomerations: a small world?

Figure 2.15 Top 10 percent co-invention ties among GIHs and SNCs, 2011–2015

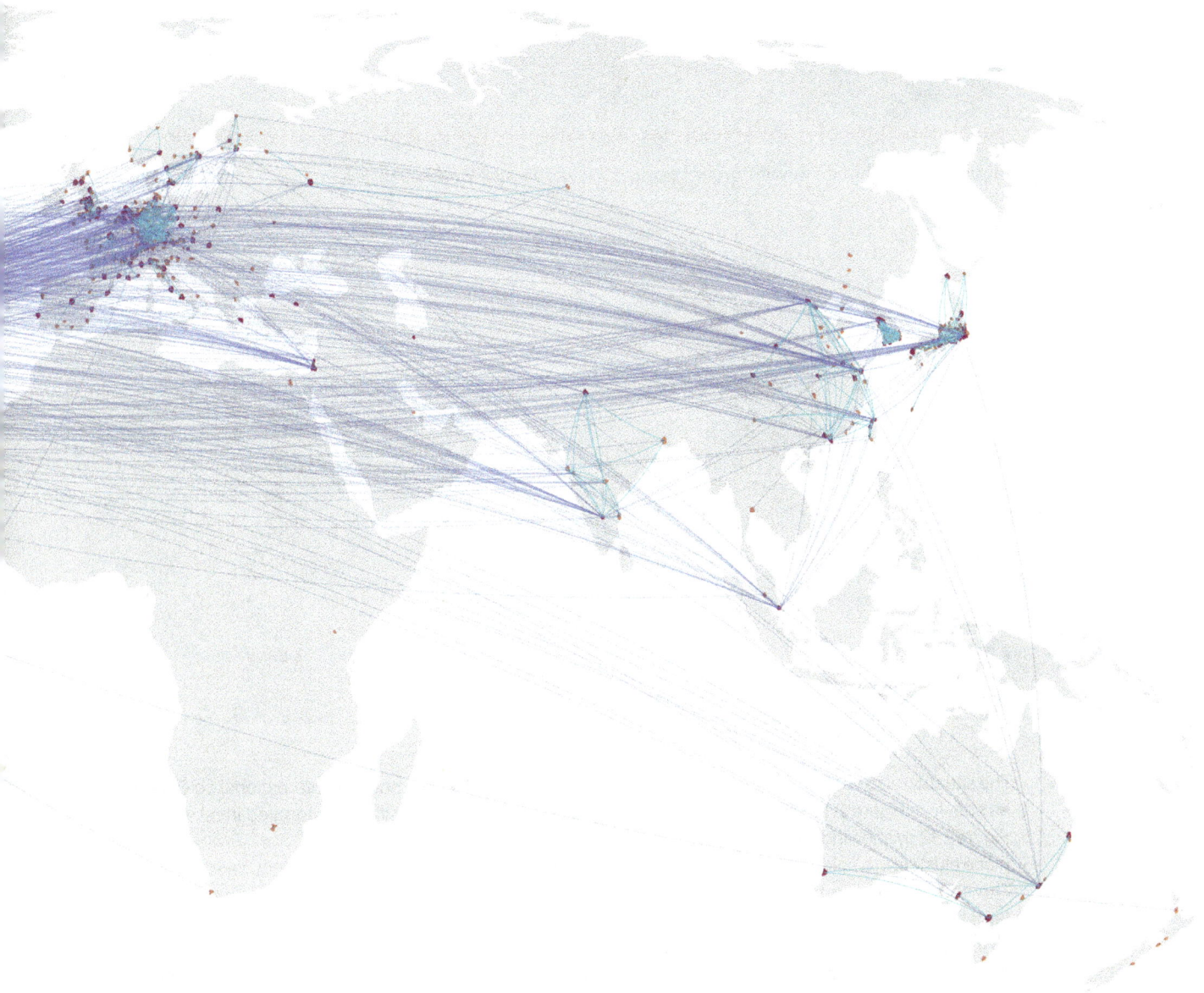

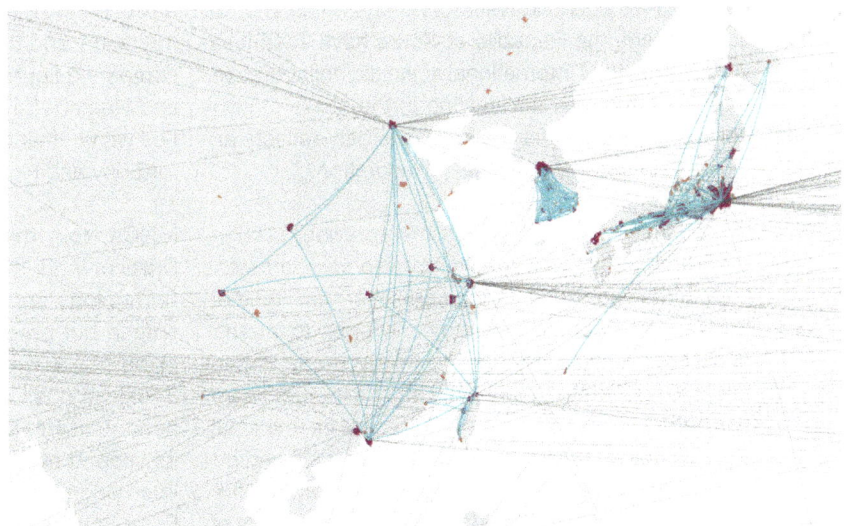

Source: WIPO based on PATSTAT,
PCT and Web of Science data
(see Boxes 2.1 and 2.2).
Notes: Only the world's
10 percent largest links reported.
Green lines connect GIHs/SNCs
from the same country and purple
lines connect those from different
countries. Bubbles represent
the top 10 hotspots in terms
of connectivity volume. Patent
figures based on international
patent families.

Agglomerations in a few economies are central to the global innovation network

Figure 2.16 Patent co-invention network, 2001–2005 and 2011–2015

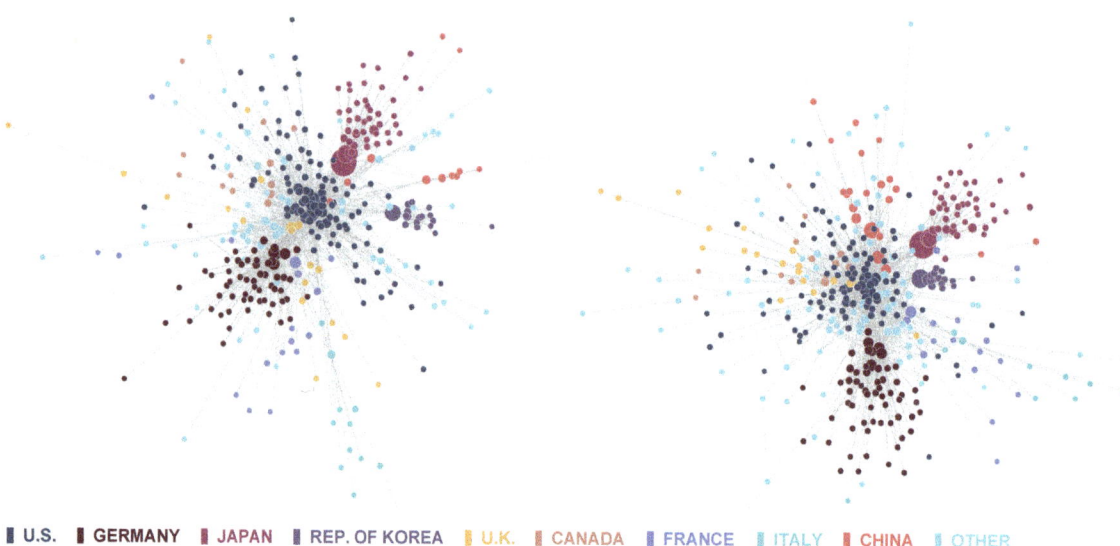

▌ U.S. ▌ GERMANY ▌ JAPAN ▌ REP. OF KOREA ▌ U.K. ▌ CANADA ▌ FRANCE ▌ ITALY ▌ CHINA ▌ OTHER

Source: WIPO based on PATSTAT, PCT and Web of Science data (see Boxes 2.1 and 2.2).
Notes: Only the world's 10% largest links reported. Bubble size reflects patent volume. Bubbles positioned according to their network centrality.
Patent figures based on international patent families.

The situation also varies considerably across countries, as shown in Figure 2.13, which extends the analysis of Figure 2.12 by showing the breakdown for hotspots and niche clusters in a selection of top innovating countries. The country-specific trends for scientific publication largely follow what was observed in Figure 2.12, with virtually all countries showing similar patterns and increases in collaboration. There are some differences, however. In the U.S., Japan, Germany and Switzerland, the increasing share of international co-publication is the principal cause of a reduction there in non-collaborative scientific research. China, India and, to some extent, the Republic of Korea have seen less vibrant growth of international scientific collaboration. In these countries, the decline in the share of non-collaborative scientific publication largely reflects an increase in national and local collaboration.

In line with the trends for MNCs in the previous section, the trends for patent co-inventorship vary substantially across countries. Some countries – like India or Switzerland – can be extraordinarily open to international co-invention, with the Republic of Korea, Japan and, more recently, China at the other extreme. There has been a noticeable drop in the share of international teams in patent production in some countries, particularly in China, due in the latter case to a sharp growth in local-only co-invention. However, for the majority of

countries, the share of international co-inventions has grown or only slightly stagnated in recent years.

MNCs can have very different needs and strategies for where to source for talent, and these can change over time (Figure 2.14). For example, in the 2010s, San Jose–San Francisco accounted for 53 percent of Google's patents. Similarly, Nuremberg – the most important source of patents for Siemens – accounted for 32 percent during the same period. As expected, Tokyo and Shenzhen–Hong Kong are the most important sources of invention for Sony and Huawei, concentrating 71 and 81 percent, respectively. Interestingly, comparing figures for the 2010s to the 2000s, Google and Siemens have concentrated more inventive activities within their top hubs, whereas the reverse holds for Sony and Huawei.

MNCs from middle-income countries – such as Brazil or India – also seek out talent in different ways. Technology services company Infosys has a widespread but predominantly Indian network. Brazilian plane-maker Embraer remains very concentrated in São José dos Campos, which is also the company's headquarters. But in the 2010s, Embraer replaced its second main national hub, São Paulo, with more international connections, including San Jose–San Francisco, Los Angeles or Seoul, among others.

Size plays a role in network centrality, but it is not everything

Figure 2.17 SNC network and the global innovation subnetworks of Los Angeles and Daejon, 2011–2015

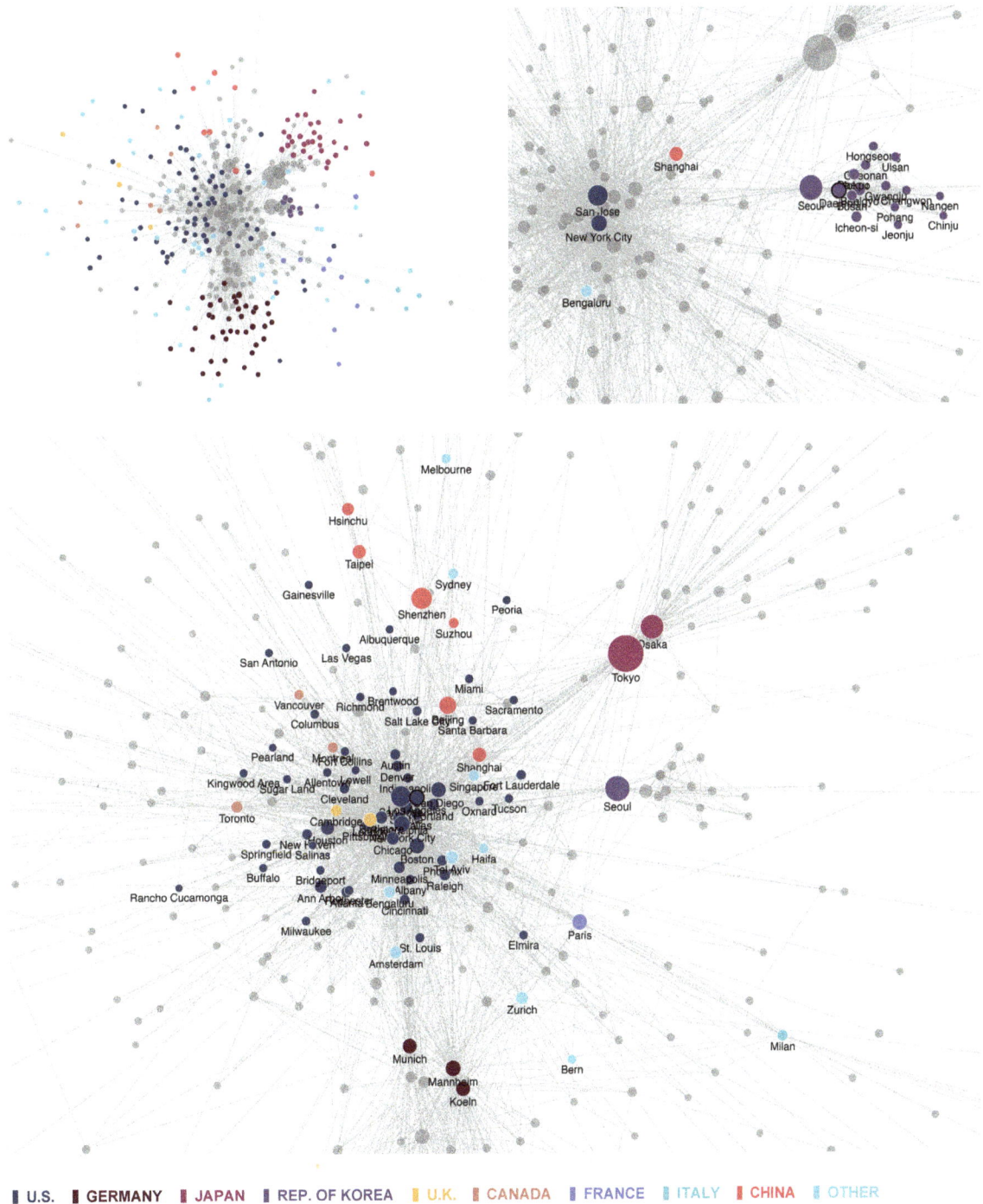

U.S.   GERMANY   JAPAN   REP. OF KOREA   U.K.   CANADA   FRANCE   ITALY   CHINA   OTHER

Source: WIPO based on PATSTAT, PCT and Web of Science data (see Boxes 2.1 and 2.2).
Notes: Bubble size reflects patent volume. Bubbles positioned according to their network centrality. Grayed bubbles do not belong to the subnetwork.

Global network of hotspots and niche clusters

Innovation-dense agglomerations worldwide form a network – within and outside their own countries – that concentrates most inventive and scientific activities, to the possible detriment of non-agglomerated actors.[16] In particular, these innovative agglomerations form a thick web of national and international ties between hotspots and niche clusters in the U.S., Europe and Asia. Only 10 hotspots account for 26 percent of all international co-inventions between hotspots of the world (Figure 2.15). These are San Jose–San Francisco, New York, Frankfurt, Tokyo, Boston, Shanghai, London, Beijing, Bengaluru and Paris.

Figure 2.15 also depicts the top 10 percent co-invention links between all the world's global innovation hotspots and specialized niche clusters. Even in the U.S., niche clusters and smaller hotspots often have only national connections. But despite their extensive geographical spread, global innovation hotspots and specialized niche clusters in the U.S. form a far denser national innovation network than is the case in the rest of the world. Nevertheless, in the U.S., the larger hotspots concentrate the greater portion of both national and international connections with other hotspots and niche clusters.

In Europe, a similar pattern can be detected. A few large hotspots in each country act as gatekeepers that connect the national innovation system to global innovation networks. Clear examples can be found in France, with Paris connecting other French cities with the rest of the world, and in the U.K., with London being a central actor. Germany shows some hierarchical structure too, though access points to the global innovation networks are more numerous and the national innovation network is very dense. Japan and the Republic of Korea also stand out, with very dense national innovation networks, although their international connections are less widespread and mostly directed to the U.S. and the main Western European hotspots.

Hotspots and niche clusters in the remaining regions of the world have substantially fewer connections than those in the U.S., Western Europe, Japan and the Republic of Korea, although among those that do, China, India, Canada and Australia stand out. China has a dense national innovation network where a hierarchical structure is also evident, with Shanghai, Beijing and Shenzhen–Hong Kong acting as the top

international gatekeepers. With obvious proximity advantages, Canada has a national network well integrated to the U.S. one. The role of Canadian hotspots in the overall North American network contrasts with the absence of equivalent Mexican co-invention ties.

Notwithstanding the dominance of Bengaluru, India has a fairly active national innovation network, with several hubs directly connecting internationally. Similarly, despite its remote location and vast territory, Australia manages to have several hotspots that connect internationally and a fairly interconnected national network. One region less connected than the rest is Latin America, where the large majority of connections of its few hotspots and niche clusters are with leading economies outside the region. There are no national or regional networks in Latin America comparable to those depicted for other regions and countries.

The above discussion demonstrates that it is not only geography that shapes the global innovation networks. From a network analysis perspective, an innovation agglomeration is more "central" within a global network the more international connections it concentrates. Figure 2.16 depicts such centrality by grouping the hotspots and niche clusters with most connections in the center and scattering the less connected ones.

As noted, U.S. agglomerations are among the more connected nodes, hence more central in the networks in both of the periods (Figure 2.16). In the center of the picture are other global innovation hotspots which are arguably highly connected, such as Tokyo, London, Shanghai, Beijing, Seoul or Paris. But they are much less central than the U.S. hotspots. The network also evolved over time, getting more nodes and more connections and denser at its center.

Size plays only a limited role. Smaller clusters are connected to big and highly connected ones in the same country, reflecting the hierarchical pattern discussed earlier. This is clearly the case for agglomerations in the U.K., Japan and the Republic of Korea. On the other hand, several hotspots that are larger or similar in size to the top U.S. agglomerations – for example, Tokyo – fail to occupy the same kind of central position in the global network. This reflects the lower international connectivity of Japanese hotspots.

Figure 2.17 depicts subnetworks of the same 2011–2015 co-invention network presented in Figure 2.16. It shows the subnetwork of all niche clusters by graying the network connections of all hotspots. As is apparent, these specialized innovation-dense areas cannot compete with the hotspots in volume of connections. The few connections among niche clusters are virtually always within the same country.

The figure also depicts the specific subnetworks of two hotspots – Los Angeles and Daejeon in the Republic of Korea – which are of equivalent size in terms of the number of patents they generate. The Los Angeles hotspot is highly connected – both nationally and internationally – making it a relatively centered node in the global network. Daejeon is not as central, because it is mostly connected only to other Korean agglomerations. Daejeon's international connections are largely limited to Shanghai, San Francisco and New York.

Geography alone, therefore, does not determine the importance, or the "centrality," of a top innovation agglomeration within a network. Many other factors also have to be considered.

2.4   Conclusions

This chapter exploited a rich data set of patent applications and scientific publications in order to answer several questions arising from two current phenomena connected to the way knowledge is produced and shared worldwide – its geographical spread internationally and – at the same time – its concentration in a few geographical hotspots.

The production of patents and scientific articles has not stayed within the traditional knowledge-producing economies (Europe, Japan and the U.S.). This is a notable development as knowledge-related phenomena, such as patenting, scientific production, R&D investment and so on, have always been more concentrated than other aspects of globalization, like trade or FDI.

Yet, a few Western economies, plus Japan and the Republic of Korea, account for almost 80 percent of internationally-oriented patent activity and around 57 percent of all scientific publication, which is a lot. In fact, it seems that by far most of the spread in knowledge production is due to a handful of developing, middle-income economies, notably China. At the same time, large areas of the world, notably in Africa and Latin America, are left out of the full process of knowledge globalization.

Part of this limited geographical spread of knowledge activities is due to the emergence of global innovation networks, which first link more traditional innovation countries and then bring in middle-income economies. However, networks among core countries dominate and innovation networks involving only non-core economies are of marginal importance for patents. For scientific publication, some middle-income economies, and even subnetworks among these, are beginning to play a larger role.

Overall, knowledge production and interactions are becoming increasingly global in terms of their reach, through the spread of knowledge-creating hubs and the formation of international teams. There has been some stagnation of co-inventorship networks, reflecting a more general slowdown on globalization, but no let-up in international teamwork for the publishing of scientific articles. However, as discussed in Chapter 1, truly global innovation networks cannot be confined to networks based mostly in a few high-income countries. Several regions of the world still have much work to do to integrate themselves into international networks and, eventually, become part of global innovation networks. Certainly, international collaboration with top innovation hotspots is a way forward. It has worked to some extent for East Asian economies, notably China.

Another important message relates to the geographical distribution of knowledge production within countries (both within well-established knowledge producers and emerging ones). Despite the increasing worldwide spread of knowledge production, there is no equivalent spreading within countries; there is even increased concentration in some. This may have, of course, important consequences for the distribution of economic benefits within countries, which will need to be addressed properly (see Chapter 5).

These agglomerations – identified as hotspots and niche clusters – do not only keep concentrating a larger share of the production of innovative ideas. They also increasingly concentrate connections with other hotspots, both within their own countries and across borders through a global innovation network of relatively few hotspots. This is bad news for areas of a country that not only produce less innovation, but also lack the necessary connectivity to the outside world. Lack of connectivity can leave countries or areas locked into non-innovative development paths.

Notes

1   This chapter draws on Miguelez *et al.* (2019).

2   The data work relies on the research efforts and generosity conducted by many others. In particular, it relies on geocoded patent data from Yin and Motohashi (2018), Ikeuchi *et al.* (2017), Li *et al.* (2014), de Rassenfosse *et al.* (2019), Morrison *et al.* (2017) and PatentsView (www.patentsview. org, accessed March 2019).

3   See Miguelez *et al.* (2019).

4   Amendolagine *et al.* (2019).

5   Alcácer and Zhao (2016).

6   See a review in Miguelez *et al.* (2019).

7   See Ester *et al.* (1996).

8   See Technical Notes for further information.

9   Economists have found that nightlight data is a relatively good proxy for population and establishment density (see Mellander et al., 2015), but there are also limitations. There is a known weaker link with other economic indicators – for example, wages – and some known technical distortions in relation with overglow, gas flares, the aurora and zero lights.

10 UNCTAD (2005) and Cantwell and Janne (1999).

11 For a discussion on this co-inventorship slowdown see Miguelez *et al.* (2019).

12 Branstetter *et al.* (2015).

13 He *et al.* (2017) and UNCTAD (2005).

14 Branstetter *et al.* (2018).

15 See Miguelez *et al.* (2019) for full series.

16 See Chaminade *et al.* (2016).

References

Alcácer, J. and M. Zhao (2016). Zooming in: a practical manual for identifying geographic clusters. *Strategic Management Journal*, 37(1), 10–21. doi.org/10.1002/smj.2451

Amendolagine, V., C. Chaminade, J. Guimón and R. Rabellotti (2019). Cross-Border Knowledge Flows Through R&D FDI: Implications for Low- and Middle-Income Countries. Papers in Innovation Studies No. 2019/09. Lund: CIRCLE, Lund University.

Branstetter, L., B. Glennon and J.B. Jensen (2018). Knowledge Transfer Abroad: The Role of US Inventors within Global R&D Networks. Working Paper No. 24453. Cambridge, MA: National Bureau of Economic Research.

Branstetter, L., G. Li and F. Veloso (2015). The rise of international co-invention. In Jaffe, A.B. and B.F. Jones (eds), *The Changing Frontier: Rethinking Science and Innovation Policy*. Chicago: University of Chicago Press, 135–168.

Cantwell, J. and O. Janne (1999). Technological globalisation and innovative centres: the role of corporate technological leadership and locational hierarchy. *Research Policy*, 28, (Issues 2–3), 119–144. doi. org/10.1016/S0048-7333(98)00118-8

Chaminade, C., C. De Fuentes, G. Harirchi and M. Plechero (2016). The geography and structure of global innovation networks: global scope and regional embeddedness. In: Shearmur, R., C. Carrincazeaux and D. Doloreux (eds), *Handbook on the Geographies of Innovation*. Cheltenham: Edward Elgar, 370–381.

de Rassenfosse, G., J. Kozak and F. Seliger (2019). Geocoding of worldwide patent data. papers.ssrn. com/sol3/papers.cfm?abstract_id=3425764

Ester, M., H.-P Kriegel, J., Sander and X. Xu (1996). A density-based algorithm for discovering clusters in large spatial databases with noise. *Proceedings of the 2nd International Conference on Knowledge Discovery and Data Mining* (KDD-96), Portland, Oregon, August 2–4, Menlo Park, CA: AAAI Press, 226–231.

He, S., G. Fallon, Z. Khan, Y.K. Lew, K.H. Kim and P. Wei (2017). Towards a new wave in internationalization of innovation? The rise of China's innovative MNEs, strategic coupling, and global economic organization. *Canadian Journal of Administrative Sciences*, 34(4), 343–355. doi. org//10.1002/CJAS.1444

Ikeuchi, K., K. Motohashi, R. Tamura and N. Tsukada (2017). Measuring Science Intensity of Industry using Linked Dataset of Science, Technology and Industry. *RIETI Discussion Paper Series*, 17-E-056. www.rieti.go.jp/en/publications/summary/17030073.html

Li, G.-C., R. Lai, A. D'Amour, D.M. Doolin, Y. Sun, V.I. Torvik and L. Fleming (2014). Disambiguation and co-authorship networks of the U.S. patent inventor database (1975–2010). *Research Policy*, 43, 941–955.

Mellander C., J. Lobo, K. Stolarick and Z. Matheson (2015). Night-time light data: a good proxy measure for economic activity? *PLoS ONE* 10(10): e0139779. doi.org/10.1371/journal. pone.0139779

Miguelez, E., J. Raffo, C. Chacua, M. Coda-Zabetta, D. Yin, F. Lissoni and G. Tarasconi (2019). Tied In: The Global Network of Local Innovation. *WIPO Working Paper No. 58*, November. Geneva: WIPO.

Morrison, G., M. Riccaboni and F. Pammolli (2017). Disambiguation of patent inventors and assignees using high-resolution geolocation data. *Scientific Data*, 4. doi.org/10.1038/sdata.2017.64

UNCTAD (2005). World investment report 2005: transnational corporations and the internationalization of R&D – overview. *Transnational Corporations*, 14(3), 101–140.

Yin, D. and K. Motohashi (2018). Inventor Name Disambiguation with Gradient Boosting Decision Tree and Inventor Mobility in China (1985–2016), *RIETI Discussion Paper Series*, 18-E-018. www.rieti.go.jp/en/publications/summary/18030018.html

Collaboration between car manufacturers and tech companies is beginning to shift the geography of innovation in the sector.

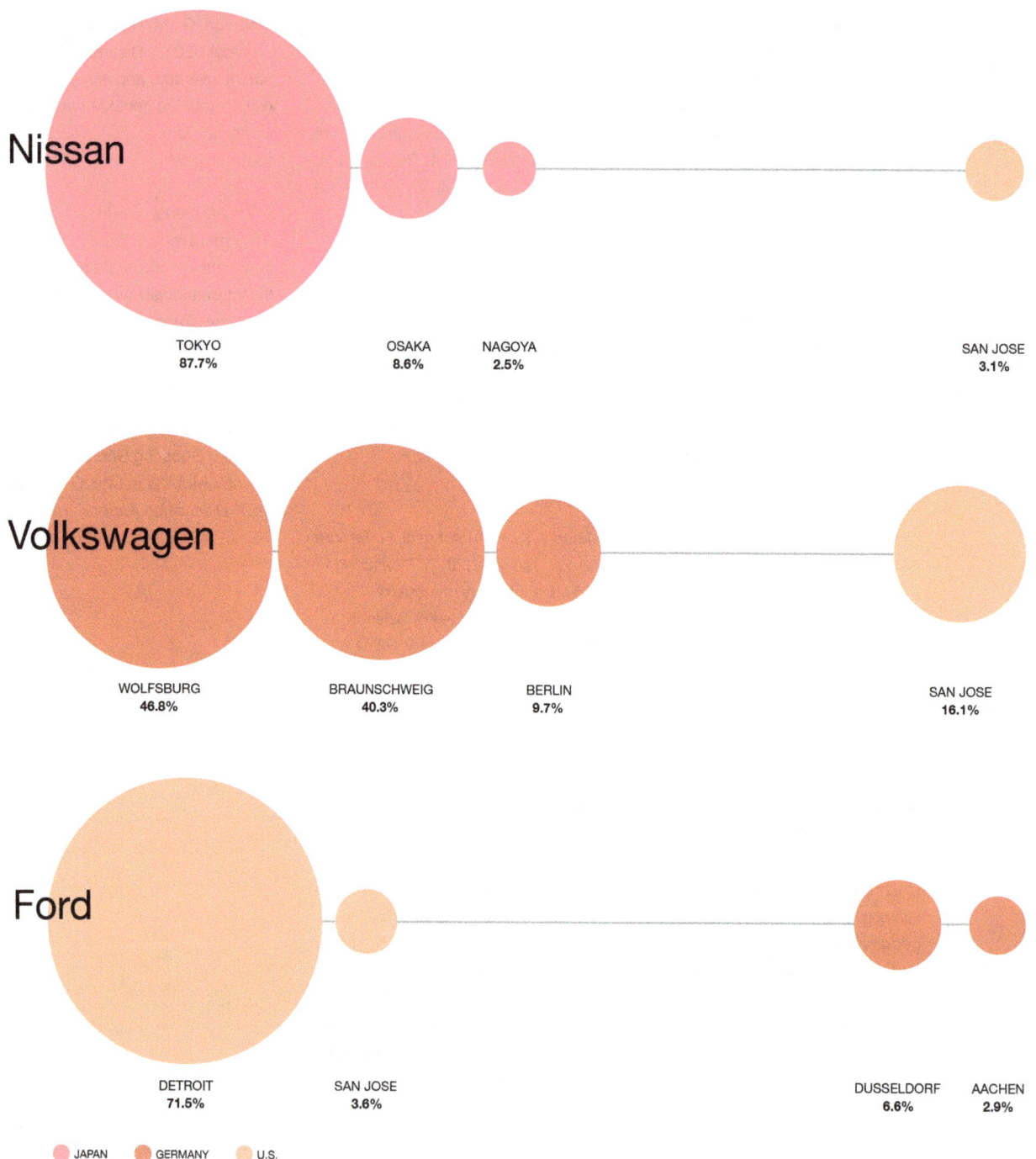

Nissan

TOKYO
87.7%

OSAKA
8.6%

NAGOYA
2.5%

SAN JOSE
3.1%

Volkswagen

WOLFSBURG
46.8%

BRAUNSCHWEIG
40.3%

BERLIN
9.7%

SAN JOSE
16.1%

Ford

DETROIT
71.5%

SAN JOSE
3.6%

DUSSELDORF
6.6%

AACHEN
2.9%

● JAPAN ● GERMANY ○ U.S.

Chapter 3

Auto and tech companies – the drive for autonomous vehicles

In 2004, the United States (U.S.) Defense Department staged a novel off-road race in the Mojave Desert. The novelty lay in it being open only to driverless or self-drive cars. First prize for winning the "Grand Challenge" over the 240km course was $1 million. Nobody lifted the prize, because nobody finished the race.[1]

But a year later, the Department's Defense Advanced Research Projects Agency (DARPA) staged the competition again and doubled the prize. It attracted dozens of entrants and this time a number completed the course. The desert race was won by "Stanley," an autonomous vehicle (AV) entered by Stanford University, with vehicles from Carnegie Mellon University (CMU) taking second and third places.

The automobile industry has been envisioning self-driving[2] or autonomous vehicles at least since General Motors presented its "Futurama" concept at the 1939 World's Fair. Even in those early days, GM was not the only one dreaming of a self-driving future, and several attempts toward realization of AVs were made in subsequent years. But it is since the mid-2000s that huge advances in robotics and, particularly, artificial intelligence (AI)[3] have begun to turn a long-held aspiration into something closer to reality.

The AV industry is still in its infancy and fully autonomous vehicles (Level 5) are years from reaching the market. Nevertheless, robotics and AI are already reshaping the car industry – so much so that new technologies are posing a significant existential threat to the incumbent automakers. AI, data analytics and a slew of connected devices and components are reformulating the industry's business model toward services and the so-called "platform economy."

Traditional automakers fear being supplanted and reduced to bit-players in their core competency – the making and marketing of cars. To tackle these challenges a menu of options is available to them – from investing in internal knowledge development, recruiting human capital and strategic alliances, to acquisitions of new entrants, or a combination of these.[4] It is not clear which single or combination of the above strategies will yield the most successful results. What is clear though is that neither the incumbents nor the new entrants, on their own, currently have all the required competencies for producing AVs. They either need to join forces or else develop internally the respective skills they now lack.

Against this background, this chapter seeks to analyze current innovation clusters in the automotive industry and understand how AV is affecting the geographical spread and concentration of innovation (see Chapter 1). Understanding the relationship between the new entrants and the incumbents can offer pointers to the evolution of current innovation clusters. How firms react to AV technology will determine which firms will be the market leaders and which regions will be the AV technological hubs.

In the following sections the chapter looks into the contemporary evolution of AV technology and its key players. It also briefly discusses two other related technologies: mobility and connectivity. Next, it explores the impact of AV technology on the automotive industry from two perspectives. First, whether AV technology is changing the nature of innovative collaborations between and within incumbents and entrants. Second, whether it is changing the geography of innovation. It concludes with a discussion on potential positive and negative impacts.

3.1   Definitions

Basic components of a driving automation system

There are three basic functional components of any computer-automated system: monitoring, agency, and action – as depicted in Figure 3.1. Monitoring can be understood as sensing and paying attention, while agency consists of decision-making, and action involves implementing decisions. Furthermore, automated systems can also include various feedback loops, possibly including machine learning.

Levels of driving automation

The established Society of Automotive Engineers (SEA) industry standard for terms relating to automated vehicles is *Taxonomy and Definitions for Terms Related to Driving Automation Systems for On-Road Motor Vehicles* (SAE J3016). It was initially published in 2014 and substantially revised in 2018.

The SAE standard introduced and defined six levels of driving automation (Figure 3.2), including level 0 for systems that perform no sustained dynamic driving tasks. Levels 1 and 2 are termed driver assistance and partial driving automation, respectively. The lower levels of automation require the driver to at least actively supervise the driving automation system. Driving automation systems that assume the entire dynamic driving task are classified as SAE levels 3, 4 and 5 and are collectively described as automated driving systems (ADS). While the main focus of this chapter is on level 3+ technologies, in the empirical analysis we do not exclude the historical innovations of the 1980s,

Core aspects of computer-backed driving

Figure 3.1 Three basic functional components of any computer-automated system

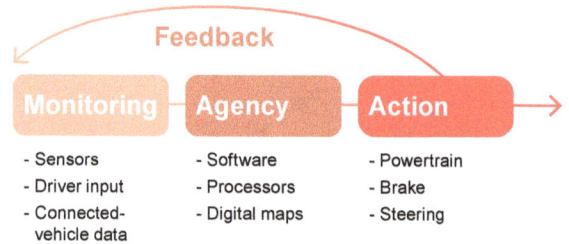

Source: Center for Automotive Research (CAR).

1990s and early 2000s that were the building blocks of modern AV technology.

3.2   Technological evolution of the automotive industry

Industry evolution literature[5] divides the life cycle of any given industry into five stages: the introductory embryonic stage, growth, shakeout, maturing and decline. The early stages are ripe with high uncertainty and numerous entries and exits. Later on, the emergence of a dominant design will leave only a handful of firms standing. Names like Sprite, Unito, Wolfe, Angus, Empire do not exactly ring a bell and that is because these early car companies were some of the thousands that exited the industry more than a century ago when the first automobiles started mesmerizing the world.

Until a few years ago, the automotive sector was considered a mature industry with well-established players and for which the key technological questions had been answered in the 1930s.[6] The initial innovations were fundamental as they defined the basic structure of the automobile. These included the development of water-cooled engines placed in the front of the car, shaft-driven transmissions, streamlined bodies and pressed steel frames.[7] The remaining product and process innovation in the years after the Second World War, and particularly after the 1970s, was attributed to rising oil prices, cost pressure arising from intensifying international competition and changes in consumer demands.

At the turn of the millennium this picture changed; the increasing processing power of computers in

From manual to fully automated

Figure 3.2 Six levels of driving automation

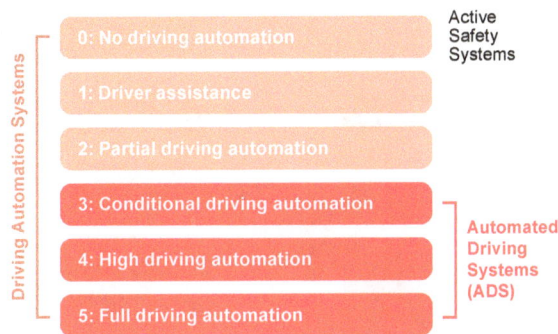

Source: Center for Automotive Research (CAR) based on SAE 2016.

conjunction with the widespread adoption of the Internet and, consequently, smartphones, opened several avenues for innovation. Many established old-line industries – like newspapers, the music business, TV and retail – woke up to the waves of technological disruption that advances in software and the hardware side of computer technology had triggered. These affected not only their core competencies, but also their complementary assets – those needed to commercialize and market products – and their distribution channels. Many of these industries were rattled and reshuffled by the digital era. The automotive industry – although with some lag – has not been untouched by the waves. For instance, in 2018, the global electric vehicle fleet exceeded 5.1 million,[8] achieving almost 2.1 percent of market share. This number is expected to increase to around 30 percent by 2030.

Industry life-cycle literature discusses how industries, as they reach maturity, are subject to new technological shocks which can be the seeds for the beginning of a new cycle. Whether the new cycle is actually realized or not depends on the existence of various technological and non-technological competencies. The participants in the new cycle may be from within the same industry or from previously non-competing industries whose competencies meet the technological requirements for entering the new cycle.

Competencies required for the development of AVs have allowed players from the tech industry to enter the automotive sector, with the ultimate goal of creating fully autonomous vehicles that require no driver. The main ingredients for the realization of AVs are both the "V" and the "A." An AV unit is basically chassis and engine, plus an intelligence that brings full autonomy to the physical aspect. The incumbent automakers' core competency[9] lies with the "V." Creating all the software (e.g., artificial intelligence) and hardware elements (e.g., sensors and cameras) required for autonomy – the "A" – is within the core competencies of the tech companies.

The incumbent automakers' core competencies are mass manufacturing, mechanical engineering and jumping through the thousands of regulatory hoops that lead to the final car being on the road. They are the result of decades of accumulated tacit knowledge – knowledge that is not easily replicable – and know-how. Mastering these competencies is not immediate and straightforward.

New entrants' technological competencies are in hardware and software, especially the deep-learning and real-time control algorithms needed for vehicle autonomy. They are beyond the spectrum of expertise of most automakers and their suppliers, which have little prior knowledge of them.

Core competencies of the automakers are more or less familiar to most people, but not so the technological waves that are transforming the industry. The following sections will briefly discuss three technological waves that are somewhat related. A fourth wave, electric vehicles, although equally affecting the industry, is not within the focus and scope of this chapter.

Autonomous vehicles: scientists behind their contemporary rise

The genesis of a set of AV-related startups and tech firms stems from the Massachusetts Institute of Technology (MIT). MIT has been a global leader in robotics technology for decades and has contributed to an agglomeration of firms specializing in AV-related robotics technology in the Cambridge and Boston area. MIT graduates have also produced several robotics-related spin-offs, including a few specifically interested in deploying autonomous vehicles.

In 2007, DARPA held a follow-up competition to its "Grand Challenge," this time providing a 60-mile course through a simulated urban traffic environment, including interaction with other vehicles and compliance with traffic laws. CMU and Stanford again led the pack,

Grand challenge scientists and their spin-offs

Figure 3.3 Many leading players in today's AV industry started in the DARPA grand challenges

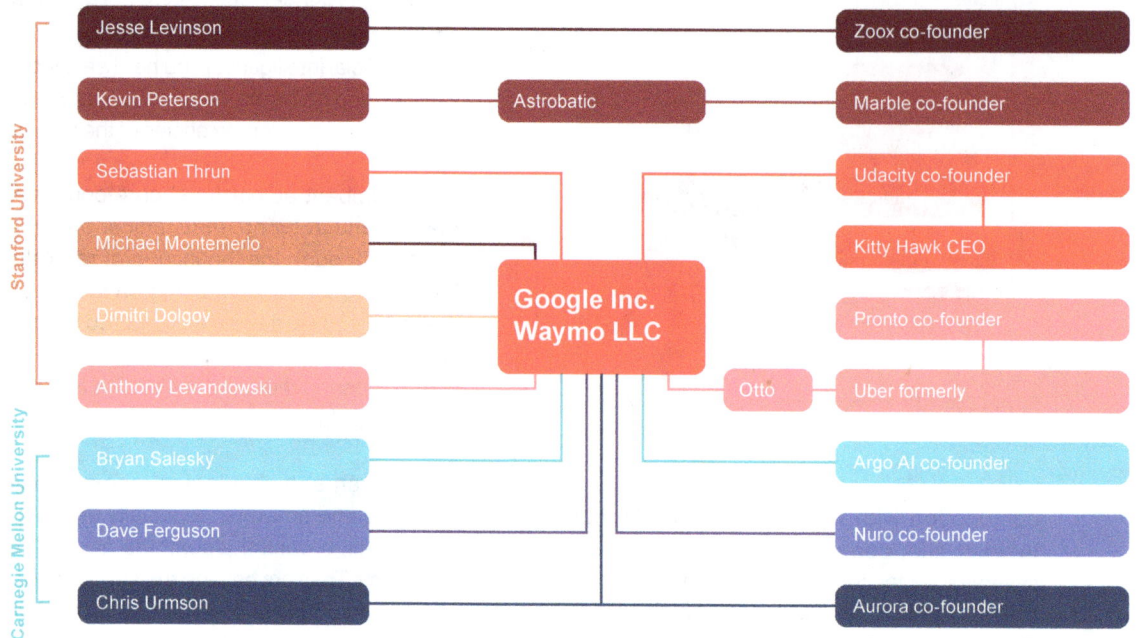

Source: Stanford and Carnegie Mellon University

with CMU's "Boss" taking first place. In all, six teams completed the 2007 course – demonstrating the rapid development of self-driving technology within several universities. Silicon Valley tech giants, notably Google, later recruited many Stanford and CMU participants of the DARPA challenges. (Waymo originated as a self-driving project of Google before it became a stand-alone subsidiary.) Most of the scientists involved subsequently have founded their own spin-offs, including such tech startups as Aurora, Udacity, Nuro and Argo AI, all of which are at the forefront of the AV industry (see Figure 3.3).

The DARPA challenges have been a milestone in the history of modern AV technology. Although there's no evidence of their causal effect, we observe an increasing trend in innovative activity in AV technology (measured by patents, see Box 3.1) in the mid-2000s that coincides with the DARPA initiatives, with a major innovative spike after 2010. Despite this upward trend, AV technology is still very niche and comprised less than 0.1 percent of total patent filings globally even at the height of that spike in 2016 (see Figure 3.4).

Box 3.1 The AV patent mapping strategy and its limitations[10]

The AV industry is a combination of various technologies applied to a specific use – automating the operation of ground-based vehicles. Thus, search strategies to identify AV-related technologies and scholarship are inherently imprecise and require creativity and several iterations. Defining clear-cut boundaries is very difficult.

Against these limitations, this chapter makes use of technological codes of the Cooperative Patent Classification (CPC), an international system for classifying patent documents. A list of CPC classes that corresponds to the technologies used in AV was compiled. The list was divided into two groups. First, the smaller number of niche classes where it is relatively safe to say the entirety were relevant to AV. Second, the classes that were broader and had patents that may not be relevant to AV. For this second group, a list of keywords was added to the search. These keywords were some permutation

AV technology has taken off since the mid-2000s

Figure 3.4 AV share of all patent first filings and key milestones over time

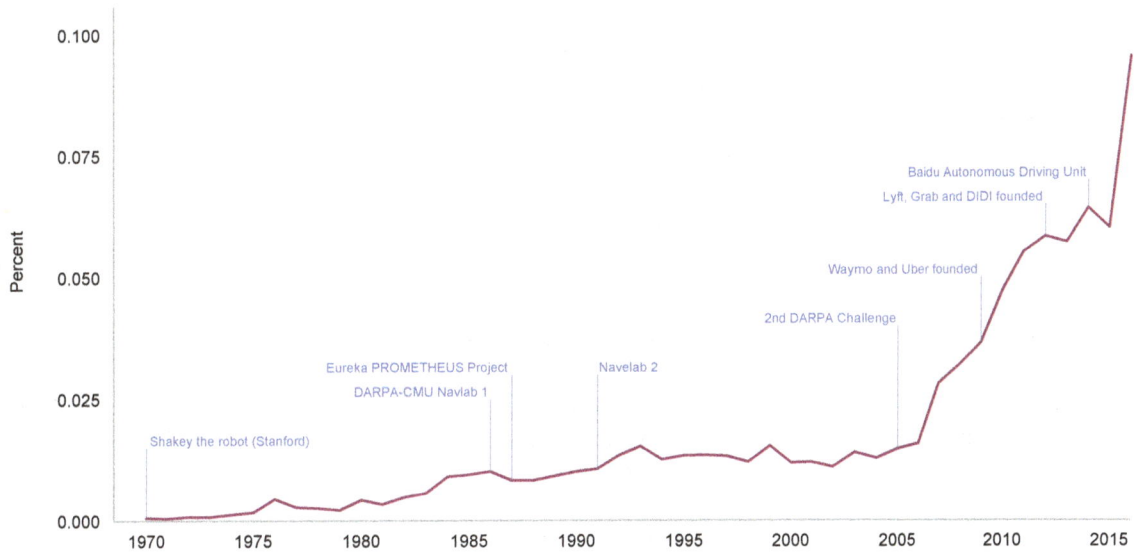

Source: WIPO based on PATSTAT and PCT data (see Technical Notes).

of autonomous vehicle, car, taxi, truck, etc. These keywords were used to identify the patents that belonged to the selected CPCs and had one of these keywords mentioned either in their patent abstract or title.

The same list of keywords was used to search for scientific publications that had mentioned some permutation of the keywords in their abstracts or titles. From these selected sets of papers a new list of keywords was compiled, for example, predictive cruise control. As publications only have broad categories, with no level of granularity similar to CPCs, the subject-level category was used to eliminate those false positive articles that belonged to areas that are intuitively far from AV technology – microbiology, zoology, etc.

Mobility as a service

Parallel to these efforts, Mobility-as-a-Service (MaaS), which integrates various transport services into a single service available on demand, became a popular concept. Companies like Uber (founded in 2009) and

Lyft (founded in 2012) in the U.S. came to fruition. Soon, others with similar business models started popping up all around the globe: Ola Cabs in India (founded in 2010), Grab (founded in 2012) in Singapore and DiDi Chuxing (founded in 2012) in China. These companies provided services like ride-hailing and/ or car-sharing. Many of them have expanded their businesses to other services, including deliveries, logistics and bike-sharing.

Uber's former CEO, Travis Kalanick, described the development of "robotaxis" (self-driving taxis) as "existential" to the company. If the future of automobiles is driverless, mobility companies have a vested interest in AV technology for multiple reasons. First, removing the driver from the equation will reduce their costs.

Second, their business model has the potential to change the economics of the automotive industry. The MaaS business model can lead to a reduction of private car ownership and a shift to a more fleet-oriented system, where the revenue model would be based on mileage instead of the number of cars sold. AV technology can enable a system where people buy access to transportation as opposed to owning vehicles. A rough calculation based on the number of cars on the road and their average annual mileage, compared to what mobility companies charge per mile, shows that if all existing cars were to convert to AVs, automakers could make a profit and charge far less than mobility companies.

Third, mobility companies are sitting on abundant data and information about customer behavior and preferences, which would give them a significant advantage in a sales environment that is increasingly about customized and bespoke experience.

Connected vehicles

Another branch of technology that has intertwined with autonomous driving is "connected vehicle technology." A vehicle can be connected without being autonomous, therefore the two terms are not interchangeable and should not be confused. The connected vehicle technologies allow vehicles to communicate with each other and the world around them. They aim to increase efficiency and road safety for both drivers and pedestrians. Popular use cases for connected vehicles are sharing braking data, real-time high-definition maps, road hazards, closure updates, fleet tracking and infotainment. All of these require minimum latency (delay in implementation of commands) and maximum precision in the transmission of data. That is why 5G cellular network technology is becoming the future of autonomous and "connected" vehicles.[11] Several tech companies, notably Huawei, Intel and Ericsson, are exploring this field.

3.3   Technological shift

The sectoral breakdown of AV patenting over time supports the idea that the rise of AI, robotics and mobility services is the main driver of the technological shift. In the years immediately after 2005 almost half of the patents seem to be from the tech sector.[12] However, the traditional auto sector later regained dominance (see Figures 3.5 and 3.6). Not surprisingly, the majority of the patent applicants are companies, roughly 20 percent are individuals and only 10 percent are universities or other public entities.

A quick look at the list of the top applicants[13] in the 1990s shows manufacturing and auto companies. Later lists tell a different story. Google, Qualcomm, Mobileye, Uber, Baidu are not among the usual suspects of the auto industry, but from the mid-2010s they appear in the top 100 AV patent applicants. These top 100

The rise of AI, robotics and mobility services is the main driver of the technological shift in the mid-2000s

Figure 3.5 Sectoral breakdown of AV-related patents by frequency

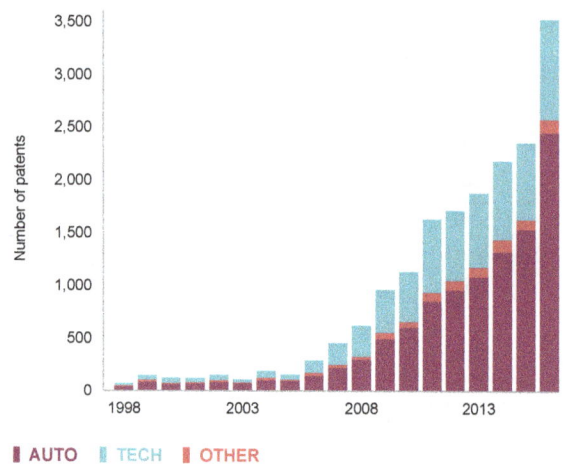

AUTO   TECH   OTHER

Source: WIPO based on PATSTAT and PCT data (see Technical Notes).

applicants, led by names such as Ford (357 patents), Toyota (320) and Bosch (277) have generated around half of the total patents. Non-automakers also feature in the list of top patent applicants. Google and its AV subsidiary Waymo lie in eighth position, with 156 patents, ahead of automakers like Nissan, BMW and Hyundai. They are followed by other companies like Uber and Delphi, which each have 62 AV patents and are ranked joint 31st.

3.4   Competition and cooperation in AV

Thus far it is established that the auto sector is in the early phases of a period of technological disruption, with several new entrants, both from the auto and the tech side, joining this bandwagon. Standardization and regulatory issues are not yet being deeply discussed and there is still no consensus on basic definitions and terminologies. AV technology is an extremely costly endeavor not only in terms of capital but also time. Therefore, players in this industry have high incentives to collaborate with each other to share the risks and costs. But who collaborates with whom? And why? Theoretically speaking, three types of collaboration can form: incumbent automakers with each other, tech firms with each other, or automakers with tech firms.

In the years immediately after 2005, the tech sector comprised almost half of the patents in AV

Figure 3.6 Sectoral breakdown of AV-related patents by share

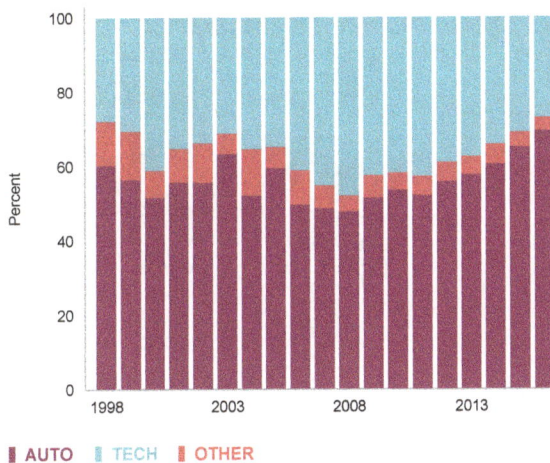

AUTO   TECH   OTHER

Source: WIPO based on PATSTAT and PCT data (see Technical Notes).

Collaboration among auto companies

In the face of the AV technological shock, auto companies have an incentive to join forces to share the costs and risks but also defend their market position, which is being threatened by outsiders. The common threat they are facing is "commoditization" of their core competency; that is, becoming simply a supplier of a commodity good, which in this case is a car. The tech companies would be the ones generating the value added and therefore reaping the largest benefits. Global automakers Daimler and BMW announced they would partner in a new long-term partnership to co-develop automated driving technologies.

The joint effort will involve 1,200 technicians from both companies. The technicians will be based at BMW's autonomous driving campus in Unterschleissheim, near Munich, its Mercedes subsidiary's technology center in Sindelfingen, near Stuttgart, and Daimler's testing and technology center in Immendingen in southern Germany. The two companies aim to launch their next-generation, self-driving passenger cars by 2024.[14] Audi, another German automaker, has announced that it is to join forces with them.[15]

While some may be surprised to see long-time foes becoming friends, it is not rare in AV development. The

enormous costs of designing and building computer-powered vehicles has already prompted Honda to pool its efforts with General Motors, while Volkswagen is pursuing talks with Ford about an alliance on autonomous cars.

Collaboration among tech companies

Tech firms also would need to collaborate with each other to share the technology's large risks and costs. Most tech firms, especially the smaller startups, occupy niches, focusing on hardware, software, mobility services, connectivity, communications and many more (see Figure 3.7 below). With the exception of Waymo – which develops all its hardware and software stack[16] in-house – no single tech company has the necessary expertise in all these areas. So, collaboration among tech companies is not uncommon. Taiwan-based VIA Technologies Inc. announced in 2018 that it is partnering with AI vision startup Lucid to deliver AI-based depth sensing in dual- and multi-camera devices for use in security, retail, robotics and autonomous vehicles.[17] This is just one of a long list of examples of collaboration between tech companies.

Some tech companies have also decided to give open access – free of cost or other access barriers – to their closely guarded data and technologies. For instance, Waymo has decide to sell one of its three LIDAR sensors – called Laser Bear Honeycomb, which uses a laser to measure distances – to third parties interested in using the technology for purposes other than self-driving cars. Some believe the LIDAR sensor development curve is similar to Moore's Law in computer chips – every 18 months, resolution will double and the price drop by half[18] – so granting open access offers the chance to scale up with reduced costs.

Waymo is making some of the high-resolution sensor data gathered by its fleet of autonomous vehicles available to researchers for free. It is not the first company to release an open dataset. In March 2019, global technology company Aptiv was one of the first large AV operators to publicly release a set of its sensor data. Uber and Cruise, the autonomous division of General Motors, have also released their AV visualization tools to the public.[19]

These decisions are in line with the "open innovation"[20] strategies that firms adopt as a response to highly complex innovative ideas.

Mapping the involvement of AV companies

Figure 3.7 Examples of companies working in various AV technologies

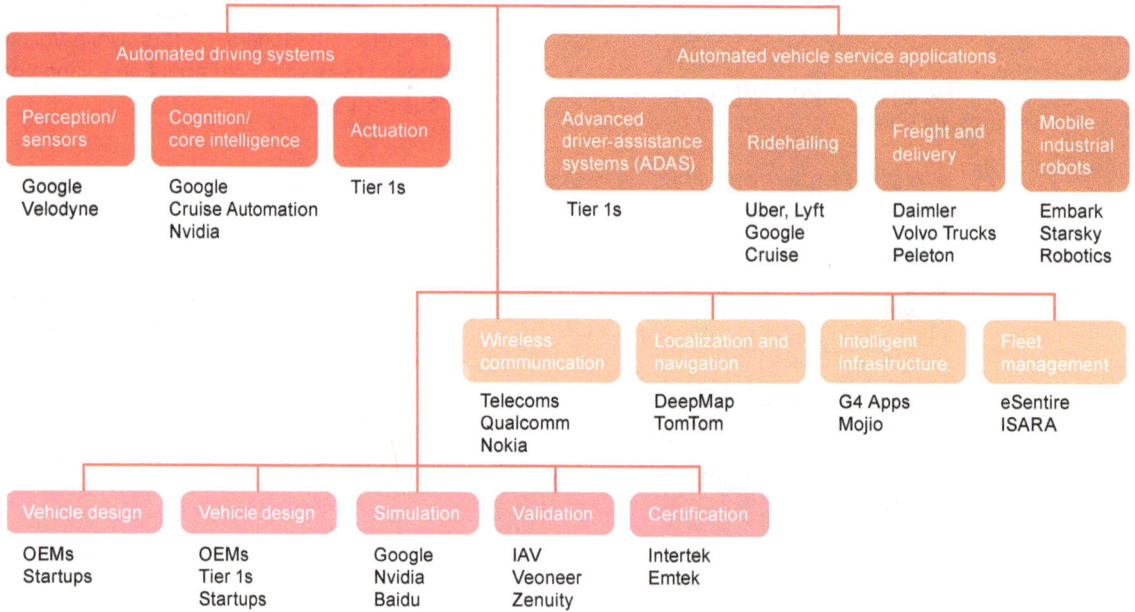

Source: Center for Automotive Research (CAR).

Collaboration between tech and auto companies

AV technology is not rendering the upstream core knowledge of automakers completely obsolete. In fact – at least for now – AV is a type of technological discontinuity that needs the incumbent's core competency to achieve its goal. Research shows[21] that – historically – incumbents can survive the discontinuity if they cooperate with the entrants challenging their core knowledge. In presence of strong "appropriability regimes," the new entrants have the incentive to license out their technologies. The literature[22] defines strong appropriability regimes as environmental factors – legal protection (e.g., patents) or the needed knowledge is difficult to pass on (tacit) or codified – that allow the tech company to recuperate its investment.

AV technology shows characteristics of strong appropriability. This allows the new entrants to cooperate with incumbents while securing their benefits without fear of imitation.[23] By partnering with tech companies, automakers gain a better understanding of the key technologies that are transforming the industry and accelerate the learning process that can keep them competitive in a rapidly changing environment.

While it seems logical for auto companies to collaborate with tech companies, the reverse is not so straightforward. Some might even argue that tech giants do not need auto companies and that they can, and will eventually, directly enter the auto sector.[24] Their argument focuses on the costs. Since IT giants like Alphabet, Amazon and Apple in the U.S. and Alibaba, Baidu and Tencent in China have deep pockets they can easily afford the costs of designing and manufacturing a car. Others do not agree.[25] Excelling at complex mass manufacturing, organizing quality value chains, dealing with complex regulatory issues is neither trivial nor negligible. U.S. energy and automotive company Tesla's financial losses and struggles to keep up with delivery schedules of its Model 3 electric sedan car attest to this issue. The ecosystem in which automakers operate and lobby is their stronghold. Even if the tech companies had the technological capacity to produce cars, they would still have difficulties challenging the current socio-technical regime unless they collaborate with the incumbent automakers.

Therefore, tech companies also have an incentive to collaborate and see where their strengths complement those of the automakers. This division of labor, at least at this stage of the industry, allows each side to focus on what they do best and is the shortest and safest route to AV success.

The types of collaboration outlined are not mutually exclusive and they coexist. The high uncertainty makes firms simultaneously bet on multiple combinations of the three options – "build," "borrow" and "buy."[26]

By default, much of the above collaboration may not be captured by patent or scientific publication data. The main reason is that most are formal partnerships and alliances, joint ventures, investments or acquisitions. Out of more than 100 formal collaborations identified,[27] in terms of frequency, the largest share belongs to auto–tech, followed by tech–tech and auto–auto. Finally, a small portion of the collaboration is between tech companies and national or regional government entities. For instance, Detroit-based Quadrobot and the Chinese Postal Service are partnering to produce autonomous delivery vans.

3.5   Role of geography in AV technology

Spread over time

Until a few years ago, no one would have associated places like Boston, San Francisco and Pittsburg, Singapore or Jerusalem with the automotive industry. The more familiar names were Detroit, Toyota City in Japan and Stuttgart in Germany. But advances in robotics and AI as general-purpose technologies,[28] with multi-faceted applications in various fields, have created avenues for new entrants. Naturally, these entrants reside in the main tech hubs, such as the U.S. Silicon Valley and others around the world. However, places like Singapore or Jerusalem, with no history in the automotive sector but with booming and vibrant tech and startup scenes, have become highly active in AV technology.

A historical look at innovative activity in AV shows its geographical evolution and global spread. Figure 3.8 displays the regions involved in patenting[29] and publishing scientific articles concerning AV-related technologies, before and after 2005. Not surprisingly, in the earlier period, regions that traditionally led the auto market also show high patenting activity. But even then, there was significant patenting activity from Silicon Valley and Singapore. The focus in the earlier period was still on areas like advanced driver assistance systems (ADAS) and automated highway systems (AHS), technologies that are not directly related to AI/robotics approaches. These patents were closer to the operations of the traditional automobile and mainly related to level 1 or 2 of driving automation (See Figure 3.2).

In the later years, we observe some developing countries that are not traditional automaking countries also engaging in this technology. The most noticeable change is the emergence of China and India. As discussed earlier, the changing nature of technology can be one explanation of this expansion. The new sets of technologies – AI and robotics – allow for "leapfrogging" of countries/regions with no longstanding ties to the auto-manufacturing sector.[30] Despite this, the top countries involved are still the U.S., Japan, Germany, the Republic of Korea and Sweden, with the U.S. and China latterly being the most active.

When looking at scientific publication we observe that more developing countries in the Middle East, Latin America and Africa – that are not captured in the patenting data – are highly active in generating basic research and scientific articles. Iran would be an example of a country highly active in scientific publication but with almost no patenting presence in this field. Scientific publication data complements patents in giving a better picture of the innovation landscape in AV technology.

3.6   AV innovation, countries and cities

North America

Boston, Massachusetts

Boston is not a traditional automotive industry cluster. However, the Massachusetts Institute of Technology (MIT) has been a global leader in robotics technology for decades and has contributed to an agglomeration of firms specializing in AV-related robotics technology. One major company that has taken advantage of the Boston robotics cluster for AV development is the Toyota Research Institute (TRI), which located one of its three offices in Cambridge (the other two offices are in Michigan and California). TRI sponsors MIT's Computer Science and Artificial Intelligence Laboratory (CSAIL), where researchers study various aspects of AI and machine learning applied to vehicle automation.[31]

MIT has produced several robotics-related spinoffs, including a few specifically interested in deploying

East Asia has become very active in AV technology in recent years

Figure 3.8 Geographical distribution of AV-related patents (this page) and publication (next page) in selected regions, pre- (left) and post-2005 (right)

North America

Europe and the Middle East

East Asia

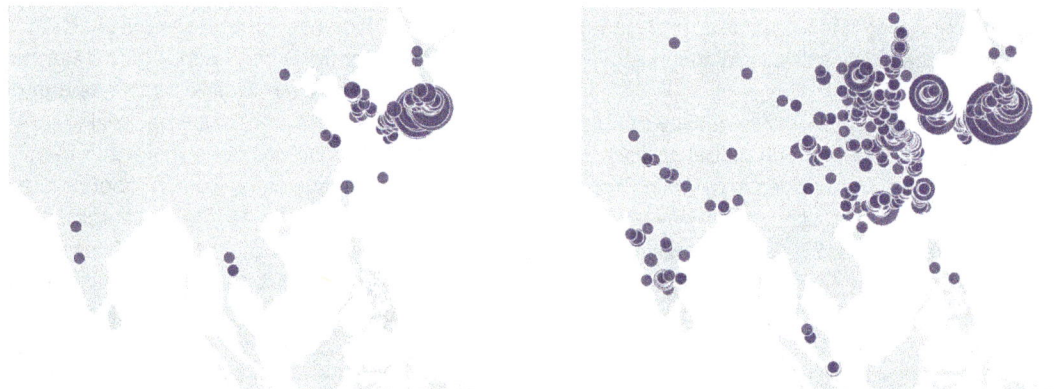

▌ PATENTS   ▌ SCIENTIFIC PUBLICATIONS

Source: WIPO based on PATSTAT, PCT and Web of Science data (see Technical Notes).

North America

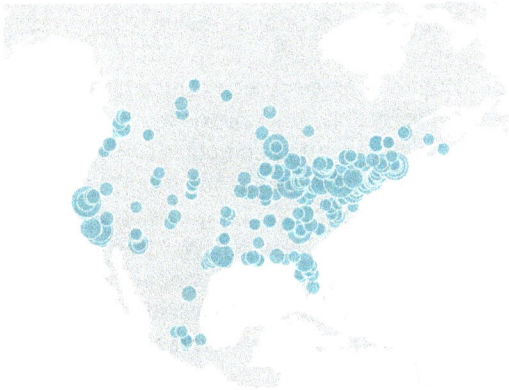 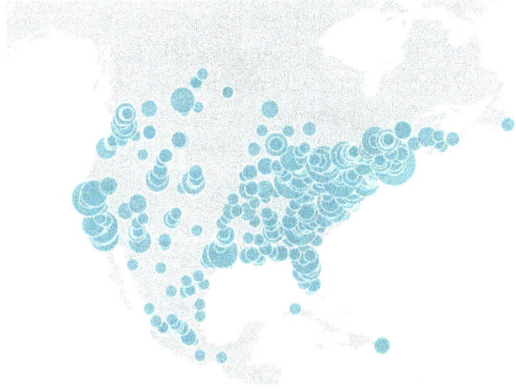

Europe and the Middle East

 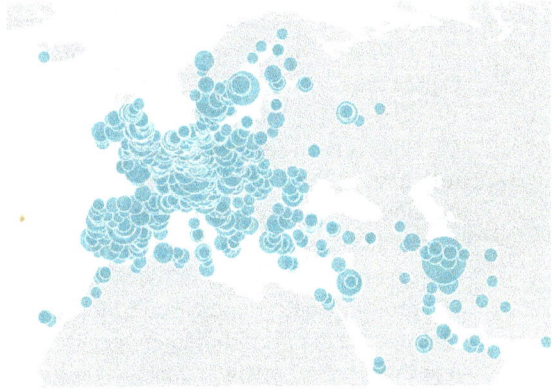

East Asia

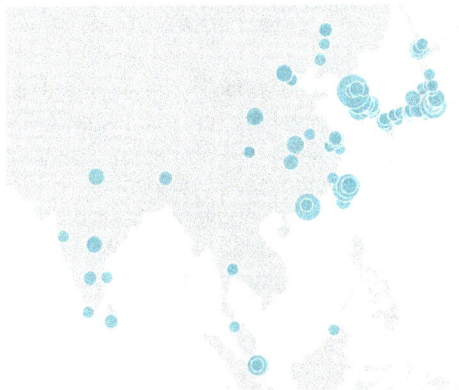 

autonomous vehicles. One of these, nuTonomy, was purchased in 2017 by Aptiv – a global tier-1[32] automotive supplier historically tied to Detroit and General Motors.[33] Aptiv maintains a technology center in Boston, along with centers in Pittsburgh and California.[34] nuTonomy is running trials in Boston and Singapore, where the state Economic Development Board has taken a stake in the company.[35] Another MIT spinoff, Optimus Ride, has partnered with multiple Silicon Valley and automotive firms to deploy low-speed, self-driving shuttles in defined geo-fenced routes.[36]

Detroit, Michigan

Detroit is the historical center of the North American automotive industry. General Motors and Ford maintain headquarters and multiple research centers in the Detroit metropolitan area, as do several international automakers (Fiat Chrysler Automobiles (FCA), Hyundai/Kia and Toyota) and dozens of large automotive suppliers. Nearly all automakers involved in the North American market have some presence in the Detroit area.

Michigan is not a historical locus for robotics. However, it is among the top areas worldwide for research, development, design and manufacturing of advanced automotive systems. While Detroit-based firms have opened regional offices in robotics hubs, such as Pittsburgh, Boston and Silicon Valley, AV-focused startups have opened offices near Detroit to leverage the local expertise in engineering and validating robust automotive-grade systems. The automotive focus of the technology is also leading to increased investment in software development facilities in the Detroit area, including significant investments by Ford, GM and Toyota.

Waymo – perhaps the most advanced autonomous vehicle developer in the industry – plans to renovate a historic Detroit facility to fit vehicles with its proprietary automotive technology.[37] Waymo is partnering with Magna International – a tier-1 automotive supplier based in Aurora, Canada, with multiple facilities in the Detroit area.[38] Previous to the partnership with Magna, Waymo contracted with another major Detroit-area engineering firm – Roush.[39] Roush, meanwhile, has expanded its involvement in automated-vehicle engineering, opening a new research center focused on AV software and systems integration.[40]

Ontario, Canada

The interest in automated vehicle systems has brought additional attention to centers of software development and artificial intelligence. One research cluster that has benefited is the Canadian province of Ontario, including Toronto, Waterloo and Ottawa.

Ontario is an established automotive industry cluster, owing mainly to its proximity to Detroit. Ontario is also strong in the computer software industry. The University of Waterloo, for example, has outstanding math and computer programs. The Waterloo Centre for Automotive Research (WatCAR) has several distinct groups researching advanced vehicle and mobility technology.[41] The University of Toronto also has programs focused on vehicle automation, connectivity and cyber-security.[42]

Pittsburgh, Pennsylvania

Carnegie Mellon University (CMU) in Pittsburg has been a center of autonomous driving technology for decades. CMU researchers tested the very first prototype on-road hands-free driving automation system in 1986, the Navlab 1 project,[43] which was followed by Navlab 2 in 1990. CMU teams also were among the most successful in the DARPA grand challenges that helped usher in the current era of AV research.[44] To some extent, the CMU robotics program has been a victim of its success, as dozens of established researchers have been hired away by AV startups. The most notable example of this is Uber, which first began a strategic partnership with CMU and opened a nearby research center. However, eventually, it hired over 50 CMU researchers away from the university.[45]

CMU has also spawned some AV startups, such as Argo.AI, of which Ford has purchased an ownership stake and announced it will deploy a robotaxi service in 2021.[46] Boston-based nuTonomy, now owned by tier-1 auto supplier Aptiv, has facilities in Pittsburgh and is actively expanding. Many other CMU robotics alumni are now scattered throughout the AV diaspora, including some of the most significant names in the industry, as shown earlier. CMU's Robotics Institute carries on, though with less emphasis on driving automation than in previous decades.[47] Meanwhile, Pittsburgh has become one of the world's most popular cities for on-road testing and development of prototype autonomous vehicles.[48]

Silicon Valley, California

It now feels as though Silicon Valley (the area surrounding San Francisco, California), has always been the center of the AV industry. However, it began with Google (now Waymo) taking an interest in on-road autonomous vehicles following the DARPA grand challenges. Google started to hire grand challenge participants in 2009, including CMU team leader Chris Urmson, who became chief technology officer (CTO) of the project. Other researchers were available locally. Stanford University had an established robotics and automated-driving research program on the same level as CMU and otherwise unparalleled in the world.

Google announced its self-driving project in 2010 with a compelling video of a blind man taking a self-driving car to a Taco Bell restaurant. The video did not convey the extent of preparation required for the demonstration, but it did show a level of driving automation capability that surprised the automotive industry and sparked a movement of industry stalwarts and startups to catch up and get in on the self-driving action.

Google's self-driving car project, combined with the pre-existing pool of AI and software engineers, catalyzed the development of Silicon Valley as a global leader in AV development.

It would be difficult to tabulate the number of firms pursuing automated driving in the Valley. But as of early 2019, 62 entities have received a permit from the California Department of Motor Vehicles to test prototype ADS on public roads in the state.[49]

China

The three waves of technological disruption discussed earlier (AV, MaaS and connected cars), have created a window of opportunity for Chinese auto firms as they have no legacy disadvantage vis-à-vis foreign multinationals.[50] Even in China, however, local tech giants have the upper hand over the auto sector. Chinese tech giants, such as search engine company Baidu, e-commerce concern Alibaba and ride-hailing firms Didi Chuxing, Dida and Ucar are more or less on par with their foreign counterparts. With regard to connectivity, Baidu's CarLife – a system that allows mobile phones to control the infotainment in a car – has been up and running since 2015. Baidu's voice assistant technology is called DuerOS. Alibaba has also rolled out an embedded control system, AliOS, and a smart assistant called Tmall Genie. Tencent, another tech giant, has its own system called "AI in Car."

Moreover, the Government's New Generation Artificial Intelligence Development Plan,[51] announced in 2017, shows China's determination to become a global leader in artificial intelligence, including autonomous driving technology. China also heavily invests in infrastructure and building roads and streets that are compatible with connected and autonomous vehicles. Roads in Beijing's E-Town[52] are among 44 roads (total 123 km) marked out for testing AVs. Besides Beijing, extensive testing is also taking place in 15 other cities around China, including Shanghai, Shenzhen and Guangzhou in Guangdong province, Hangzhou in Zhejiang province, Wuhan in Hubei province and Chongqing.[53]

Baidu, Pony.ai and WeRide are the leaders in self-driving technology in China.[54] However, even Baidu is not yet considered to be among the top 10 globally. In California, Baidu's test vehicles required human intervention every 41 miles driven, compared with every 5,596 miles driven by Waymo's vehicles.[55] The Baidu Apollo Automated Vehicle Platform has, however, attracted more than 100 global partners. Apollo has an AV simulation system, vehicle test data and high-definition maps.[56] Both CarLife and DuerOS are incorporated in Apollo. Further, Baidu has pledged to deploy self-driving taxis in geo-fenced areas of Changsha, Hunan Province, in 2019.[57] Baidu is attracting the majority of investment and attention in the Chinese market for autonomous driving. However, the city government of Beijing, which has begun requiring reporting for testing of automated vehicles on city streets, has received reports from seven other companies in addition to Baidu.[58] Many Chinese companies also maintain research facilities in Silicon Valley, including Baidu.[59] Chinese companies, including Baidu, NIO, Tencent, Alibaba, FAW, SAIC, ChangAn, BAIC, Great Wall, GAC, Dongfeng, Geely, BYD and Lifan have started testing their vehicles in China. Waymo has also opened a subsidiary in Shanghai, although the filing says the subsidiary will focus on logistics consulting, supply chain and AV parts and product design and not AVs.[60]

Japan

Japan's AV work was slow to start due to particularly restrictive laws on self-driving. However, with the 2020 Olympics approaching, there has been an explosion in the AV industry in order to show off the country's cutting-edge technology. Japan has introduced legislation to ease restrictions on self-driving cars and it intends to use Toyota autonomous self-driving shuttles at the 2020 Olympics to transfer competitors around the athletes' village. Evidently, Toyota has become a large part of Japan's foray into AV tech, but Toyota and other Japanese companies are doing much more than just the Olympics push.

Within Japan, Toyota has partnered with Japanese tech investment firm Softbank, most known for its USD 100 billion Vision Fund to buy stakes in fast-growing technology companies, to create a joint venture – MONET – that will focus on development of driverless technology and MaaS solutions in Tokyo. Additionally, MONET has investment from Japanese automakers Honda and Hino. Waymo has partnered with Renault and Nissan, a Franco-Japanese alliance, to bring its AV mobility services to France and Japan. Also, ZMP, a Japanese AV company, and Hinomaru Kotsu, a Japanese taxi company, have paired to develop an autonomous taxi, which they are hoping will be ready for the 2020 Olympics. However, the Japanese AV space isn't just populated by private companies. Both the University of Tokyo and Keio University have smart/advanced mobility projects developing AV technology.

Internationally, the main player is Toyota, again. It has partnered and invested internationally for AV advancements with a myriad of companies, including Uber, May Mobility, Hui, Grab, Getaround, Nvidia and AT&T. Furthermore, on the international front, Softbank has invested USD 2.25 billion in GM's Cruise Automation, a robotaxi firm, and was involved in providing USD 1 billion in funding for Uber to use on its AV division. Chinese company SenseTime is one of the world's highest-valued AI startups, and they have opened a self-driving facility in Joso, just outside of Tokyo.

United Kingdom (U.K.)

The U.K. is an established hub of automotive and engineering talent. The Government has taken a keen interest in autonomous vehicles and has worked to leverage existing capabilities to remain a significant contributor to an emerging AV industry. For example, the U.K. Autodrive project funded trials of prototype automated vehicles made by several manufacturers.[61] The UK CITE Consortium is an industry-led group focused on connected vehicle technology but with an eye toward automation.[62] The U.K. has also published an advisory document to guide testing automated-driving technologies on public roads.[63]

The U.K. has also benefited from EU-funded research programs, such as the EU GATEway project. That project funded U.K.-based Oxbotica – an Oxford University spin-off – to deploy a low-speed autonomous shuttle on a mixed-use pathway.[64] Another U.K. project supported the development of an automated podcar,[65] which operates on purpose-built guideways, to be developed by the U.K.-based RDM group, an automotive supplier. That project resulted in RDM spinning-off an independent company, Aurrigo, which now has facilities in the U.S., Canada and Australia.[66]

Cambridge is a global center of innovation for AI – dating back to 1936 when Alan Turing invented the "universal computing machine" at Kings College.[67] Cambridge is also the home of ARM – a global leader in high-performance processors – which has taken an interest in automated driving.[68]

Other U.K. universities are heavily invested in developing an AV cluster. The universities of Warwick, Birmingham and others contribute to the AI talent pipeline supporting clusters. Oxford University boasts an exceptionally strong robotics program and, as previously mentioned, gave birth to Oxbotica.

France

France's automobile industry is doing its part to remain engaged in the development of next-generation automated vehicles. Renault has pledged "eyes-off/hands-off" functionality in production vehicles as soon as 2021.[69] The Groupe PSA (whose brands include Peugeot, Citroen and DS) is pursuing its Autonomous Vehicle for All (AVA) program.[70] PSA is testing AV technology on roads in Europe and China.[71] The global automotive tier-1 supplier Valeo is also investing heavily in driving automation.[72] Valeo is building a research center for AI in Paris and has secured multiple research partnerships. Such efforts have been buoyed by a national effort to make France an AI leader.[73]

Europe has seen dozens of low-speed autonomous shuttle trials deployed by several firms. France is a center of R&D for autonomous shuttles. One of the largest and best-known companies, Navya, was founded in France in 2014. It has pilot deployments of shuttles around the globe and has a facility in Michigan. Well over 100 shuttles have been produced.[74] Keolis, a France-based private operator of public transit systems, operates many of these deployments.[75]

Another of the world's largest autonomous shuttle companies is EasyMile. It was founded in Toulouse in 2014 following the EU-funded CityMobile2 Project. Over 100 EasyMile shuttles have been produced and used in test deployments around the globe.[76] TransDev, another France-based private operator of public transit systems, manages many of these deployments.[77] TransDev has also partnered with U.S.-based Torc Robotics to test autonomous shuttles in France.[78]

Many French companies are making efforts to expand in the North American market.[79] While many of the French AV-focused companies remain small, many are actively partnering with other companies and institutions, which demonstrates their global ambitions.

Germany

Germany may be second only to the U.S. as a well-spring of innovation and development of AV technology. The EU-sponsored PROMETHEUS research program in the 1980s paralleled DARPA-sponsored research and established German institutions, such as Universität der Bundeswehr München (UBM), as sources of AI and AV expertise.[80] The very first consumer-available level 2 driving automation system, which provides such things as steering, braking and acceleration support to the driver, was introduced by Mercedes Benz and was a legacy of the PROMETHEUS program.[81]

The German auto industry, including Daimler, BMW and Volkswagen, has created numerous partnerships inside and outside of Germany in efforts to bring about a new era of autonomous shared mobility. These activities include not only minor research partnerships and investment tie-ins, but also large consortia.[82] The German automakers have been among the most aggressive in communicating goals for public deployment of automated driving. VW's Audi brand announced that the 2018 Audi A8 would have an option for the world's first consumer-available level 3 ADS, called "Traffic Jam Pilot,"[83] which would allow for highly automated driving. But it later cited regulatory barriers as delaying its appearance.[84] Mercedes has announced its flagship S-Class sedan will include

level 3 automation in 2020[85] and BMW is targeting deployment of consumer-available autonomy in 2021.[86]

German tier-1 suppliers are also very active in this space. Tire company Continental has long manufactured components of vehicle automation and has even constructed its own autonomous shuttle.[87] Conti also aspires to provide an ADS platform as a supplier to automakers.[88] German firm ZF has been partnering and maneuvering for years to become integrated into a global supply chain for AVs and is also developing a prototype vehicle.[89] Bosch is another major tier-1 with ambitions to provide AV technology and is working with Daimler among others to deploy the technology in future consumer vehicles.[90] The maturity of this cluster has supported dozens of autonomy and mobility-related startups.[91]

Israel

The agglomeration of technology companies in this small country is remarkable. By one count, as of mid-2018, nearly 1,000 Israeli startups were using or developing AI technology, and well over a dozen new firms were being established every month.[92]

Global AI and software firms have maintained facilities in Israel for some time to take advantage of this ecosystem, and the auto industry has followed. For example, General Motors was once notable for having no significant presence in Silicon Valley (this is no longer the case after GM acquired Cruise Automation), but it established a research center for automated vehicle technology in Israel in 2008 and expanded it in 2016.[93] Several other automakers have expanded or opened research centers in Israel since 2016.[94]

Perhaps the best-known Israeli firm contributing to the global AV ecosystem is Mobileye – a supplier of vision systems for multiple automakers. Mobileye started in 1999. It had its initial public offering (IPO) in 2014 and was acquired by Intel in 2017 for USD 15 billion. As an established supplier, Mobileye claims that its technology has been embedded in over 27 million vehicles across 25 different brands.[95] Mobileye is now the face of Intel's foray into the automotive supply chain and is pursuing fully autonomous driving in earnest. Intel has announced a partnership with Israel's Champion Motors and Volkswagen to deploy driverless taxis in Israel with commercialization scheduled for 2022.[96] Beyond its supplier role, Intel/Mobileye's activity in strategic R&D partnering has become increasingly extensive and global.[97]

3.7   Is AV technology changing the geography of innovation in the automotive industry?

Innovation has a geographical dimension.[98] Research has shown that industries tend to co-locate in the vicinity of each other (see Chapters 1 and 2). The two types of players in the auto industry, the incumbents and the new entrants, have their own geographical clusters. The new entrants belong to the tech clusters of the world (e.g., Silicon Valley), whereas the incumbent automakers are well established in their manufacturing clusters (e.g., Detroit). The key question is whether the emergence of AV has made the automakers and tech companies seek greater geographical proximity. If the answer is yes, in which direction? The automakers are appearing in the tech clusters or vice versa.

While it is too early to give a definitive answer to the above questions, evidence based on patent data can shed some light. This section looks at the top global auto industry companies' patents, selected from three geographical areas: the U.S. (Ford and GM), Germany (Daimler, BMW, Audi, Volkswagen and Bosch) and Japan (Toyota, Honda and Nissan). These companies' total patent portfolio was examined, and a subset of patents related to AV technology identified and flagged. Based on this data the share of each company's total patenting for different clusters is calculated together with that of AV patents. For instance, 72.6 percent of Daimler's total patents are in Stuttgart, with 76.9 percent of its AV patents also being there.

The major chunk of automakers' AV patents is still generated in the same main clusters where most of their patenting happens. Nevertheless, there are also important variations. More than 82 percent of Japanese automakers' total and AV patents belong to their primary, Japan-based clusters, a far higher percentage than that of the two U.S. companies, as can be seen from Table 3.1 below.

A quick look at the list below of second-line clusters reveals some interesting differences. A number of clusters, such as San Jose, Berlin, Los Angeles and Osaka, have strong AV specialization (in the sense that their AV share is large relative to their total patent share). For Volkswagen, for example, San Jose and Berlin each

have 16.1 and 9.7 percent of AV patents but only 1 and 4.8 percent, respectively, of general patents.[99]

In order to test whether tech companies have moved physically closer to automakers, the same exercise was repeated[100]. The selected companies were Google, Waymo, Delphi, Mobileye, DeepMap, Magna Electronics, Qualcomm, Uber and Apple. No systematic trend toward auto clusters was observed. As with automakers, the lion's share of both total and AV patenting happens in the same top cluster.

The geography of Uber's AV patents is interesting. While 39.6 percent of its patents are in San Francisco, Silicon Valley is not its top cluster when it comes to AV. Around 48.5 percent of Uber's AV patents are in Pittsburgh, where it has been hiring and collaborating with CMU researchers. Uber has also been testing AVs in Pittsburg since late 2018.

These results indicate that, while there is some shifting geography at the margin, auto and tech companies' innovation is still largely home based. However, the evidence available, although interesting, should be treated with caution. The numbers, particularly for AV patents, are very limited and the weight of this limited set of patents may distort the overall picture. Moreover, patent data is made public with at least 18 months' delay after being first filed. And the actual innovation may have been developed months, if not years, before the patent request was made. Finally, applicants' name disambiguation issues may have impacted the results for some companies.

3.8   Potential positive and negative impacts of AVs

Despite the high anticipation that surrounds them, fully autonomous vehicles are, if not decades, definitely years away.[101] Multiple intertwined technological advances are creating new rules for an industry that had not changed its way of doing business for almost a century. Key players from the tech and traditional automobile sectors – although with different incentives – are pooling resources to realize the goal of self-driving cars. However, the obstacles are not simply technical. Every technological shock at the early stages faces some level of socio-technical inertia in the sense that new technology requires organizational changes that also affect the interaction of people and technology. Oftentimes, change is not easily welcomed.

While there is some shifting geography at the margin, auto and tech companies' innovation is still largely home-based

Table 3.1 Comparison of the total share of patents with the AV patents of selected automakers in different clusters

Cluster name	Total share (%)	AV share (%)	Cluster name	Total share (%)	AV share (%)
Audi			**GM**		
Ingolstadt	60.1	60	Detroit–Ann Arbor	45.3	54.7
Munich	10.7	18.8	Waterford	5.1	11.3
Frankfurt	3.9	6.2	Los Angeles	4.5	8.5
San Jose–San Francisco	0.4	6.2	Frankfurt	16.6	7.5
BMW			**Honda**		
Munich	72.5	84.1	Tokyo	90.8	82.3
Nürnberg	1.3	6.1	Los Angeles	0.2	3.7
Würzburg	0.4	3.7	Osaka	2.6	2.4
San Jose–San Francisco	0.4	3.7	Nagoya	3.1	1.8
Bosch			**Nissan**		
Stuttgart	69.1	77.6	Tokyo	97.0	87.7
Munich	2.6	5.0	Osaka	1.5	8.6
San Jose–San Francisco	1.0	4.6	San Jose–San Francisco	0.0	3.1
Braunschweig	0.5	4.1	Nagoya	1.2	2.5
Daimler			**Toyota**		
Stuttgart	72.6	76.9	Nagoya	95.4	93.7
Ulm	5.8	7.4	Tokyo	5.4	5.2
Frankfurt	5.1	4.1	Osaka	2.3	3.0
Aachen	0.7	4.1	Shizuoka	0.2	1.1
Ford			**Volkswagen**		
Detroit-Ann Arbor	65.0	71.5	Wolfsburg	47.9	46.8
Cologne–Dusseldorf	8.8	6.6	Braunschweig	37.1	40.3
San Jose–San Francisco	1.4	3.6	San Jose–San Francisco	1.0	16.1
Aachen	4.8	2.9	Berlin	4.8	9.7

Note: The sum of the percentages may be more than 100 percent, due to the fact that a single patent can be assigned to more than one cluster so there is double counting.

The current ecosystem of the automotive industry – its market power and its social and political position, for example – has been in place for decades and is very strong. This ecosystem is not so likely to change easily unless the key players in the industry change (i.e. existing automakers exit the market or the market is totally taken over by the tech companies), there is a drastic transformation of policy and regulatory issues or customer demand and preferences shift considerably. At the same time, public opinion is still split over AV.

Advocates of AV technology see it solving several grave urban problems. For example, it could reduce traffic jams and air pollution and improve road safety. Increased precision in the movement of vehicles and the elimination of human error can reduce traffic fatalities. Connected "smart" vehicles can safely travel much closer together – a technique known as "platooning." This, together with automated highway systems, should increase road capacity and lead to other efficiency gains, such as lower fuel consumption and better energy efficiency, which will also have a positive impact on the environment.

Hours would no longer be wasted "behind the wheel" and those who would once have been driving could instead dedicate time to relaxing, working or even sleeping. Children, senior citizens and disabled people would have more independence and mobility. Land currently devoted to parking lots could be put to other uses.

Not everyone is so positive about self-drive cars, however. In 2018, the death of a pedestrian in Arizona in an accident involving a test vehicle operating in self-driving mode was a huge setback. Some companies temporarily halted road testing. Whatever the state of play technologically, the general public may not yet be ready for AVs to go mainstream. Some critics question whether AVs would really help solve urban issues such as traffic jams and pollution. The new technology could simply increase the number of vehicles on the road, and therefore congestion. And with cars being self-driving, commuters might be prepared to "drive" further to work rather than take a train, which is less polluting.

Privacy and cyber-security are also major concerns. Data about drivers collected through autonomous, connected vehicles and other "intelligent transport system" applications could potentially be used for purposes not related to driving. The ability of hackers to crack the system, and alter information or the identity of another vehicle is one of the many serious security worries. Legal and regulatory systems already have trouble keeping up with the fast pace of change in the automotive industry. It is still not clear, in the case of an accident, who would be legally liable – the company that runs the software system, the hardware or the mobility platform.

Moreover, countries and regions are at different levels of infrastructure readiness for AVs. Uneven degrees of preparedness may exacerbate inequality between richer and poorer areas within countries and between regions. All these changes will ripple through other industries – from insurance to repair, trucking to taxi driving. AV technology has an impact that goes beyond the boundaries of a single industry.

Until the auto and tech world can address all these technical, ethical, security and legal issues, the AV future will continue to be a dream.

Notes

1 This section draws on Dziczek *et al.* (2019).

2 In this chapter, terms like autonomous vehicle, self-driving, driverless, etc. are used interchangeably and are meant to refer to the same phenomenon.

3 See WIPO Technology Trends 2019 - Artificial Intelligence

4 See Tripsas (1997) on internal knowledge development strategies, Zucker and Darby (1997) on recruiting human capital, Rothaermel (2001) on strategic alliances, Higgins and Rodriguez (2006) on acquisitions of new entrants, and Rothaermel and Hess (2007) for combinations of these strategies.

5 See Klepper (1997), Audrestsch and Feldman (1996), Abernathy and Utterback (1978), Jovanovic and MacDonald (1994).

6 See Abernathy and Clark (1985) and Klepper (1997).

7 See Klepper (1997).

8 See IEA (2019).

9 See Prahalad and Hamel (1997).

10 See Zehtabchi (2019) for more detailed information about AV patent and scientific publication search strategy.

11 See Intel (n.d.).

12 Tech includes: electronics, ICTs, semiconductors and audio-visuals. Auto includes: instruments, material, machines, engines and transport, civil engineering. Others include: biopharma, chemicals and environment and consumer goods.

13 See Zehtabchi (2019).

14 See Hummel (2019).

15 See Reuters (2019).

16 A technology stack is the list of all the tools and technologies used to build and run a single product.

17 See VIA Technologies (2018).

18 See Randall (2019).

19 See Hawkins (2019).

20 See Chesbrough (2003)

21 See Arora and Gambardella (1990).

22 See Teece (1986).

23 See Gans and Stern (2003) and Cozzolino and Rothaermel (2018).

24 See Perkins and Murmann (2018).

25 See MacDuffie (2018), Jiang and Lu (2018), Teece (2018).

26 See Capron and Mitchell (2012).

27 The majority of the data was collected from the latest media and company announcements. However, at times this info may be misleading as other motivations like market signaling and gaining venture capitalist attention might be behind the announcements.

28 See Bresnahan and Tratjenberg (1995).

29 The patent and scientific publication data used in this section are a sub-sample of those explained in Chapter 2. For more information about detailed search strategy and data collection please check the respective working papers.

30 See Lee and Lim (2001).

31 See Toyota Research Institute-CSAIL (n.d.).

32 See Stone (2018).

33 See Abuelsamid (2017).

34 See nuTonomy (2017).

35 See Singapore Economic Development Board (2016).

36 See Engel (2017).

37 See Bigelow (2019a).

38 See Bigelow (2019b).

39 See Nicas (2017).

40 See Snavely (2017).

41 See University of Waterloo (n.d.) and McKenzie and McPhee (2017).

42 See University of Toronto (2019).

43 See Carnegie Mellon (1986).

44 See U.S. Defense Advanced Research Projects Agency (n.d.).

45 See Lowensohn (2015).

46 See Vasilash (2018).

47 See Carnegie Mellon University (n.d.).

48 Wiggers (2019).

49 See California Department of Motor Vehicles (n.d.).

50 See Teece (2019).

51 See full translation: FLIA (2017).

52 Economist (2019).

53 See Feifei (2019).

54 See Silver (2018).

55 See Teece (2019) and Jing (2018).

56 Visit apollo.auto.

57 See Xinhua (2019).

58 See Liao (2019).

59 Visit research.baidu.com.

60 See Korosec (2018).

61 Visit www.ukautodrive.com/the-uk-autodrive-project.

62 See Fleet News (2018).

63 See U.K. Department for Transport (2015).

64 See Dennis and Brugeman (2019).

65 Personal Rapid Transit (PRT), also referred to as podcars, is a public transport mode featuring small automated vehicles operating on a network of specially built guideways.

66 See Dennis and Brugeman (2019).

67 See Taylor (n.d.).

68 See ARM (n.d.).

69 See Poulanges (2017).

70 See PSA Groupe (n.d.).

71 See PSA Groupe (n.d.).

72 See Valeo (2015).

73 See Ministère de l'Enseignement supérieur, de la Recherche et de l'Innovation (2019).

74 See Dennis and Brugeman (2019).

75 Visit www.keolis.com/en.

76 See Dennis and Brugeman (2019).

77 Visit www.transdev.com/en.

78 See McQuilkin (2019).

79 See UBI Mobility-Connected Cars France (2018).

80 See Dickmanns (2002).

81 See Gregor *et al.* (2002), Daimler (2016), Oagana (2016).
82 See Taylor and Wissenbach (2019).
83 See Audi (2017).
84 See Ulrich (2019).
85 See Hetzner (2018).
86 See DeMattia (2018).
87 See Continental AG (n.d.).

88 See Continental AG (2018).
89 See Behrmann and Rauwald (2018).
90 See Daimler (n.d.).
91 See Initiative for Applied Artificial Intelligence (n.d.).
92 See Singer (2018).
93 See South Africa Israel Chamber of Commerce (2016).

94 See Leichman (2017).
95 See Scheer (2018).
96 See Intel (2018).
97 See Reichert (2019).
98 See Saxenian (1996) and (2007).
99 See Zehtabchi (2019).
100 See Zehtabchi (2019).
101 See Ghemawat (1991).

References

Abernathy, W.J. and K.B. Clark (1985). Innovation: mapping the winds of creative destruction. *Research Policy*, 14(1), 3–22.

Abernathy, W.J. and J.M. Utterback (1978). Patterns of industrial innovation. *Technology Review*, 80(7), 40–47.

Abuelsamid, S. (2017). Delphi acquires nuTonomy for $450M, advancing push for automated Driving. *Forbes*, October 24. www.forbes.com/sites/samabuelsamid/2017/10/24/delphi-acquires-automated-driving-startup-nutonomy-for-450m

ARM. (n.d.). Automotive Autonomous Drive. www.arm.com/solutions/automotive/autonomous-car

Arora, A. and A. Gambardella (1990). Complementarity and external linkages: the strategies of the large firms in biotechnology. *The Journal of Industrial Economics*, 38(4), 361–379.

Audi. (2017). *Audi piloted driving*. media.audiusa.com/models/piloteddriving

Audretsch, D.B. and M.P. Feldman (1996). Innovative clusters and the industry life cycle. *Review of Industrial Organization*, 11(2), 253–273.

Behrmann, E. and C. Rauwald (2018). ZF plans $14 billion autonomous vehicle push, concept van. *Automotive News*, September 19.

Bigelow, P. (2019a). Waymo firms up plans for autonomous car assembly plant in Detroit. *Automotive News*, April 23.

Bigelow, P. (2019b). Waymo to build self-driving cars in Detroit, invest $13.6 million in factory. *Crain's Detroit Business*, April 23.

Bresnahan, T.F. and M. Trajtenberg (1995). General purpose technologies 'Engines of growth'? *Journal of Econometrics*, 65(1), 83–108.

California Department of Motor Vehicles. (n.d.). Testing of autonomous vehicles with a driver. www.dmv.ca.gov/portal/dmv/detail/vr/autonomous/testing

Capron, L. and W. Mitchell (2012). *Build, Borrow, or Buy: Solving the Growth Dilemma*. Cambridge, MA: Harvard Business Press.

Carnegie Mellon. (1986). NavLab 1. Robotics Institute History of Self-Driving Cars. YouTube video, www.youtube.com/watch?v=ntlczNQKfjQ

Carnegie Mellon University. (n.d.). No Hands Across America. www.cs.cmu.edu/~tjochem/nhaa/nhaa_home_page.html

Chesbrough, H.W. (2003). *Open Innovation: The New Imperative for Creating and Profiting from Technology*. Cambridge, MA: Harvard Business Press.

Continental AG (2018). Continental expands automated driving tests on the autobahn. Press Release, April 26. www.continental.com/en/press/press-releases/cruisingchauffeur-128928

Continental AG. (n.d.). Driverless mobility. www.continental-automotive.com/en-gl/Landing-Pages/CAD/Automated-Driving/Hidden-Pages/Driverless-Mobility

Cozzolino, A. and F.T. Rothaermel (2018). Discontinuities, competition, and cooperation: Cooperative dynamics between incumbents and entrants. *Strategic Management Journal*, 39(12), 3053–3085.

Daimler. (2016). The PROMETHEUS project launched in 1986: Pioneering autonomous driving. Press release, September 20.

Daimler. (n.d.). Reinventing safety: a joint approach to automated driving systems. www.daimler.com/innovation/case/autonomous/reinventing-safety-2.html

DeMattia, N. (2018). Klaus Fröhlich talks about BMW iNEXT. *BMW Blog*, September 24. www.bmwblog.com/2018/09/24/klaus-frohlich-to-talks-about-bmw-inext

Dennis, E.P. and V.S. Brugeman (2019). *Automated and Connected Vehicle Deployment Efforts: A Primer for Transportation Planners*. Ann Arbor, MI: Center for Automotive Research; Lansing, MI: Michigan Department of Transportation.

Dickmanns, E. (2002). The development of machine vision for road vehicles in the last decade. In *Proceedings Intelligent Vehicle Symposium 2002*, Versailles, June 17–21. Piscataway, NJ: IEEE, 268–281.

Dziczek, K, E.P. Dennis, Q. Hong, Y. Chen, V. Sathe-Brugeman and E. Marples (2019). Automated Driving Technology Report. Unpublished background report for the World Intellectual Property Organization.

Economist (2019). Chinese firms are taking a different route to driverless cars. *The Economist*, October 12. www.economist.com/business/2019/10/12/chinese-firms-are-taking-a-different-route-to-driverless-cars

Engel, J. (2017). Optimus Ride drives off with $18M for autonomous vehicle tech. *xconomy*, November 2. xconomy.com/boston/2017/11/02/optimus-ride-drives-offwith-18m-for-autonomous-vehicle-tech

Feifei, F. (2019). Autonomous vehicles gaining more ground. *China Daily*, January 15. www.chinadaily.com.cn/a/201901/15/WS5c3d2bb0a3106c65c34e46e2.html

Fleet News (2018). UK CITE enters second phase of Coventry autonomy testing with Jaguar Land Rover. *Fleet News*, July 2. www.fleetnews.co.uk/news/environment/2018/07/02/uk-cite-enters-second-phase-of-coventry-autonomy-testing-with-jaguar-land-rover

Foundation for Law and International Affairs (FLIA) (2017). China's New Generation of Artificial Intelligence Development Plan. flia.org/notice-state-council-issuing-new-generation-artificial-intelligence-development-plan

Gans, J.S. and S. Stern (2003). The product market and the market for "ideas": commercialization strategies for technology entrepreneurs. *Research Policy*, 32(2), 333–350.

Ghemawat, P. (1991). Market incumbency and technological inertia. *Marketing Science*, 10(2), 161–171.

Gregor, R., M. Lutzeler, M. Pellkofer, K-H. Siedersberger and E. Dickmanns (2002). MS-Vision: a perceptual system for autonomous vehicles. *IEEE Transactions on Intelligent Transportation Systems*, 3(1), 48–59.

Hawkins, A.J. (2019). Waymo is making some of its self-driving car data available for free to researchers. *The Verge*, August 21. www.theverge.com/2019/8/21/20822755/waymo-self-driving-car-data-set-free-research

Hetzner, C. (2018). Mercedes plans advanced self-driving tech for next S class. *Automotive News*, October 11.

Higgins, M.J. and D. Rodriguez (2006). The outsourcing of R&D through acquisitions in the pharmaceutical industry. *Journal of Financial Economics*, 80(2), 351–383.

Hummel, T. (2019). BMW, Daimler seal self-driving tech partnership. *Automotive News Europe*, July 4. europe.autonews.com/automakers/bmw-daimler-seal-self-driving-tech-partnership

Initiative for Applied Artificial Intelligence. (n.d.). German Startup Landscape of Autonomous Driving. appliedai.de/insights/autonomous-driving

Intel. (n.d.). 5G Is key to fully realizing connected and autonomous vehicles. www.intel.com/content/www/us/en/communications/5g-connected-vehicle.html

Intel. (2018). Volkswagen, Mobileye and Champion Motors to invest in Israel and deploy first autonomous EV ride-hailing service. *Intel Newsroom*, October 29. newsroom.intel.com/news-releases/volkswagen-mobileye-champion-motors-invest-israel-deploy-first-autonomous-ev-ride-hailing-service/#gs.bt6x8i

International Energy Agency (IEA). (2019). *Global EV Outlook 2019*. Paris: IEA. www.iea.org/publications/reports/globalevoutlook2019

Jiang, H. and F. Lu (2018). To be friends, not competitors: a story different from Tesla driving the Chinese automobile industry. *Management and Organization Review*, 14(3), 491–499.

Jing, M. (2018). Baidu's self-driving cars require more human intervention than Alphabet's Waymo. *South China Morning Post*, May 7. www.scmp.com/tech/enterprises/article/2144863/baidus-self-driving-carsrequire-more-human-intervention-alphabets

Jovanovic, B. and G.M. MacDonald (1994). The life cycle of a competitive industry. *Journal of Political Economy*, 102(2), 322–347.

Klepper, S. (1997). Industry life cycles. *Industrial and corporate change*, 6(1), 145–182.

Korosec, K. (2018). Waymo opens subsidiary in China. *TechCrunch*, August 24. techcrunch.com/2018/08/24/waymo-opens-subsidiary-in-china

Lee, K. and C. Lim (2001). Technological regimes, catching-up and leapfrogging: findings from the Korean industries. *Research Policy*, 30(3), 459–483.

Leichman, A.K. (2017). Porsche invests 8-figure sum in Israeli auto innovation. *Israel21c*, June 4. www.israel21c.org/porsche-invests-8-figure-sum-in-israeli-auto-innovation

Liao, R. (2019). Search giant Baidu has driven the most autonomous miles in Beijing. *TechCrunch*, April 2. techcrunch.com/2019/04/02/baidu-self-driving-2018

Lowensohn, J. (2015). Uber just announced its own self-driving car project. *The Verge*, February 2. www.theverge.com/2015/2/2/7966527/uber-just-announced-its-own-self-driving-car-project

MacDuffie, J.P. (2018). Response to Perkins and Murmann: Pay attention to what is and isn't unique about Tesla. *Management and Organization Review*, 14(3), 481–489.

McKenzie, R. and J. McPhee (2017). Research and educational programs for connected and autonomous vehicles at the University of Waterloo. *Mechanical Engineering*, 139(12), S21–S23. www.memagazineselect.asmedigitalcollection.asme.org/article.aspx?articleid=2676826

McQuilkin, K. (2019). Blacksburg's Torc Robotics is launching autonomous shuttle buses in France. *RichmondInno*, January 8. www.americaninno.com/richmond/tech-news-richmond/blacksburgs-torc-robotics-is-launching-autonomous-shuttle-buses-in-france

Ministère de l'Enseignement supérieur de la Recherche et de l'Innovation (2019). Lancement de 4 Instituts Interdisciplinaires d'Intelligence Artificielle (3IA) et ouverture de deux appels à projets complémentaires. Press release, April 24. www.enseignementsup-recherche.gouv.fr/cid141320/lancement-de-4-instituts-interdisciplinaires-d-ia-3ia-et-ouverture-de-deux-appels-a-projets-complementaires.html

Nicas, J. (2017). Google parent retires 'Firefly' self-driving prototype. *Wall Street Journal*, June 13.

nuTonomy. (2017). Aptiv opens Boston Technology Center. Press release, December 12. www.aptiv.com/media/article/2017/12/12/aptiv-opens-boston-technology-center

Oagana, A. (2016, January 25). A short history of Mercedes-Benz autonomous driving technology AutoEvolution. Retrieved from www.autoevolution.com/news/a-short-history-ofmercedes-benz-autonomous-driving-technology-68148.html

Perkins, G. and J.P. Murmann (2018). What does the success of Tesla mean for the future dynamics in the global automobile sector? *Management and Organization Review*, 14(3), 471–480.

Poulanges, M. (2017). Renault presents eyes-off/hands-off technology for the autonomous vehicle of the future. Groupe Renault, June 28. group.renault.com/en/news/blog-renault/renault-presents-eyes-offhands-off-technology-for-the-autonomous-vehicle-of-the-future

Prahalad, C.K. and G. Hamel (1997). The core competence of the corporation. In *Strategische Unternehmungsplanung/Strategische Unternehmungsführung*. Heidelberg: Physica, 969–987.

PSA Groupe. (n.d.). On the road to the autonomous car! www.groupe-psa.com/en/story/en-route-vers-la-voiture-autonome

Randall, T. (2019). Waymo starts selling sensors to lower cost of self-driving cars. *Bloomberg Hyperdrive*, March 6. www.bloomberg.com/news/articles/2019-03-06/waymo-starts-selling-sensors-to-lower-cost-of-self-driving-cars

Reichert, C. (2019). CES 2019: Mobileye inks autonomous vehicle deals across China. *ZD Net*, January 8. www.zdnet.com/article/ces-2019-mobileye-inks-autonomous-vehicle-deals-across-china

Reuters (2019). Audi to join Mercedes, BMW development alliance: paper. www.reuters.com/article/us-volkswagen-audi-bmw-daimler/audi-to-join-mercedes-bmw-development-alliance-paper-idUSKCN1VC0YT

Rothaermel, F. T. (2001). Incumbent's advantage through exploiting complementary assets via interfirm cooperation. *Strategic management journal*, 22(6-7), 687--699.

Rothaermel, F.T. and A.M. Hess (2007). Building dynamic capabilities: innovation driven by individual-, firm-, and network-level effects. *Organization Science*, 18(6), 898–921.

Saxenian, A. (1996). *Regional Advantage*. Cambridge, MA: Harvard University Press.

Saxenian, A. (2007). *The New Argonauts: Regional Advantage in a Global Economy*. Cambridge, MA: Harvard University Press.

Scheer, S. (2018). Mobileye gets self-driving tech deal for 8 million cars. *Automotive News Europe*, May 17. europe.autonews.com/ article/20180517/ANE/180519817/ mobileye-gets-self-driving-tech-deal-for-8-million-cars

Silver, D. (2018). Baidu brings the Waymo model to China. *Forbes*, November 1. www.forbes.com/ sites/davidsilver/2018/11/01/ baidu-brings-the-waymo-model-to-china/#d0b52193d961

Singapore Economic Development Board. (2016). World's first driverless taxi system comes to Singapore. www.edb.gov.sg/en/news-and-events/insights/innovation/world-s-first-driverless-taxi-system-comes-to-singapore.html

Singer, D. (2018). Israel's artificial intelligence start-ups. *StartupHub. ai*. www.startuphub.ai/israels-artificial-intelligence-startups-2018

Snavely, B. (2017). Roush expands in Troy, will hire 150 engineers of self-driving tech. *Detroit Free Press*. May 9.

South Africa Israel Chamber of Commerce. (2016). Autonomous cars herald new era for Israeli high-tech. saicc.co.za/general-motors-to-triple-size-of-rd-israelicentre

Stone, A. (2018). What the three tiers of automotive marketing mean today. *Forbes*, June 28. www.forbes.com/sites/ forbesagencycouncil/2018/06/28/ what-the-three-tiers-of-automotive-marketing-mean-today/#c449dec26510

Taylor, M. (n.d.). AI in Cambridge: the machine learning capital of the U.K.? *Luminous PR*. luminouspr.com/ cambridge-the-ai-capital-of-the-uk

Taylor, E. and I. Wissenbach (2019). As Google races ahead, German carmakers look to go faster on autonomous driving. Reuters, January 23. www.reuters.com/article/ us-germany-autos/as-google-races-ahead-german-carmakers-look-to-go-faster-on-autonomous-driving-idUSKCN1PH18C

Teece, D.J. (1986). Profiting from technological innovation: implications for integration, collaboration, licensing and public policy. *Research Policy*, 15(6), 285–305.

Teece, D.J. (2018). Tesla and the reshaping of the auto industry. *Management and Organization Review*, 14(3), 501–512.

Teece, D.J. (2019). China and the reshaping of the auto industry: a dynamic capabilities perspective. *Management and Organization Review*, 15(1), 177–199.

Toyota Research Institute-CSAIL. (n.d.). *Joint Research Center*. toyota. csail.mit.edu

Tripsas, M. (1997). Unraveling the process of creative destruction: complementary assets and incumbent survival in the typesetter industry. *Strategic Management Journal*, 18(S1), 119–142.

UBI Mobility-Connected Cars France (2018). French delegation: Connected autonomous vehicles. 1419891vq14j2fapah1bpghjzyq. wpengine.netdna-cdn.com/ wpcontent/uploads/2018/05/French-delegation_Ubimobility-2018-Detroit-Final.pdf

U.K. Department for Transport. (2015). *The Pathway to Driverless Cars: Code of Practice for Testing*. assets.publishing.service. gov.uk/government/uploads/system/ uploads/attachment_data/file/446316/ pathway-driverless-cars.pdf

Ulrich, L. (2019). 2019 Audi A8 review: Tech-packed flagship delivers almost everything, except level 3 autonomy. *The Drive*, January 31. www.thedrive. com/new-cars/26252/2019-audi-a8-review-tech-packed-flagship-sedan-delivers-almost-everything-except-level-3-autonomy

University of Toronto. (2019). News: Self-driving cars. www.utoronto.ca/ news/tags/self-driving-cars

University of Waterloo. (n.d.). *Centre for Automotive Research*. uwaterloo. ca/centre-automotive-research/ research-expertise/connected-andautonomous

U.S. Defense Advanced Research Projects Agency. (n.d.). The grand challenge. www.darpa.mil/about-us/timeline/-grand-challenge-for-autonomous-vehicles

Valeo (2015). *The Autonomous Car Takes to the Road*. Retrieved from www.valeo.com/en/the-autonomous-takes-to-the-road

Vasilash, G. (2018). Argo AI and getting Ford to Level 4 autonomy. *Autoblog*, September 8. www. autoblog.com/2018/09/08/argo-ai-ford-level-4-autonomy-self-driving-car

VIA Technologies (2018). VIA partners with Lucid to develop industry-leading VIA Edge AI 3D developer kit powered by Qualcomm APQ8096SG embedded processor. www.viatech.com/en/2018/11/via-partners-with-lucid-to-develop-industry-leading-via-edge-ai-3d-developer-kit

WIPO (2019. WIPO Technology Trends 2019. *Artificial Intelligence*. Geneva: WIPO.

Wiggers, K. (2019) 5 companies are testing 55 self-driving cars in Pittsburgh. *Venture Beat*, April 26. venturebeat.com/2019/04/26/5-companies-are-testing-55-self-drivingcars-in-pittsburgh

Xinhua (2019) Baidu's self-driving taxis to run in Changsha in late 2019. Xinhuanet.com, April 5. www.xinhuanet.com/english/2019-04/05/c_137952253.htm

Zehtabchi, M. (2019). Measuring Innovation in the Autonomous Vehicle Technology. *WIPO Economic Research Working Paper No. 60*. Geneva: World Intellectual Property Organization.

Zucker, L.G. and M.R. Darby (1997). Present at the biotechnological revolution: transformation of technological identity for a large incumbent pharmaceutical firm. *Research Policy*, 26(4–5), 429–446.

The impact of plant biotech
innovation reaches far beyond
the lab. Innovation produced
in a metropolitan hotspot can
benefit 75 times its land mass.

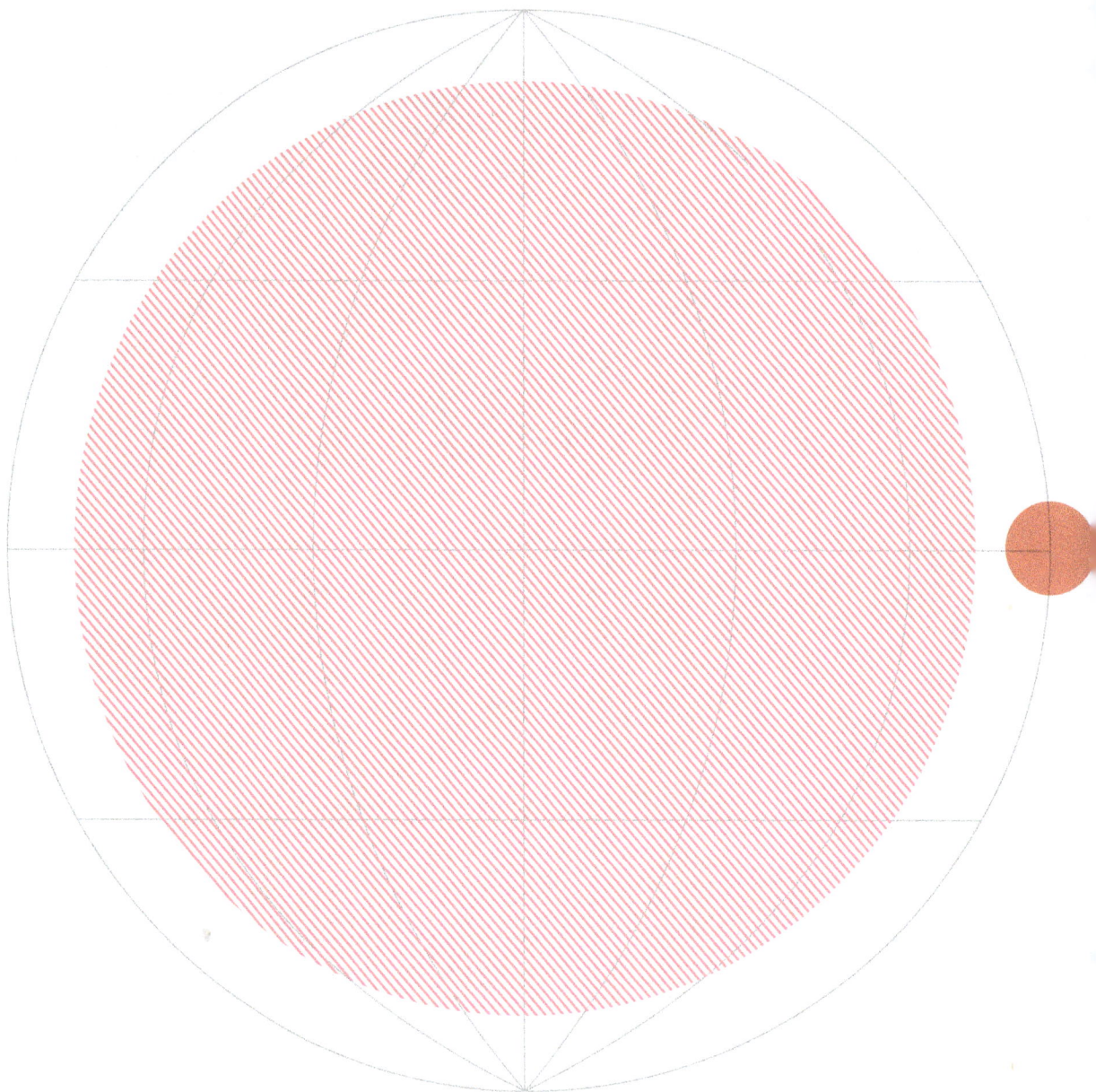

■ 200,000 km²

● METROPOLITAN HOTSPOT

▨ AGRICULTURAL LAND

Chapter 4

Plant biotechnology – connecting urban innovation and rural application

Humans began making genetic improvements to plants thousands of years before anyone even knew what a gene was. Starting circa 10,000 BCE, they initially began by selecting and domesticating crops from the natural biological diversity of plants. These crops differed from their wild predecessors through the propagation of carefully chosen specific plant materials, which were cultivated for human consumption and use.[1]

The techniques used to select and propagate crop varieties with desirable traits – known as cultivars – can generally be divided into three categories: the traditional, which began with domestication, the conventional and the modern. All three methods are in use today to varying degrees.

15,000,000 km²

Conventional breeding of new crop varieties and traits involves the sexual reproduction of two compatible crop varieties to produce a mutated offspring with the desired biological traits.[2] This method often requires many crosses to get to the right combination of genes to produce the desired crop. It also needs the crops to be sexually compatible.

Today, new crop varieties can be achieved by biotechnology. This modern technique relies on an understanding of a plant's genetic make-up and uses different methods of genetic engineering to make changes to its deoxyribonucleic acid (DNA), molecules of nucleotides which carry the genetic instructions for the development, functioning, growth and reproduction of all known organisms.

Biotechnology refers to "any technological application that uses biological systems, living organisms, or derivatives thereof, to make or modify products or processes for specific use."[3] It can also involve the implementation of advanced molecular and cellular technologies and techniques. In both the broader and narrower sense of its application, agricultural biotechnology relies on the discoveries and research tools of a relatively new science field.

It is changing the agriculture industry.[4] Advances have produced crops that are resistant to certain diseases, that result in higher yields than before, that can grow in extreme soil conditions, such as in arid and salty environments, and that are even infused with nutrients.[5]

Biotechnology innovation has the potential to increase agricultural productivity and quality, ultimately raising incomes for farmers across the world. It can also address environmental concerns about the use of chemical pesticides. Klümper and Qaim (2014) show that genetically modified technology had increased farmer profits worldwide by 68 percent, crop yields by 22 percent and reduced use of chemical pesticides by 37 percent. Brookes (2018) estimates that each extra U.S. dollar spent on transgenic soy seed – seed containing genes from another organism – relative to conventional seed raises a farmer's income by USD 3.88. The gains reflect higher yields and lower costs from using fewer pest and weed controls. Moreover, the technology is seen as a potential solution to global issues of hunger and poverty.

This chapter uses the case of agricultural biotechnology, specifically plant biotechnology, to illustrate the workings of a global innovation network.[6] It relies on information contained in patent documents and scientific publications to identify the actors and locations of innovation. It further exploits these two complementary measures of innovative activities to demonstrate how different innovation clusters link to one another.

The first section of this chapter describes the evolution of the plant biotechnology industry and identifies the factors that drive innovation. The second looks at how the industry's innovation landscape has evolved and how more countries are involved in innovation than ever before. The penultimate section examines the links between innovation centers in different parts of the world. The chapter concludes with how the plant biotechnology's global innovation landscape as well as the network may change due to new developments in the industry.

4.1 The rising importance of plant biotechnology

Plant biotechnology generally involves three areas of the farming industry: (i) plant breeding and seeds, (ii) soil health and fertility and (iii) pest control and pesticides.

The application of biotechnology in plant breeding and seeds refers to the development of new varieties and traits through hybridization, outcrossing (interbreeding), mutation, tissue culture, grafting and cloning of plants, genetic engineering and editing of the genome, which is the whole of the hereditary information encoded in a plant's DNA, to name a few. Most innovation is in this area.

For soil health and fertility, biotechnology involves using biofertilizers – the culturing and use of microbes for soil amendment and plant growth. Lastly, biotechnology for pest control and pesticides deals with biocontrol strategies, biopesticides, breeding and genetic engineering of pest resistance traits in crops, as well as mutation and genetic engineering for herbicide tolerance.

How biotechnology found its way into agriculture

The origin of agricultural biotechnology can be traced back to 1866 when an Augustinian friar, Gregor Mendel, postulated the fundamental laws of genetic inheritance, based on his work on pea plants. He laid the groundwork for scientific breeding and genetic engineering.

Subsequent breakthroughs and discoveries in the 1920s and 1930s on methods of chromosome and gene mutation, followed by the discovery of the double helix structure of DNA in 1953, at Cambridge and London in the United Kingdom (U.K.), led to an explosion in research in genetics – the study of genes, genetic variation and heredity in organisms.

However, it was the development of recombinant DNA (rDNA) technologies – the splicing together of strands of DNA from one organism to another – in bacteria in 1974 by researchers at Stanford University and the University of California, San Francisco, in the United States of America (U.S.), that cleared the way for genetic engineering to take place in plants and other organisms.

Table 4.1 lists a few breakthrough discoveries as well as innovations that form the basis of biotechnology methods and their application in plant biotechnology today.

The commercial application of biotechnology tools and techniques first found its way into the field of medicine in the mid-1970s; agricultural use began a few years later.[7] This was primarily because molecular biology was mainly developed in medical schools and universities, which were not much concerned with agriculture.[8]

However, as the use of biotechnology in medicine and for human health became more prominent, scientists began to apply biotechnology to veterinary science for animal health and then to plant breeding. Animals came first, because of their relative genetic proximity to humans.[9]

By the mid-1980s, the crop biotechnology industry had begun to grow. Several landmark legal decisions in the U.S. regarding whether living organisms may be patented led to the granting of patents on genetically engineered plants.[10] Toward the end of the decade, field trials of transgenic plants were underway in Australia, Canada, the U.S. and some European countries. Mexico, a developing economy, also began conducting field trials of transgenic crops around the same

A brief history of key scientific biotech advances

Table 4.1 Selected discoveries or scientific breakthroughs in crop biotechnology

Year	Discovery/scientific breakthrough	Affiliation
1974	Stanley Cohen and Herbert Boyer developed a technique – rDNA – that would splice together strands of DNA from more than one organism, paving the way for genetic engineering	Stanford University and University of California, San Francisco, California, U.S.
1977	DNA sequencing methods were independently devised by Walter Gilbert with graduate student Allan Maxam, and Frederick Sanger	Harvard University, Cambridge, Massachusetts, U.S., and Cambridge University, U.K.
1981	George Willems and Robert Schilperoort genetically engineered first plant (tobacco) using the bacterium Agrobacterium (see Box 4.1)	University of Leiden, Leiden, Netherlands
2000	Complete sequencing of Arabidopsis thaliana (a small plant) genome, published in 2000 as part of the Arabidopsis Genome Initiative	Consortium of universities as well as public research institutions in the U.S., Japan and Europe
2012	A new genome editing technique, CRISPR-Cas9, is developed	University of California, Berkeley, California, the U.S; and University of Vienna, Austria; Massachusetts Institute of Technology and Harvard, Cambridge, Massachusetts, the U.S.; Vilnius University, Lithuania

Source: Graff and Hamdan-Livramento (2019).

time.[11] Meanwhile, China became the first country to commercially farm a pest-resistant, transgenic tobacco plant in 1988. However, Chinese farmers stopped farming the plants in the mid-1990s as many tobacco-producing companies expressed concerns about using these genetically improved organisms (GIOs) in their products. In particular, consumers were apprehensive about consuming GIO cigarettes. These landmark events coincided with a rise in the number of specialized agricultural biotechnology startups, particularly in the U.S., during the 1980s and 1990s.

Figure 4.1 plots the rising global demand for patents for plant biotechnology inventions from 1970 to 2016. The red line shows the total number of patent applications in the field filed at different intellectual property (IP) offices worldwide.[12] By contrast, the dark red line represents the number of initial filings for new plant biotechnology patents, also known as *first filings*. The difference between the total number of patent filings and the first filings is referred to as the *subsequent filings*. The subsequent filings represent the number of applications filed in multiple countries, or jurisdictions, for the same inventions. The widening gap between the two lines from the 1980s onward shows how inventors increasingly requested patent protection for their inventions from competitors in more than one market. More importantly, it illustrates the growing commercial importance of plant biotechnology inventions globally.

What shapes innovation in the field?

Policies, rules and regulations shape and affect innovation in the plant biotechnology industry. They include the availability of IP rights as a mechanism for ensuring a return on investment in innovation, and regulations on health and safety and on protecting the environment, among others.

Appropriate returns on investments

Most jurisdictions do not allow for the patentability of things that exist in nature, including biological organisms. However, the lines have become blurred with new technological advances in biotechnology.[13]

Concerns with patentability on agricultural biotechnology innovation are similar to those expressed about patenting in the biotechnology field generally.[14] Granting exclusive rights on research tools may dampen follow-on innovation.[15] In crop biotechnology, patents could make it difficult for poorer economies to benefit from research that could alleviate poverty and address world hunger problems. In addition, critics have argued that most of the patents granted are too broad and are likely to infringe on other proprietary technology, resulting in the relatively high amount of litigation seen in the industry.

The rise of genetic engineering coincided with an increase in subsequent patent filings

Figure 4.1 Total patent filings of plant biotechnology, 1970–2016

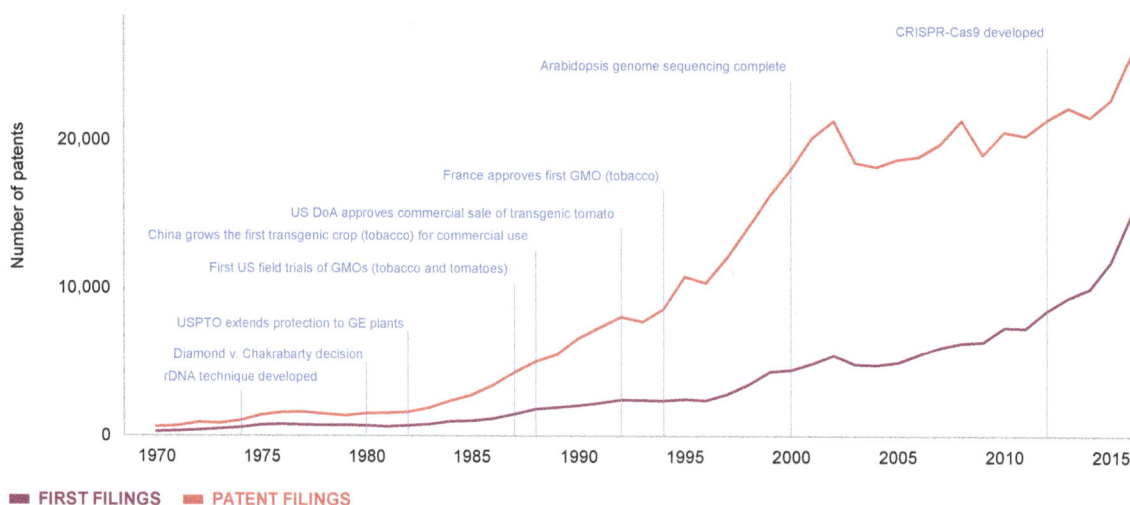

Source: WIPO based on PATSTAT and PCT data (see Technical Notes).

In the U.S., two changes related to IP policy in the 1980s played pivotal roles in shaping the agricultural biotechnology industry there. In particular, they led to the increasing reliance on IP as a way to ensure appropriate returns on investing in innovation.[16]

The first was the passing of the Bayh–Dole Act in 1980. The Bayh–Dole Act allows for the patenting of research from universities, even if it is funded by taxpayers. The second was the extension of patent protection to genetically modified organisms (GMOs) through a landmark case – *Diamond v. Chakrabarty* – decided by the U.S. Supreme Court of Justice, also in 1980.[17] By 1985, the U.S. Patent and Trademark Office (USPTO) had extended patent protection to genetically engineered plants. Europe and the rest of the world soon followed suit.

At the same time, the launch of the World Trade Organization (WTO) in 1995 included internationally binding rules for the protection of IP rights in signatory countries. This opened the way for many multinational companies (MNCs) to file for patent protection on their plant biotechnology inventions. But some developing economies, like Brazil, restrict the patenting of certain plant biotechnology products, particularly those that relate to seeds or new plant varieties. Instead, the private sector in Brazil relies on *sui generis* rights to protect their innovations.[18] Some file for patents on the development process itself, rather than the

biotechnological result, or on complementary assets – infrastructure, capabilities or other inventions – that lead to the final crop biotechnology product.[19]

Protecting consumers and safeguarding the environment

The increasing potential commercial importance of plant biotechnology led government regulators and the public to question when and how to ensure that these purposely transformed, or transgenic, crops would not harm human health or the environment.

There are several layers of regulations on the use of plant biotechnology, at both the national and international levels.[20] They help ensure that GIOs meet biosafety, food safety and consumer protection standards. For example, at the international level, the United Nations' Codex Alimentarius sets the guidelines for food safety standards, the Cartagena Protocol on Biosafety, an international agreement, provides guidelines for biosafety regulations, and another international pact, the Aarhaus Convention, gives the general public a right to access information about policy decisions affecting the environment.[21]

At the national level, there are generally at least three regulatory processes before a new transgenic plant can be commercially farmed. They include:

Box 4.1 Key differences between breeding techniques

There are two ways to introduce desired traits into plants and they differ according to plant type. Dicots, or broad-leaved crops, such as cotton, soybean and tomato, rely on the transformation brought about by a bacterium known as *Agrobacterium tumefaciens*. In nature, this bacterium infects plants, inserting some of its own DNA directly into the DNA of the plant. By modifying the bacterium to exclude its unwanted traits and include the gene of interest, a crop may be transformed through bacterial infection. The cells containing the new gene subsequently can be identified and grown using plant cell-culture technology into a whole plant that now contains the new transgene incorporated into its DNA.

Monocots, or grass species, such as maize, wheat and rice, are transformed by physically shooting small tungsten balls coated with an external DNA into the plant's genome. Some of the DNA comes off and is incorporated into the DNA of the recipient plant. Those cells can also be identified and grown into a whole plant that contains the foreign DNA.

The differences between traditional and conventional breeding and their modern counterpart boil down to the control over the breeding process. The outcomes of plants bred through the traditional and conventional methods are often unpredictable. Breeders choose the parents with the desired traits to cross but the progeny may not carry the genotype with the desired traits or display it, the phenotype.

Modern breeding techniques, such as genetic engineering, allow for targeted transfer of desirable crop traits – the transgene – and the breeding of new transgenic plants in an efficient and fast manner. These transgenic crops are also known as GMOs. The modern techniques simplify the breeding process by bypassing the need for the sexual compatibility of the plants with the desired traits and allow for the selection of desirable traits from any living organism. The desired traits can come from the same species or a cross-species; they can even come from a modification of the expression of the plant's own genes. Targeting of the desired gene, tracking it and inserting it into a crop's DNA ensures a clean breed of the crop and excludes the potential for unwanted, ancillary traits, which are often a by-product of traditional and conventional breeding. Moreover, there is a faster turnaround in the development of new crop varieties in modern breeding techniques than its predecessors.

Source: FAO (2004). and Persley and Siedow (1999).

(i) approvals to conduct field tests, (ii) approvals to farm for commercial purposes and (iii) approval to sell and market to consumers. In the U.S., the agencies include the U.S. Department of Agriculture (USDA) and the U.S. Environmental Protection Agency (EPA) for field trial approval and the U.S. Food and Drug Administration (FDA) for commercial approval.

Europe was responsible for some important break-throughs in plant biotechnology. In the early 1990s, Belgium, France and the U.K. were among the top five countries in the industry, which together accounted for nearly 95 percent of transgenic crops released – the other two were Canada and the U.S. However, by the turn of the century, European sentiment toward transgenic crops had changed significantly.[22]

Between 1998 and 2004, the European Commission (Commission), the European Union's executive arm, and five EU member states imposed a de facto moratorium on the approval of GMOs.[23] From 2003, the Commission then put in place several regulations and directives on GMOs.[24] During the moratorium, the Commission differentiated between plants whose genes had been edited with conventional breeding methods and those that had been genetically edited using biotechnology tools (see Box 4.1). The measures established specific requirements for conducting field tests and planting of transgenic crops, their import and use and the labeling of GMO products.

Several commercial explanations have been put forward for this change in the continent's attitude toward transgenic crops, besides the strong political campaigns against GMOs mounted by environmental and consumer groups. Graff and Zilberman (2007) argue that Europe's strong agrochemical businesses enjoyed a comparative advantage in chemistry and wanted to prevent their competitors from entering the market. Sheldon (2004) proposed that EU farmers saw the measures limiting the approval of genetically engineered plants as an opportunity to prevent agricultural commodities from the rest of the world from entering the market.

Crop biotechnology patent filings from the U.S. have grown faster than from Europe

Figure 4.2 Share of plant biotechnology filing over total patent filings by origin (%), 1970–2016

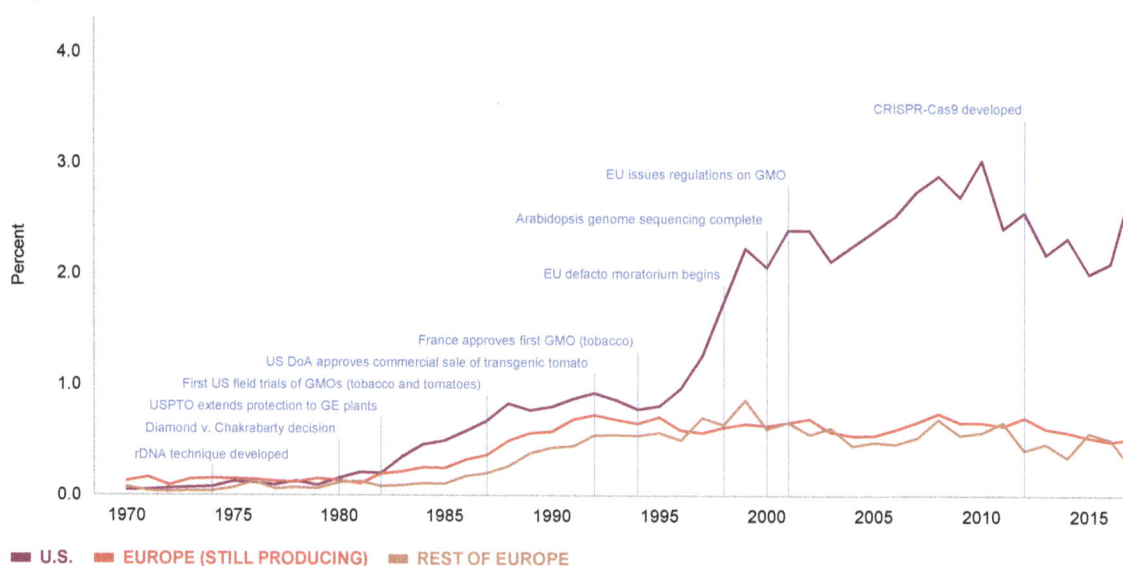

Source: WIPO based on PATSTAT and PCT data (see Technical Notes).

Regardless, the EU regulations have arguably had a cooling effect on research and development of agricultural biotechnology on the continent.

Figure 4.2 shows the share of patent filings by the U.S. (in dark red) and several European countries (in red and light red) of the total plant biotechnology filings worldwide.[25] Until the late 1990s, the share of plant biotechnology patents filed in the U.S. and the EU rose more or less in parallel. However, from 1997 onward there is a widening gap between patent filing growth rates in the U.S. and the EU. It is difficult to say conclusively if this is due to Europe's de facto moratorium. But since 1998, EU countries have been filing crop biotechnology patents at a relatively similar – if not slower – rate than the total patent filing rate.

Industry has reported that the EU stance on transgenic crops has affected companies' business strategies. A study conducted by the USDA Foreign Agricultural Service showed that many European companies have shifted their research and development (R&D) outside of Europe, relocating to places such as the U.S. While public institutions and universities in Europe continue to conduct basic research into plant genetics, the likelihood of these outputs reaching the EU market is small. In addition, the report noted that many European biotechnology firms have shifted their focus away from

agricultural uses toward medicinal and biofuel industrial applications.[26] One of the major European MNCs in the industry, BASF, a German chemical firm, halted the development and marketing of its transgenic crops for the EU in 2012.[27]

Who drives innovation?

Innovation in the plant biotechnology industry is driven by investments by both the public and private sectors.

Strong public sector push in agricultural research

The public sector plays a pivotal role in plant biotechnology research by funding and providing important infrastructure necessary for research. In Europe as well as the U.S., key policy documents and published reports underscore the importance of investing in genetic engineering research.[28]

Scientists and researchers in public research institutions have made important discoveries that paved the way to genetic engineering. The importance of basic science to innovation in the plant biotechnology field continues today. For example, fundamental advances in molecular biology and genetics have created more efficient ways to identify and target specific genotypes in organisms. Moreover, the development of CRISPR-Cas9, a gene editing technology, has significantly cut costs in the field of genetic engineering.[29]

Agricultural research centers and universities specializing in agricultural science play a pivotal role in adapting research and diffusing crop biotechnology innovations. These research centers are mandated to conduct and develop work that would improve agronomics and advance genetic improvements in crops and agricultural innovation in general. Moreover, support for their research work includes funding from governments, foundations and various intergovernmental and not-for-profit organizations and agencies. The strong mandate and financial support help ensure the continuity and importance of these institutions' work.

In the U.S., the 1862 Morrill Act established Land-Grant colleges by allocating 30,000 acres (nearly 121.5 km^2) of federal land across the country to build colleges and universities that would teach and promote the development of agriculture, among other things. The second Morrill Act, passed in 1890, ensured that these colleges had regular federal funding.

The success of Land-Grant colleges laid the foundation for establishing similar research centers in emerging economies.[30] The International Maize and Wheat Improvement Center (CIMMYT) in Mexico City, Mexico, and the International Rice Research Institute (IRRI) in Los Baños, the Philippines, were the first two such establishments. These two national agriculture research systems (NARS) would later become part of the Consultative Group for International Agricultural Research (CGIAR), an umbrella organization of 15 independent, non-profit research centers focused on innovation in agriculture. The CGIAR has shaped the historical evolution of innovation in agricultural biotechnology, particularly in crop genetic development.

Agriculture requires innovation to be adapted to different regional agro-ecological conditions, which include the combinations of soil, landform and climatic characteristics.[31] This means that transgenic crops should be bred with local cultivars and tested in local fields. In many developing countries these cultivars and germplasms – living genetic resources held for animal or plant breeding or preservation – are kept by public institutions, such as the NARS or international agriculture research centers (IARCs).[32]

Collaboration between public institutions is important, especially when trying to commercialize GIOs in less developed economies. Most of the transgenic crops planted in these economies during the late 1990s were locally adapted germplasms of their North American counterparts.[33] In poorer countries, IARCs can act as nodes in global networks of innovation by connecting agricultural scientists and breeders across many NARS, including agricultural research universities in the world.

Plant biotechnology innovation has the potential to address food scarcity and food security issues.[34] Thus, advances find strong support from the public sector, including intergovernmental organizations and not-for-profit institutions and agencies, to promote their diffusion to the rest of the world.[35]

Governments fund most of the agricultural research in many emerging economies. In a few cases, such as China, India and Brazil, public sector R&D spending in agriculture has increased rapidly. From 1990 to 2013, China's public sector agricultural R&D spending grew nearly tenfold, from USD 1 billion to more than USD 9 billion.[36] At the same time, India's spending tripled, from less than USD 1 billion to almost USD 3 billion and Brazil's almost doubled, from less than USD 2 billion to almost USD 3 billion. By contrast, public sector spending in agriculture in the U.S. grew only moderately from about USD 4 billion in 1990 and declined from 2003 onward.

But many emerging economies, especially those with limited capacities to innovate in plant biotechnology and/or those that lack the financial resources to conduct research in the field tend to rely on the work of NARS and/or IARCs.[37]

Incentives backed by market consolidation

Small, university-based startups initially dominated the plant biotechnology market in the early years. However, from the 1990s onward, MNCs bought many of them out. One study estimated that nearly 90 percent of all research and development agreements on agricultural biotechnology were between startups and large MNCs.[38]

At the same time, firms in the seed, chemical and fertilizer industries, both in richer and poorer countries, have experienced significant market concentration.[39] There are many reasons. The high fixed costs of commercializing transgenic plants require large financial resources, which many startup companies may not have. Second, the high fixed costs also necessitate increasing reliance on IP rights to ensure a return on investment. Accumulated proprietary technologies in plant biotechnology can be a barrier to innovation, as they are in the semiconductor industry. Firms that collaborate are less likely to infringe on one another's IP. For example, Monsanto, BASF, Dow, Bayer, DuPont and Syngenta cross-licensed one another's IP rights on transgenic crops.[40]

By 2001, 30 separate firms in the seeds and agrochemical industries had been reduced to six – Monsanto, DuPont, Swiss-based Syngenta, Bayer, Dow and BASF. The four biggest account for almost 60 percent of the agricultural biotechnology market. The major agrochemical-seed groups are: Bayer CropScience and BASF in Germany, Corteva Agriscience in the U.S. and ChemChina, which purchased Syngenta in 2017, in China.

This consolidation of crop biotechnology innovation in the hands of a few has not necessarily translated into a reduction of innovative activities in this field.[41]

Table 4.2 lists selected alliances, including mergers and acquisitions, of the multinational seed and agrochemical companies. It shows how the industry has become more concentrated since the 1990s.

Need for public–private collaboration

Zilberman *et al.* (1997) conducted a survey of plant biotechnology firms in the U.S. and found many cases of collaboration between the public and private sectors. In particular, they reported that in most patterns of plant biotechnology innovation the universities made the important discovery and the private sector then developed and commercialized the innovation. This pattern of collaboration between the private and public sectors continues.

Large chemical and seed MNCs commercialized and cultivated all of the major transgenic crops bred through genetic modifications in the early years.[42] The only exception was *Bacillus thuringiensis* (*Bt*) cotton, which was developed by a Chinese public research institution, the Biotechnology Research Center of the China Academy of Agricultural Sciences (CAAS) in Shenzhen. However, CAAS entered into a joint venture with U.S.

Industry has seen significant concentration

Table 4.2 Selected alliances in the industry, 1996–2016

Bayer [Germany] purchases Monsanto [U.S.] (2016)	
Monsanto [U.S.] (merged with Pharmacia March, 2000; spun off entirely August, 2002)	**Bayer (Bought Aventis Crop Sciences, 2001) [Germany]**
Biotechnology • Agracetus [U.S.] (1995) • Calgene [U.S.] (1996) • Ecogen [U.S.] (2003) • Joint venture with Millennium Pharmaceuticals [U.S.] (1998) • Paradigm Genetics [U.S.] (2000), name changed to Icoria (2004) **Seeds** • DeKalb [U.S.] (1996) • Asgrow [U.S.] (1997) • Holden's Foundation Seeds [U.S.] (1997) • Cargill International Seeds, Plant Breeding International [U.S.] (1998) • Delta and Pineland [U.S.] (alliance, 1994; bought 2007) • Sensako [South Africa] (2002); Carnia [South Africa] (2002); later merged under DaKalb brand • Seminis [U.S.] (2005) • Emergent Genetics [U.S.] (2005) • Acquired De Ruiter [Netherlands] (2008); and Peotec Seeds S.r.l. [Italy] (2008) via Seminis	**Agricultural chemicals** • Hoechst [chemical, Germany] merged with Schering [pharmaceutical, Germany] to create Hoechst Schering AgrEvo (1994) [Dusseldorf, Germany] • Hoechst (Agrevo) and Rhône-Poulenc [pharmaceutical, France] merged (and their agrochemicals division became) to Aventis CropScience (1999); • Bayer buys Aventis CropSciences in August 2002 **Biotechnology** • Plant Genetics Systems (PGS) (acquired by AgrEvo in 1996; became part of Monsanto in 2002) [Belgium] • PlanTech [Japan] (1999) • Lion Biosciences (11.3%, 1999) • Limagrain (purchased the Canadian seeds activity; 2001) [France] **Seeds** • Nunhems [Netherlands], Vanderhave [Netherlands], Plant Genetic Systems [Belgium], Pioneer Vegetable Genetics, Sunseeds (1997) [U.S.] • Nunza (vegetables), Proagro (India) and two Brazilian seed companies (1999) • Fibermax (joint venture with Cotton Seed Inc. of Australia, 2000)

Notes:
a The corporate entities as they currently exist.
b The corporate entities as they had existed up to their latest merger, acquisition or takeover.
Source: Updated, based on Pray and Nassem (2003).

| ChemChina [China] purchases Syngenta [Switzerland] (2017) | Corteva Agriscience [U.S.] spinoff created in (2019), result of DuPont and Dow merger (2015) | | BASF [Germany] |

Syngenta [Switzerland]

Dow Chemicals [U.S.]; Dow AgroSciences [US]

DuPont [U.S.]

Agricultural chemicals

- Ciba-Geigy and Sandoz merged to form Novartis [Switzerland] (1996)
- Novartis [Switzerland] buys Merck's pesticide business for USD 910 million (1997)
- Merger of Novartis agriculture division [Switzerland] and AstraZeneca's Ag. Chemicals [U.K.] to form Syngenta [Switzerland] (1999)

Biotechnology

- Zeneca Ag. [U.K.] bought Moden International N.V. [Netherlands] (1997)
- Alliance with Japan Tobacco [Japan] on rice (1999)
- Alliance with Diversa [U.S.] (2003)
- Zeneca [pharmaceutical, U.K.] buys PSA Genetics (via Garst subsidiary, 1999)

Seeds

- Merger between Northrup-King and Ciba Seeds brings together S&G Seeds, Hilleshog and Rogers Seed Co. under one umbrella (1997)
- ICI (Imperial Chemical Industries, pharmaceuticals and agrochemcials) [U.K.] splits into Zeneca (inclduing ICI seeds) and ICI PLC (1993)
- Garst [U.S.] reborn as a Zeneca company (1996)
- Zeneca [U.K.] via Garst [U.S.] buys Agripro Seeds [U.S.] (1998), Gutwein Seeds (2000)

Agricultural chemicals

- Dow purchases Eli Lilly's [U.S.] 40% share of Dow Elanco for USD 900 million (1997)
- Rohm and Hass Ag. Chem [U.S.] (2001)

Biotechnology

- Mycogen (1996) [U.S.]
- Ribozyme Pharmaceuticals Inc. [U.S.] (1999)
- Contract with Proteome Systems Limited [Australia] (1999)

Seeds

- Mycogen buys Agrigenetics [U.S.] (1992)
- United AgriSeeds [U.S.] becomes part of Mycogen (1996)
- Joint venture of Mycogen [U.S.] with Boswell [U.S.] on cotton seed to form Phytogen (1998)
- Joint venture with Danisco Seeds [Denmark] (1999)
- Agreement with Illinois Foundation Seed [U.S.] (1999)
- Cargill Hybrid Seeds [U.S.] (2000)

Agricultural chemicals

- Hoechst [chemical, Germany] merged with Schering [pharmaceutical, Germany] to create Hoechst Schering AgrEvo (1994) [Dusseldorf, Germany]
- Hoechst (Agrevo) and Rhône-Poulenc [pharmaceutical, France] merged (and their agrochemicals division became) to Aventis CropScience (1999);
- Bayer buys Aventis CropSciences in August 2002

Biotechnology

- Alliances with Human Genome Sciences [U.S.] (1996)
- Alliance with Curagen [U.S.] (1997)
- Purchased Verdia from Maxygen [U.S.] for USD 65 million (2004)

Seeds

- Pioneer [U.S.] (1997, 20%)
- Hybrinova [France] (1999)

Agricultural chemicals

- Bought corn herbicide business from Sandoz [Switzerland] (1996)
- American Cyanamid [U.S.], crop protection subsidiary from American Home Products for USD 3.8 billion (2000)

Biotechnology

- Joint venture with Institute of Plant Genetics and Crop Plant Research [Germany] to create SunGene [Germany] (1998)
- Joint venture with Max Planck Institute [Germany] and Metanomics [Germany] (1997)

Seeds

- Bought 40% of Savlöf Weibell [Sweden] (1999)

firms, Monsanto and Delta and Pineland, and China's Heibei Provincial Seed to bring *Bt* cotton to market. The transgenic crop was made available to Chinese farmers in 1997.[43]

The need for access to complementary assets in innovating in agricultural biotechnology necessitates collaboration between innovators. Commercialization of research work from universities, or public research institutions, both in developed and developing economies, may require further assistance from the private sector. This was the case for the Chinese *Bt* cotton and continues to be the case for many joint research projects between university research labs and private companies.

In many developing economies, there are a few instances of collaboration between the NARS and large MNCs to develop transgenic crops adapted to the region.[44] These public institutions may need access to proprietary biotechnological research tools to conduct their research work, and thus would need the collaboration of the IP owners. One such example is through licensing in proprietary technologies held by private companies.[45] Another is through purchasing the technology at an agreed cost. The firm may be paid by funds raised by donor countries. Collaboration between the IARC and the private firm may be made available royalty-free to developing economies or on reasonable royalty terms.[46] For example, the International Potato Center (IPC) in Peru made arrangements with Plant Genetics Systems, a Belgian firm later acquired by Bayer CropScience, to use *Bt* genes to test its line of genetically engineered potatoes.[47]

Private firms may collaborate with NARS or IARCs on research in return for exclusive commercial rights on any resulting technology in developed markets. Developing economies would be entitled to the resulting technology at a preferential rate. There could also be a hybrid approach to IP, with the private company applying for patents in developed markets only.

Collaborations have also been initiated by the private sector. For example, large life sciences firms may need access to different pools of germplasms administered by various IARCs and NARS for further innovation. CGIAR has a collection of germplasm which it has committed to keep in the public domain. Access to this pool of germplasm could help in cultivating various different versions of transgenic crops for use in many parts of the world.

The increasing need for collaboration between the private and public sectors implies some changes to the use of IP. Research institutions in many emerging economies used to shy away from relying on the IP system and focused instead on ensuring that knowledge could be easily shared. This view has changed. Collaboration between the two sectors – either to help with commercialization (for the research institutions) or as sources of germplasms and cultivars (for the private sector) – necessitates a hybrid approach to IP use.

Evidence collected from patent documents shows that the number of collaborations between the private and public sectors is on the rise. On average, only 18 percent of plant biotechnology patents are inventions with co-applications.[48] However, this underestimates collaboration activities. Not all collaborations lead to patented inventions and the number does not accurately capture collaborations between subsidiaries of large MNCs in different locations, because, typically, only the headquarters appears as the applicant on many MNC patent applications. Moreover, some of the public–private collaborations take place during the commercialization stage, such as during field trials, and these are not generally captured by either patent or scientific publication data.

Figure 4.3 plots the number of co-applications involving the private and public sectors. The trend shows an increase in the share of patents filed with at least one public-sector applicant since 1999.

4.2 The innovation landscape of plant biotechnology

The global innovation landscape of plant biotechnology is spread relatively widely across the globe. Figure 4.4 plots the innovation landscape using two proxies for innovative activities – patents and scientific publication in the form of articles and conference proceedings (see Chapters 1 and 2) – for two time periods, 1998–2007 (top) and 2008–2017 (bottom).

It shows the evolution of innovative regions in the industry and illustrates how patenting and publication tend to mirror one another, at least for the top plant biotechnology clusters. The four top countries for innovation activities in plant biotechnology are China, Germany, Japan and the U.S., with Switzerland joining them in the top five for patenting and France for scientific publication.

Innovation by the private sector is the main driver of agricultural biotechnology innovation, but public–private and public–public collaborations are on the rise

Figure 4.3 Trend in patent co-application type by number (left) and share (right), 1980–2016

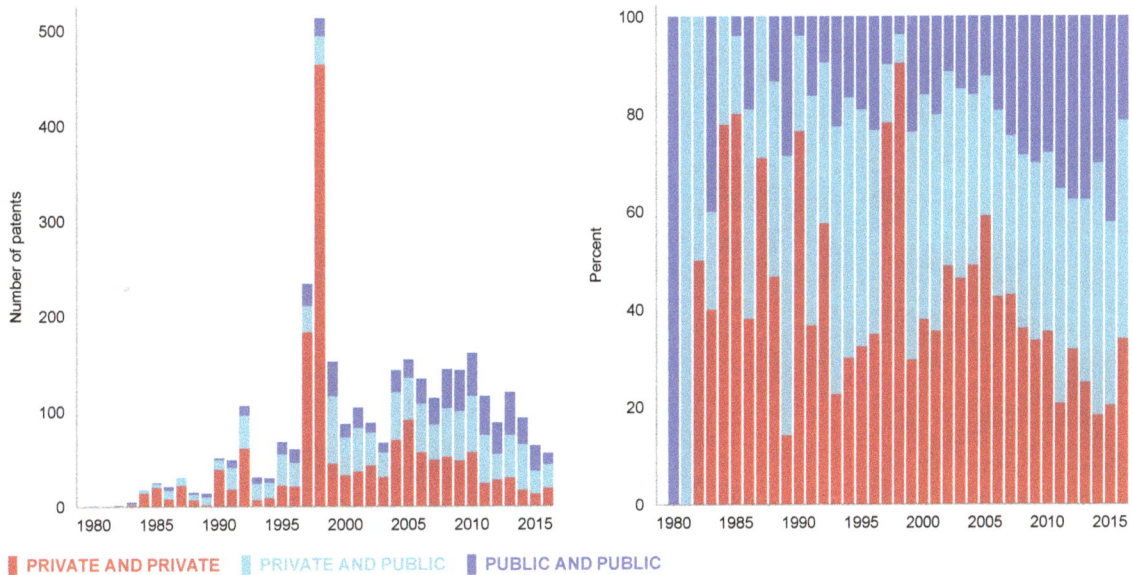

PRIVATE AND PRIVATE   PRIVATE AND PUBLIC   PUBLIC AND PUBLIC

Source: WIPO based on PATSTAT and PCT data (see Technical Notes).

In addition, Figure 4.4 also shows how some regions lean more toward patenting, while others toward scientific publication. The U.S., Europe, Japan and China show more patenting, while developing countries generally have more regions featuring scientific publication work.[49]

The difference in innovative output as captured by Figure 4.4 for patents and scientific publication can be quite significant for plant biotechnology. There are two reasons for this.

First, patenting of plant biotechnology inventions is subject to different criteria across jurisdictions. Hence, using patenting as the sole indicator of crop biotechnology innovation may miss important research work carried out by scientists in countries where patenting possibilities are limited.

Second, while both patented inventions and scientific publication are used to measure innovative activities, there are important differences. For example, inventions disclosed under patenting requirements may be closer to the commercialization stage than research published in scientific publications, which may be more "upstream" and science related.[50] Moreover, most

innovative activities in the U.S. are carried out by the private sector, which tends to rely on patents, while in China, universities and public institutions are the main sources of such activities.

Figure 4.5 maps the international and national clusters of crop biotechnology across the world. These clusters are determined by the relative significant co-location of inventors and authors of plant biotechnology outputs across countries (international clusters) and within countries (national clusters).

Box 4.2 highlights the method used to identify these clusters. It emphasizes how only international plant biotechnology clusters are comparable across countries, while national clusters are only comparable across regions in one country.

The international clusters of plant biotechnology show how geographically diverse is its innovation landscape. The clusters include the three main corridors of innovation, namely the U.S., Europe and East Asian countries, Japan and the Republic of Korea. They further include India, Israel, China and Singapore in Asia, Australia in Oceania, and Argentina and Mexico in Latin America and the Caribbean. But at the same

97

The distribution of agricultural biotech innovation has been relatively wide since the 2000s

Figure 4.4 Distribution of plant biotechnology innovation centers by patent filings (left) and publication (right), 1998–2007 (top) and 2008–2017 (bottom)

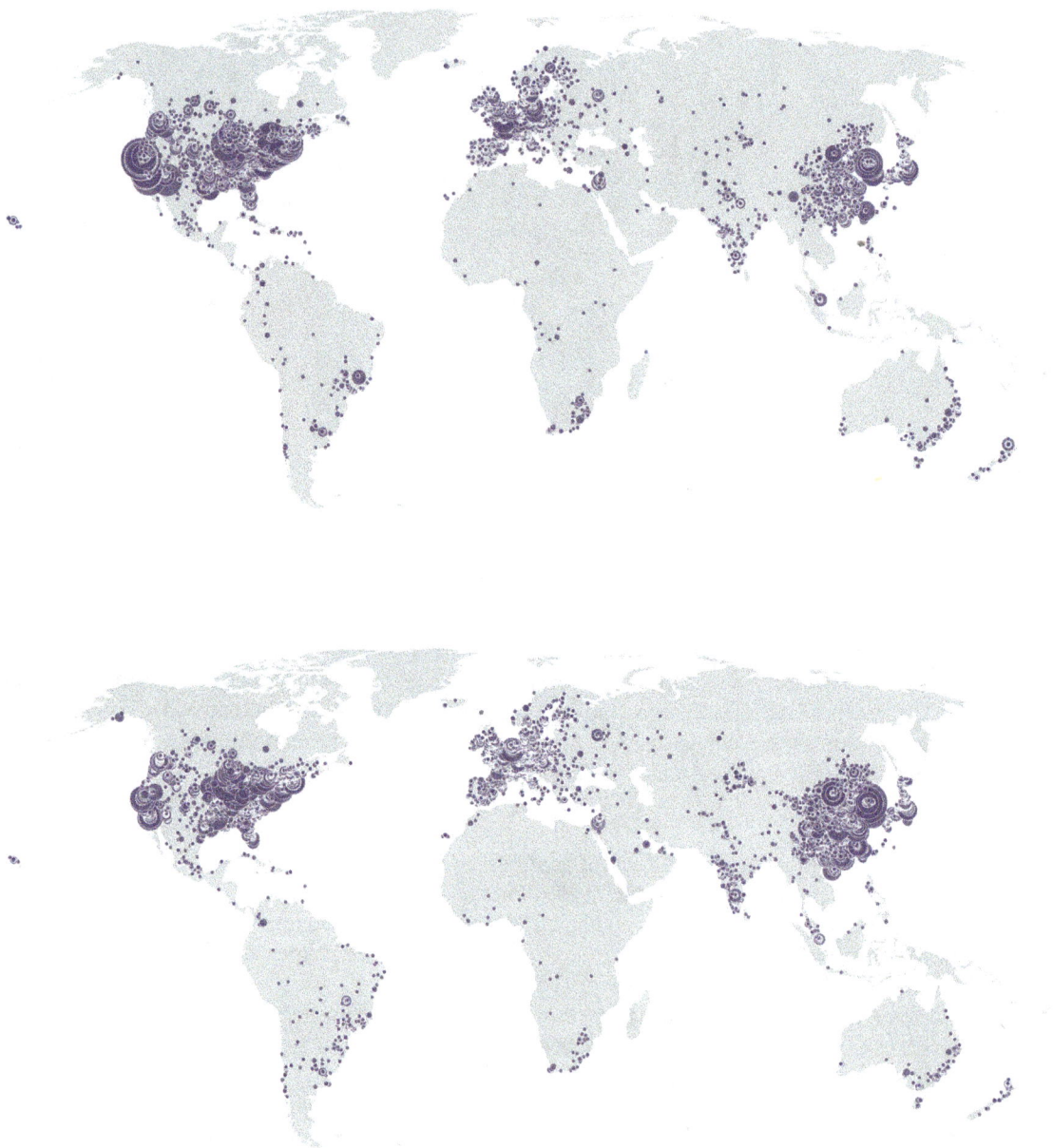

▌ PATENTS ▌ SCIENTIFIC PUBLICATIONS

Source: WIPO based on PATSTAT, PCT and Web of Science data (see Technical Notes).
Note: Size of bubbles corresponds to the relative volume of patent and scientific publications, respectively.

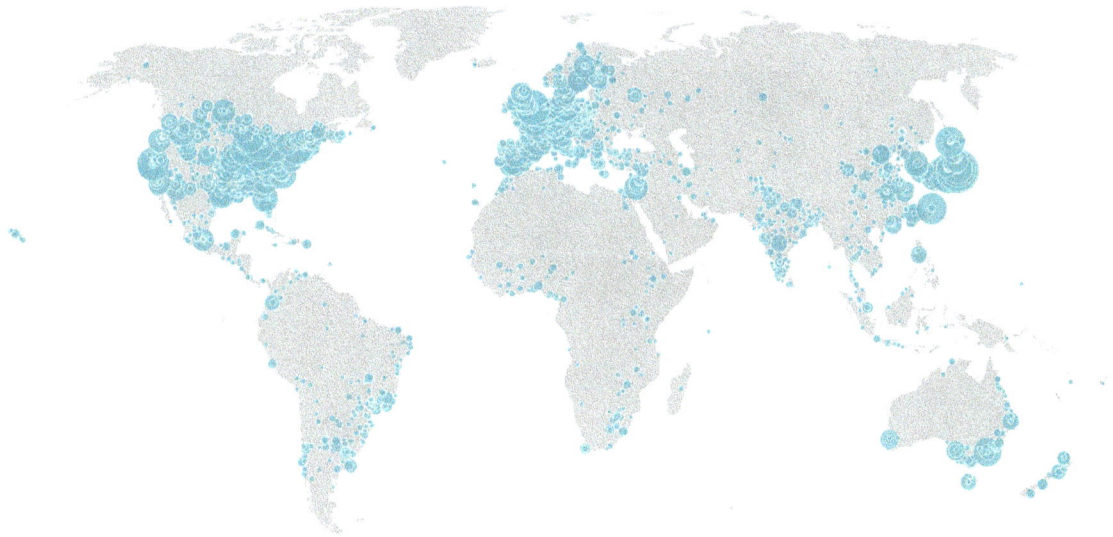

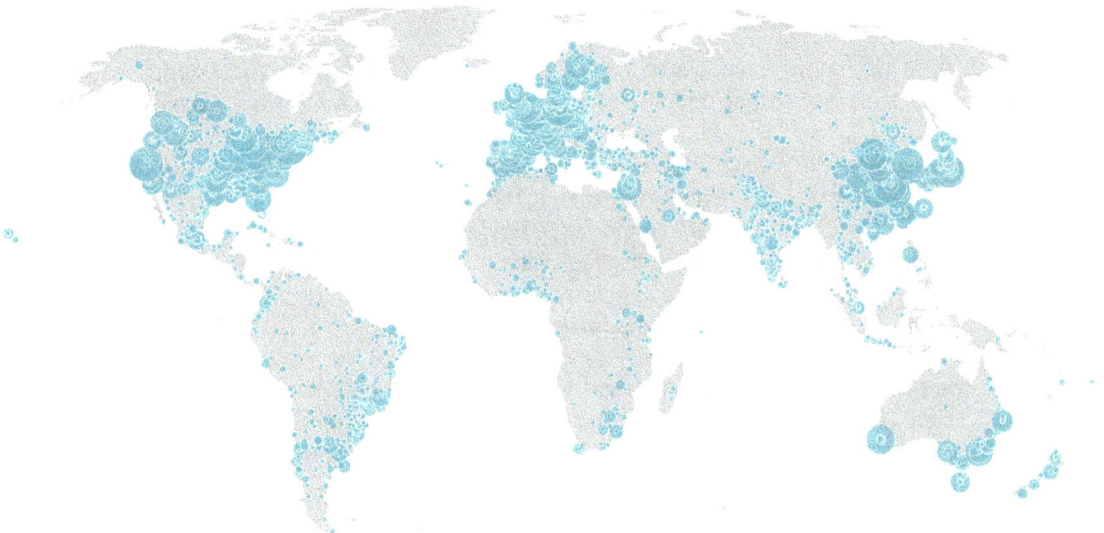

Agricultural biotechnology clusters are spread across the globe

Figure 4.5 Global distribution of plant biotechnology innovation clusters, 1970–2017

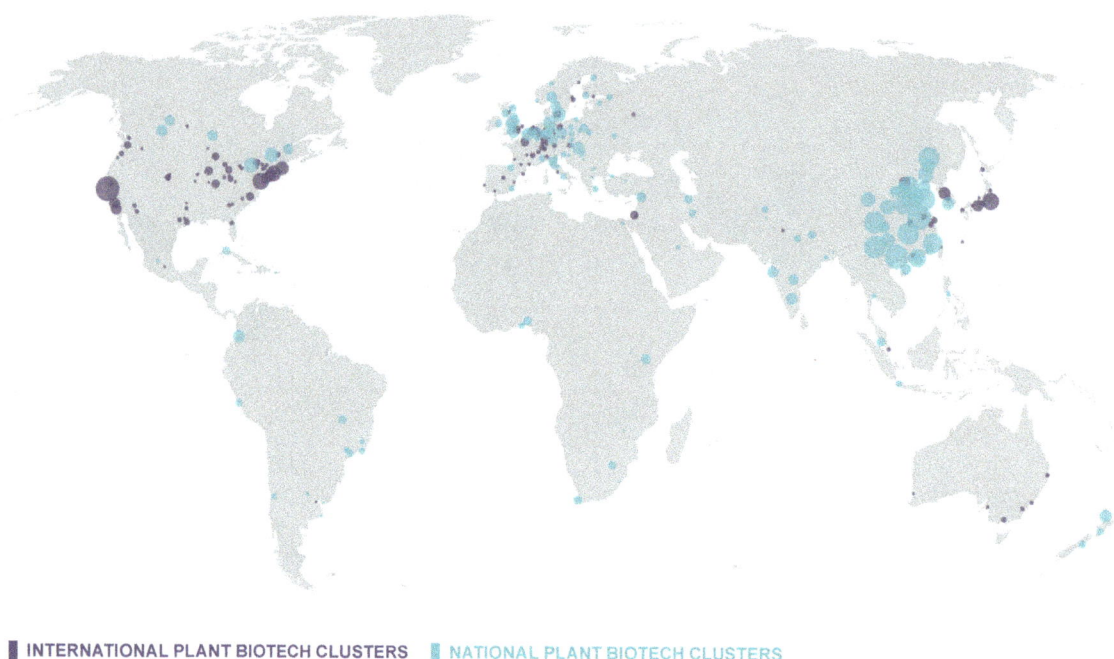

■ INTERNATIONAL PLANT BIOTECH CLUSTERS   ■ NATIONAL PLANT BIOTECH CLUSTERS

Source: WIPO based on PATSTAT, PCT and Web of Science data (see Technical Notes).

time, these international plant biotechnology clusters mirror their related biotechnology field clusters.

Not all countries with significant innovative activities have international clusters. Brazil, for example, is a leading developing economy with important innovative activities in the field, but with no international cluster. The main reason for this is that its innovative activities in plant biotechnology are spread across seven different regions that individually do not reach volume thresholds for the production of patents and scientific articles (see Box 4.2). The Brazilian Agricultural Research Corporation (EMBRAPA), its NARS, mandates that its research activities should be scattered across its different research campuses and not just concentrated in its main office in Brasilia.

There are two notable insights from the global mapping of plant biotechnology's international and national clusters. First, there is an urban–rural divide between the location of innovation centers and the farming the innovation is aimed at.[51] Most innovation in the plant biotechnology industry is conceptualized, researched and developed in urban areas rather than in farming

areas. However, field trials are conducted in rural areas, which may require some innovative activities to adapt the genetically engineered crop to local agro-ecological conditions – to the local combinations of soil, landform and climatic characteristics.[52]

Figure 4.6 maps the international and national crop biotechnology clusters against the crop areas (shaded green) of the world for four regions: North America, Europe, Asia and Latin America. Most of the international clusters tend to be in urban areas. In the U.S., for example, they are in such places as San Jose, Boston and New York City.

However, there are some clusters that are adjacent to crop areas. The location of these clusters is not an accident. Most of these clusters are located in major agriculture-related universities, for example the U.S. Land-Grant colleges already mentioned. One notable example is Des Moines, Iowa, which is both a farming area and an international plant biotechnology cluster. Des Moines is home to Iowa State University, a Land-Grant university, and Pioneer Hi-Bred, one of the first startups specializing in agriculture biotechnology.

Box 4.2 Identifying the international and national clusters of crop biotechnology

Identifying international and national clusters of agricultural biotechnology involves at least three steps.

Step 1: Identify plant biotechnology patents and scientific publication

Patents: use a combination of two international technological classification schemes, the International Patent Classification (IPC) and the Cooperative Patent Classification (CPC) codes, and keywords to arrive at crop-specific agricultural biotechnology (see Technical Notes for the complete list of codes and keywords used in the search strategy). The categories for crop patents include: (i) crops' genetic improvement; (ii) pest control in crops; (iii) soil fertility; and (iv) climate change.

Scientific publication: use a combination of well-known top journals in agricultural biotechnology, combined with relevant plant biotechnology-specific keywords (see Technical Notes for details).

Step 2: Geocoding the addresses of inventors and authors

The addresses of authors of patented inventions and scientific articles related to plant biotechnology are geocoded and mapped. Inventors' resident addresses, as listed in the patented documents, are used, while for scientific publication, the authors' addresses are usually not disclosed. Instead, the location of the authors' affiliation is employed.

Step 3: Differentiating between national and international clusters

Once the location of both patented inventions and scientific publications are mapped out, two different thresholds are used to identify international and national clusters. For international clusters, only foreign-oriented patent families are considered, in combination with published scientific articles. These patents must be either filed in an IP office different from the applicant's residence or in at least one foreign IP office, for example, at a national IP office and a foreign IP office. Patents filed at an international patent office, such as the European Patent Office or through the Patent Cooperation Treaty (PCT), are also considered as foreign-oriented patent families.

For national clusters, all patent families, along with scientific publication, are used. The patent families include singletons, which are patents filed in the same IP office as the applicant's residence and nowhere else.

Classification as an international cluster is based on a global threshold combining foreign-oriented patents and scientific publication. National clusters are based only on a country-specific threshold.

Therefore, international clusters differ from national clusters in two main ways. First, international clusters are calculated by only considering foreign-oriented patent families. National clusters, by contrast, are based on all patents filed by the residents of a country, including both singletons and foreign-oriented patents. Second, the threshold criterion determined at the international level is based on the average volume of patents and scientific articles attributed to one region, across the globe. The threshold at the national level is measured by the average volume of patents and scientific publication attributed to one region in a country.

Only the international clusters are comparable across countries.

Note: See Box 2.1 and Box 2.2 of Chapter 2. See also the glossary list in the annex of WIPO (2018).

For many developing economies, the relevant international and national clusters of plant biotechnology are close to their respective NARS, which tend to be located in farming areas. The CIMMYT in Texcoco is approximately one hour away from Mexico City, while Buenos Aires is home to the National Agricultural Technology Institute (INTA) of Argentina. The International Crops Research Institute for the Semi-Arid Tropics, a CGIAR institute, is located in Patancheru, close to Hyderabad, in India, while the IRRI in Los Baños, the Philippines, is around one hour from Dasmarinas City. In Brazil, the national clusters coincide with the locations of EMBRAPA centers. All of these NARS are within a 50-km radius of national crop biotechnology clusters.

Innovation takes place far away from cropland

Figure 4.6 Location of plant biotechnology innovation centers and croplands

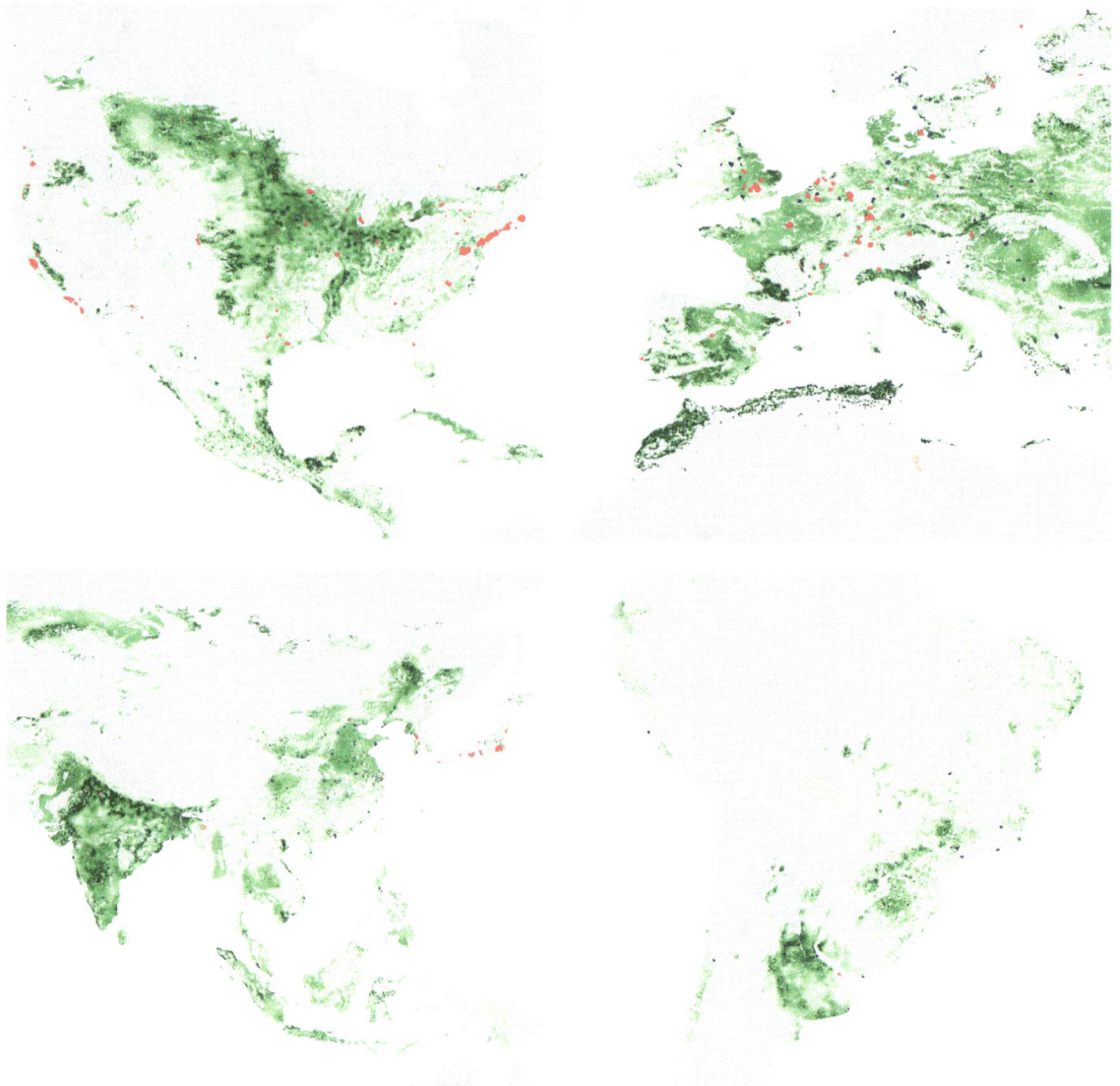

▎INTERNATIONAL PLANT BIOTECH CLUSTERS ▎NATIONAL PLANT BIOTECH CLUSTERS

Source: WIPO based on PATSTAT, PCT and Web of Science data (see Technical Notes). Cropland data from Ramankutty *et al.* (2008).
Note: Green areas represent croplands and pastures circa 2000.

The presence of these agricultural institutions is likely to create regional ecosystems that are conducive to startups as well as R&D facilities of companies in the industry. Samad and Graff (2020) show that the single most important determinant of the number of inventions to come from a given region is the number of inventions that have come from that region in the past. This relationship represents the "sticky" nature of fixed investments in regional knowledge infrastructure and human capital – the fact that knowledge, as opposed to information, does not transfer that easily between locations – as well as the localized nature of knowledge spillovers (see Chapter 1).

Second, as noted, most of the international plant biotechnology clusters are concentrated in metropolitan areas. Figure 4.7 plots the location of these international clusters alongside global innovation

Innovative activities tend to cluster, particularly in metropolitan areas

Figure 4.7 Worldwide distribution of innovation (GIHs, SNCs and international plant biotechnology clusters)

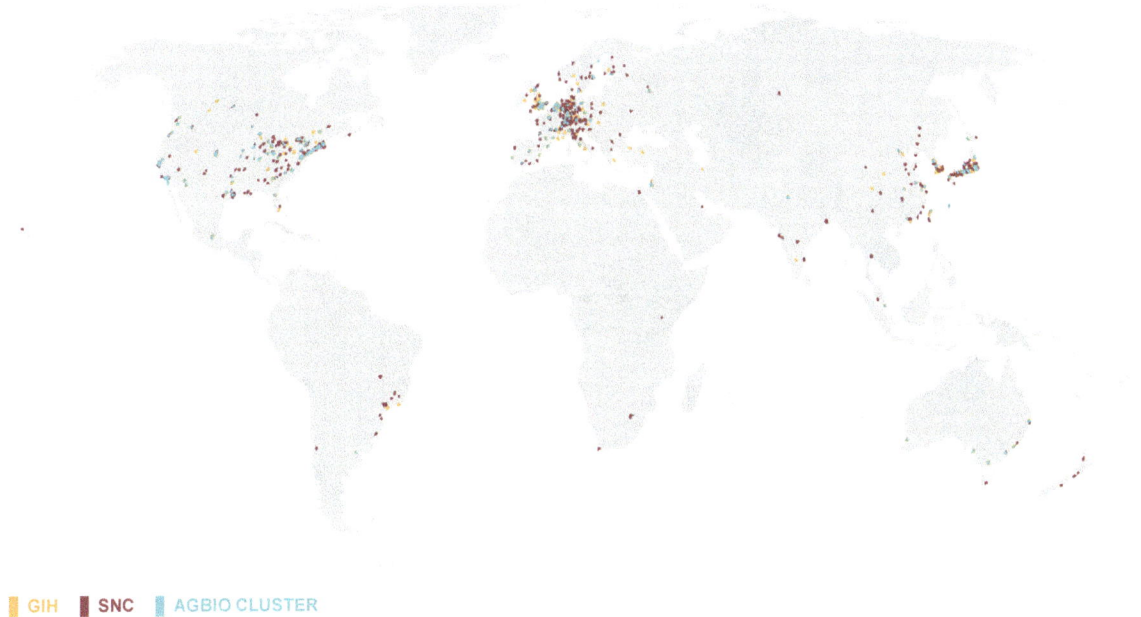

GIH   SNC   AGBIO CLUSTER

Source: WIPO based on PATSTAT, PCT and Web of Science data (see Technical Notes).

hotspots (GIHs) and specialized niche clusters (SNCs), as defined in Chapter 2 of this report.

Strong agglomerating forces determine where the innovative regions of plant biotechnology are located. By co-locating in regions where there are strong innovative activities, whether plant biotechnology specific or not, researchers in both public and private sectors are able to benefit from the knowledge spillover (see Chapter 2). For example, they can profit from the presence of other related innovating industries and specialized skilled workers, some of which could be relevant and useful and facilitate new technological advances in the crop biotechnology industry.[53]

4.3   The innovation network of plant biotechnology

The main innovation clusters in agricultural biotechnology are found, not surprisingly, in the leading countries that invest in agricultural R&D.

Figure 4.8 provides rough illustrations of how the top 30 international clusters connect to one another, based on patented inventions (left) and scientific publication (right) for 2010–2017. These links are based on co-inventorship and co-authorship across regions. The size of the bubbles in the figure represents the volume of patented inventions (or scientific publication) in that particular cluster, while the thickness of the lines represents the frequency of the interactions between them. The colors of the bubbles indicate the countries to which the clusters belong.

The U.S., Canada, Europe, particularly Germany, France, Netherlands, Denmark and the U.K., and countries in East Asia (Japan, the Republic of Korea and China) are home to most of the international clusters for patented innovation in crop biotechnology.[54] As in the case of biotechnology, distance is not necessarily the main criterion for connecting to clusters.

For example, inventors in the two largest international clusters, San Jose and New York City (nearly 4,724 km apart), interact more frequently than San Jose with San Diego (approximately 739 km apart). Inventors in Rotterdam, the Netherlands, co-invent more frequently with inventors in San Diego than with their compatriots in Eindhoven.

More openness in scientific publications than patenting? Collaboration between plant biotechnology clusters are more frequent and denser in scientific publications than in patenting activities

Figure 4.8 Linkages between the top 30 international biotechnology clusters based on patent filings (left) and scientific publications (right), 2010–2017

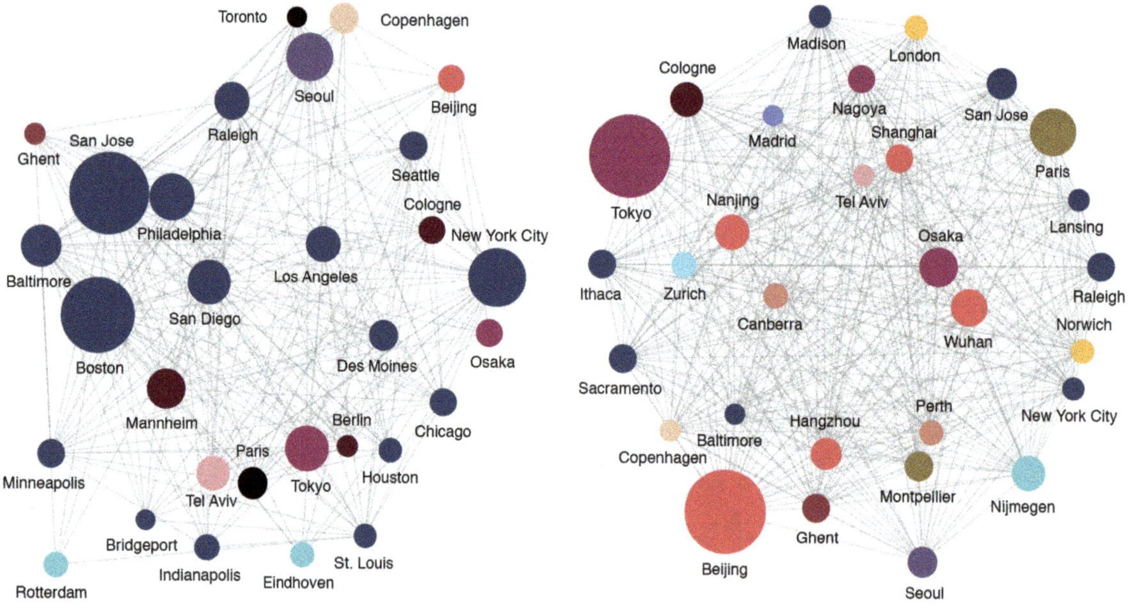

Source: WIPO based on PATSTAT, PCT and Web of Science data (see Technical Notes).
Note: Size of the bubbles corresponds to the relative volume of patent and scientific publications, respectively.

Specialized researchers in agricultural biotechnology tend to come from the U.S.

Figure 4.9 Comparison of top 10 percent applicant–inventor ties of foreign-oriented patents, 1970–1999 (left) and 2000–2017 (right)

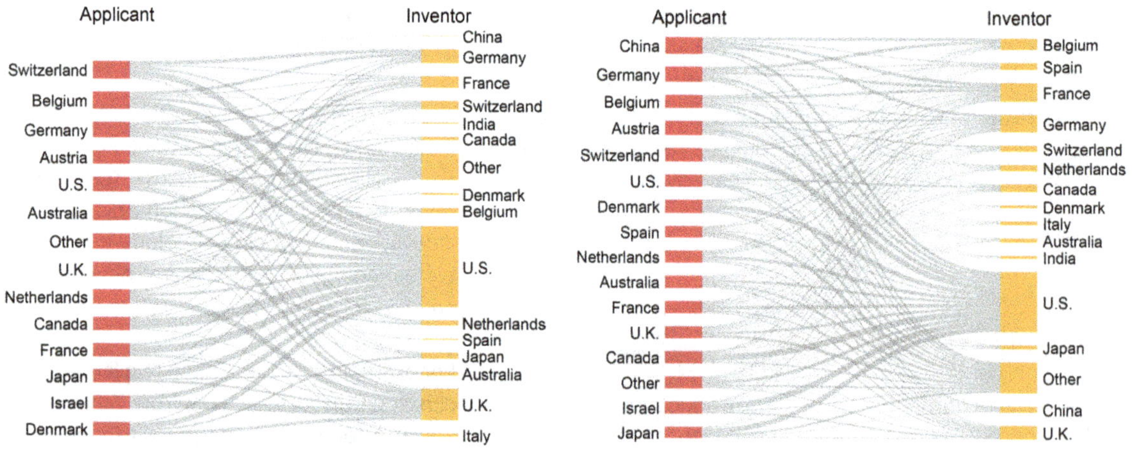

Source: WIPO based on PATSTAT, PCT and Web of Science data (see Technical Notes).
Note: Only patent families with foreign-orientation are shown. In addition, applicant-inventor ties where the applicant has a different residence than the inventor are displayed.

The picture for international clusters based on published scientific articles follows a similar pattern. However, the size of the clusters and their interactions with one another are more diverse and denser. The two biggest clusters based on publication are Beijing and Tokyo. U.S. clusters do not figure as prominently as they do for patenting.

Nevertheless, the U.S. has by far the most international clusters based on both measures of innovation: 16 clusters using patents and eight using scientific publication. It is followed by Germany with three international clusters, as measured by patents, and China with six international clusters, as measured by scientific publication.

Both measures of internationally comparable crop biotechnology clusters point to the U.S. as central to innovation in plant biotechnology. One reason for the U.S.'s importance in international clusters of plant biotechnology is the quantity and quality of its specialized inventors and researchers. When looking at where most inventors reside, especially when it is different to that of the patent applicant, we see the overwhelming centrality of the U.S. as the place to find crop biotechnology researchers.

Figure 4.9 illustrates the location of researchers in plant biotechnology by exploiting the different locations of the applicant (left) and the inventor (right) of a particular patent. The left panel provides the links between applicant–inventor pairs in the years 1970–1999, while the right panel paints the picture for the years 2000–2017. The lines connecting the applicant to the inventor are proxies for the strength of the relationship: the thicker the line the more frequent the interaction.

In both periods, many patent applicants outside the U.S. search for U.S. researchers and scientists. The fact that many of the important discoveries in agricultural biotechnology came from U.S. universities and public institutions is one reason why U.S. scientists and researchers are highly sought after. Another explanation is that private companies in the U.S. were often the first to invest strategically in the exploration of commercial applications of biotechnology in plants. These factors combine to increase the weight of the U.S. in the crop biotechnology innovation network.

4.4   Future of plant biotechnology

Three new developments in plant biotechnology could transform the current global innovation network. Recent breakthroughs in molecular biology are opening new research avenues and hence applications for plant biotechnology. The adaptation of CRISPR-Cas9 is likely to reinvigorate research on the genetic improvement of crops and livestock. Moreover, as this technology becomes more affordable, it has the potential to "democratize" innovation in agricultural biotechnology. [55] Combined with the rising role of developing economies in such innovation, this latest advance could lead to the global innovation network being more evenly dispersed. Clusters in different parts of the world could soon be making important contributions that will enhance food security in an efficient and sustainable manner.

In addition, new applications of sensors and artificial intelligence to systematize the quantification of an organism's phenotype and physical traits could enable much more powerful and precise connections to be drawn between genotype, genetic traits and phenotype than was previously possible. With the combined abilities to "read," "write" and "edit" nucleotide sequences, new technological opportunities are possible for the genetic improvement of crops and livestock.

The second development that may change the global innovation landscape and improve developing economies' participation in the global innovation network is the recent shift in CGIAR's stance on IP rights.[56] In the past, CGIAR had been committed to ensuring that its members' work could be shared and would be easily accessible to all; it had shied away from the exclusionary properties of IP rights. This stance has changed. The CGIAR has recognized the importance of collaborating with the private sector and has begun using IP rights as an incentive for such collaboration and partnerships and to encourage innovation.

Finally, in July 2018, the European Court of Justice (ECJ) ruled that plants engineered using gene-editing technologies, such as CRISPR-Cas9, would be subject to the same regulations as those applied to GMOs. The CRISPR-Cas9 technique changes a plant's make-up, its DNA, but without introducing any foreign material, and arguably might have been exempt from the regulations. However, the ECJ ruled that the technique was still subject to the European Commission directive. Scientists and researchers argue that the ruling could result in a further exodus of plant biotech R&D outside Europe. If proven true, then the ruling will further change the innovation landscape and networks of plant biotechnology.

Notes

1 This chapter draws on Graff and Hamdan-Livramento (2019).

2 Other traditional ways include hybridization as well as grafting.

3 The United Nations Convention on Biodiversity (CBD) definition. It differs slightly from that of the Biotechnology Innovation Organization (BIO), a major industry association. BIO defines biotechnology as "technology based on biology – [it] harnesses cellular and biomolecular processes to develop technologies and products that help improve our lives and the health of our planet" (www.bio.org/what-biotechnology).

4 Graff et al. (2003).

5 FAO (2003).

6 The term "agricultural biotechnology" differs from "plant biotechnology" in that the former refers to the general industry, while the latter applies to a particular field of agricultural biotechnology. "Plant biotechnology" is used interchangeably with "crop biotechnology."

7 The first licensed drug using rDNA technology was the human insulin drug, produced by Genetech and licensed to Eli Lilly and Company (Johnson, 1983).

8 Kenny (1988).

9 The proximity between humans and animals. Humans fall under the category of mammals in the animal kingdom, which allows for easier transition between human and animal health.

10 Carrer et al. (2010). The terms genetically engineered-, genetically modified- and genetically improved-organisms are used interchangeably throughout this chapter. Another term that is used alongside these is transgenic crops.

11 See Alvarez-Morales (2000).

12 Patents are territorial in nature. This means that a patent granted in one country or jurisdiction is not necessarily enforceable in another. Inventors who want to ensure that their invention is protected from imitation across countries would have to file patent applications for the same invention in those jurisdictions.

13 Other forms of IP protection on plants are plant varieties and plant patents (specific to the U.S.). However, these two IP instruments are outside the scope of this chapter and not addressed here.

14 Barton (2000).

15 See Eisenberg (1996) and Heller and Eisenberg (1998).

16 Barton and Berger (2001).

17 Brennan (1980).

18 Another instrument which protects innovation in plants is the International Union for the Protection of New Varieties of Plants (UPOV) system of plant varieties rights. This chapter does not touch on this right.

19 Figueiredo et al. (2019). See Teece (1986) and Rothaermel (2001) for importance of complementary assets.

20 See Eckerstorfer et al. (2019) for an overview of the different existing regulatory frameworks.

21 See Glowka (2003) and Komen (2012).

22 See Graff and Hamdan-Livramento (2019), and Brenner and Komen (1994).

23 See WTO dispute settlement case DS291: European Communities — Measures Affecting the Approval and Marketing of Biotech Products (www.wto.org/english/traptop_e/dispu_e/cases/e/ds291_e.htm).

24 For the list of regulations and directive on GMOs visit ec.europa.eu/food/plant/gmo/legislation_en

25 The European countries included in the figure are: EU-28 (except for missing data from Malta, Bulgaria and Poland). Portugal, Spain and the U.K. are included in the list of countries in Europe still farming transgenic crops.

26 USDA Foreign Agricultural Service (2018).

27 ISAAA (2017). In 2012, BASF announced that it was closing its SunGene, its main plant biotechnology activity in Gatersleben, Germany, to concentrate on the North and South American markets by 2013. Visit www.sungene.de

28 See European Commission (2004, 2009); National Research Council (1987, 1998); FAO (2003, 2004).

29 "CRISPR" stands for clustered regularly interspaced short palindromic repeats while "Cas9" refers to CRISPR-associated protein 9.

30 Wright (2012). See Alston et al. (2010) and Olmstead and Rhode (2011) on how these Land-Grant colleges have been useful for the agriculture industry in the U.S.

31 See Chapter 2 of FAO (1996) for further details on agro-ecological conditions.

32 Byerlee and Fischer (2002) and FAO (2004).

33 Barry and Hosch (2000).

34 See FAO (2004), and Serageldin and Persley (2000).

35 Bijman and Tait (2002).

36 Clancy et al. (2016).

37 Komen and Persley (1993), Persley (2000) and Fukuda-Parr (2006).

38 Kalaitzandonakes and Bjornson (1997) calculated the number of mergers, acquisitions and

strategic alliances between startups and MNCs at 167 between 1981 and 1985, and 801 mergers between 1991 and 1996.

39   See Kalaitzandonakes (2000); Fulton and Giannakas (2001); Tait *et al*. (2002); and OECD (2018).

40   Howard (2015).

41   See OECD (2018) and Fuglie *et al*. (2012). The OECD (2018, p. 104) reviewed the empirical literature on concentration in the seed industry and impact on innovation. The study concludes that there is little evidence for the adverse impact of concentration on innovation based on historical data.

42   Fukuda-Parr (2006).

43   Huang *et al*. (2002).

44   Byerlee and Fischer (2002).

45   See Barton and Berger (2001).

46   Pinstrup-Andersen and Cohen (2003).

47   See International Potato Center (1995).

48   Co-applications refer to patent applications where there are at least two listed applicants on the document.

49   It is plausible that there are more regions that should be included rather than those displayed in this chapter. In other words, the regions covered by scientific publication may be an underestimate. This is because identifying articles on plant biotechnology is sensitive to the method used. Here it is based on the top journals in plant biotechnology. Other journals that are not as well known, but which may have equally relevant

contributions, are excluded.

50   See Griliches (1990).

51   Samad and Graff (2020) also find this urban–rural divide when looking at the innovation centers of agriculture biotechnology regions in the U.S.

52   See Graff and Hamdan-Livramento (2019) for more information on the procedure for farming transgenic crops.

53   Hermans *et al*. (2008).

54   See annex in Graff and Hamdan-Livramento (2019) for a detailed list of the top 30 clusters by patents and scientific articles published, respectively.

55   See Mahfouz *et al*. (2014) and Shwartz (2018).

56   See CGIAR (2006, 2013).

References

Alston, J.M., M.A. Andersen, J.S. James and P.G. Pardey (2010). Persistence Pays: *US Agricultural Productivity Growth and the Benefits from Public R&D Spending*, Natural Resource Management and Policy, Zilberman, D., R. Goetz and A. Garrido (eds), Vol. 34. New York: Springer.

Alvarez-Morales, A. (2000). Mexico: ensuring environmental safety while benefiting from biotechnology. In Persley, G.J. and M.M. Lantin (eds), *Agricultural Biotechnology and the Poor: Proceedings of an International Conference, Washington, D.C., 21–22 October 1999*. Washington, D.C.: Consultative Group on International Agricultural Research.

Babinard, J. (2001). A short history of agricultural biotechnology. In Nelson, G.C. (ed.), *Genetically Modified Organisms in Agriculture*. London: Academic Press, 271–274. doi.org/10.1016/B978-012515422-2/50029-1

Barry, G. and R. Horsch (2000). Evolving role for the public and private sector in agricultural biotechnology in developing countries. In Persley, G.J. and M.M. Lantin (eds), *Agricultural Biotechnology and the Poor*. Washington D.C.: Consultative Group on International Agricultural Research, 183–185.

Barton, J.H. (2000). Intellectual property, biotechnology, and international trade: two examples. *World Trade Forum*, 3, 1–15.

Barton, J.H. and P. Berger (2001). Patenting agriculture. *Issues in Science and Technology*, 17(4). issues.org/barton

Bijman, J. and J. Tait (2002). Public policies influencing innovation in the agrochemical, biotechnology and seed industries. *Science and Public Policy*, 29(4), 245–251. doi.org/10.3152/147154302781780895

Brennan, A.A. (1980). Patentability of micro-organisms: Diamond v. Chakrabarty, 100 S. Ct. 2204. *Akron Law Review*, 14(2), 341–349.

Brenner, C., and J. Komen (1994). International Initiatives in Biotechnology for Developing Country Agriculture: Promises and Problems. *OECD Development Centre Working Papers, No. 100*. Paris: OECD Publishing. doi.org/10.1787/257557587410

Brookes, G. (2018). The farm level economic and environmental contribution of Intacta soybeans in South America: the first five years. *GM Crops & Food*, 9(3), 140–151. doi.org/10.1080/21645698.2018.1479560

Byerlee, D. and K. Fischer (2002). Accessing modern science: policy and institutional options for agricultural biotechnology in developing countries. *World Development*, 30(6), 931–948. doi.org/10.1016/S0305-750X(02)00013-X

Carrer, H., A.L. Barbosa and D.A. Ramiro (2010). Biotechnology in agriculture. *Estudos Avançados*, 24(70), 149–164. doi.org/10.1590/S0103-40142010000300010

CGIAR (2006). *CGIAR Research Strategies for IPG in a Context of IPR: Report and Recommendations Based on Three Studies*. Rome: Consultative Group on International Agricultural Research. ispc.cgiar.org/sites/default/files/ISPC_IPGStrategiesIPR.pdf

CGIAR (2013) *Implementation Guidelines for the CGIAR Principles on the Management of Intellectual Assets*.

Clancy, M., K. Fuglie and P. Heisey (2016, November 10). U.S. Agricultural R&D in an era of falling public funding. *Amber Waves*. www.ers.usda.gov/amber-waves/2016/november/us-agricultural-rd-in-an-era-of-falling-public-funding

Eckerstorfer, M.F., M. Engelhard, A. Heissenberger, S. Simon and H. Teichmann (2019). Plants developed by new genetic modification techniques – comparison of existing regulatory frameworks in the EU and non-EU countries. *Frontiers in Bioengineering and Biotechnology*, 7. doi.org/10.3389/fbioe.2019.00026

Eisenberg, R.S. (1996). Intellectual property issues in genomics. *Trends in Biotechnology*, 14(8), 302–307. doi.org/10.1016/0167-7799(96)10040-8

European Commission (2004). *Plants for the Future: A 2025 Vision for European Plant Biotechnology*, EUR 21359 EN. Brussels: European Commission Directorate-General for Research Food Quality and Safety.

European Commission (2009). Communication from the Commission to the Council, the European Parliament, the European Economic and Social Committee and the Committee of the Regions: a mid-term assessment of implementing the EC Biodiversity Action Plan. *Journal of International Wildlife Law & Policy*, 12(1–2), 108–120. doi.org/10.1080/13880290902938435

FAO (1996). *Agro-Ecological Zoning Guidelines*, FAO Soils Bulletin No. 73. Rome: Food and Agriculture Organization of the United Nations. www.fao.org/3/w2962e/w2962e00.htm#P-2

FAO (2003). *World Agriculture: Towards 2015/2030. An FAO Perspective*. Rome: Food and Agriculture Organization of the United Nations.

FAO (2004). The State of Food and Agriculture 2003–2004. *Agricultural Biotechnology: Meeting the Needs of the Poor?* Rome: Food and Agriculture Organization of the United Nations. www.fao.org/3/Y5160E/y5160e00.htm#TopOfPage

Figueiredo, L.H.M., A.G. Vasconcellos, G.S. Prado and M.F. Grossi-de-Sa (2019). An overview of intellectual property within agricultural biotechnology in Brazil. *Biotechnology Research and Innovation*, 3(1), 69–79. doi.org/10.1016/j.biori.2019.04.003

Fuglie, K.O., J.L. King, P.W. Heisey and D.E Schimmelpfennig (2012). Rising concentration in agricultural input industries influences new farm technologies. *Amber Waves*, 10(4). ageconsearch.umn.edu/record/142404

Fukuda-Parr, S. (ed.) (2006). *The Gene Revolution: GM Crops and Unequal Development*. London and Sterling: Earthscan.

Fulton, M. and K. Giannakas (2001). Agricultural biotechnology and industry structure. *AgBioForum*, 4(2), 137–151.

Glowka, L. (2003). *Law and Modern Biotechnology*, FAO Legislative Study. Rome: Food and Agriculture Organization of the United Nations.

Graff, G. and I. Hamdan-Livramento (2019). The Global Roots of Innovation in Plant Biotechnology. *WIPO Economic Research Working Paper No. 59*. Geneva: World Intellectual Property Organization.

Graff, G., A. Heiman, C. Yarkin and D. Zilberman (2003). Privatization and Innovation in agricultural biotechnology. *ARE Update*, 6(3), 5–7.

Graff, G. and D. Zilberman (2007). The political economy of intellectual property: re-examining European Policy on plant biotechnology. In J. Kesan (ed.), *Intellectual Property Protection for Agricultural Biotechnologies: Seeds of Change*. Wallingford: CABI Press.

Griliches, Z. (1990). Patent statistics as economic indicators: a survey. *Journal of Economic Literature*, 28(4), 1661–1707.

Heller, M.A. and R.S. Eisenberg (1998). Can patents deter innovation? The anticommons in biomedical research. *Science*, 280, 698–701. doi.org/10.1126/science.280.5364.698

Hermans, R., A. Löffler and S. Stern (2008). Biotechnology. In J.T. Macher and D.C. Mowery (eds), *Innovation in Global Industries: U.S. Firms Competing in a New World (Collected Studies)*. Washington, D.C.: The National Academies Press. doi.org/10.17226/12112

Howard, P.H. (2015). Intellectual property and consolidation in the seed industry. *Crop Science*, 55 (November–December). www.apbrebes.org/files/seeds/files/Howard_seed_industry_patents_concentration_2015.pdf

Huang, J., R. Hu, Q. Wang, J. Keeley, and J.F. Zepeda (2002). Agricultural biotechnology development, policy and impact in China. *Economic and Political Weekly*, 37(27), 2756–2761.

International Potato Center (1995). *Program Report 1993-1994*. Lima, Peru: International Potato Center.

ISAAA (2017). *Global Status of Commercialized Biotech/GM Crops in 2017: Biotech Crop Adoption Surges as Economic Benefits Accumulate in 22 Years* (ISAAA Briefs No. 53). Ithaca, NY: International Service for the Acquisition of Agri-Biotech Applications.

Johnson, I. S. (1983). Human insulin from recombinant DNA technology. Science, 219(4585), 632–637. doi.org/10.1126/science.6337396

Kalaitzandonakes, N. G. and B. Bjornson (1997). Vertical and horizontal coordination in the agro-biotechnology industry: evidence and implications. *Journal of Agricultural and Applied Economics*, 29(1), 129–139. doi.org/10.1017/S1074070800029187

Kalaitzandonakes, N. G. (2000). Agrobiotechnology and Competitiveness. *American Journal of Agricultural Economics*, 82(5), 1224–1233.

Kenny, M. (1988). *Biotechnology: The University-Industrial Complex*. New Haven: Yale University Press.

Klümper, W. and M. Qaim (2014). A meta-analysis of the impacts of genetically modified crops. *PLOS ONE*, 9(11), e111629. doi.org/10.1371/journal.pone.0111629

Komen, J. (2012). The emerging international regulatory framework for biotechnology. *GM Crops & Food*, 3(1), 78–84. doi.org/10.4161/gmcr.19363

Komen, J. and G.J. Persley (1993). *Agricultural Biotechnology in Developing Countries: A Cross-Country Review* (ISNAR Research Report No. 2). The Hague: International Service for National Agricultural Research.

Mahfouz, M.M., A. Piatek and C.N. Stewart (2014). Genome engineering via TALENs and CRISPR/Cas9 systems: challengesand perspectives. *Plant Biotechnology Journal,* 12(8), 1006–1014. doi.org/10.1111/pbi.12256

National Research Council (1987). *Agricultural Biotechnology: Strategies for National Competitiveness* (Report of the Committee on a National Strategy for Biotechnology in Agriculture). Washington, D.C.: National Research Council.

National Research Council (1998). *Designing an Agricultural Genome Program. Report of the Board on Biology and Board on Agriculture.* Washington, D.C.: The National Academy Press.

Organisation for Economic Cooperation and Development (OECD) (2018). *Concentration in Seed Markets: Potential Effects and Policy Responses.* Paris: OECD Publishing.

Olmstead, A.L. and P.W. Rhode (2011). Adapting North American wheat production to climatic challenges, 1839–2009. *Proceedings of the National Academy of Sciences,* 108(2), 480–485. doi.org/10.1073/pnas.1008279108

Persley, G.J. (2000). Agricultural biotechnology and the poor: Promethean science. In Persley, G.J. and M.M. Lantin (eds), *Agricultural Biotechnology and the Poor.* Washington D.C.: Consultative Group on International Agricultural Research, 3–21.

Persley, G.J. and J.N. Siedow (1999). Applications of Biotechnology to Crops: Benefits and Risks. *Council for Agricultural Science and Technology Issue Paper No. 12.*

Pinstrup-Andersen, P. and M.J. Cohen (2003). Biotechnology and the CGIAR. In Plenderleith, K. and P. De Meyer (eds), *Sustainable Agriculture in the New Millennium: The Impact of Biotechnology on Developing Countries.* Brussels: Friends of the Earth Europe.

Pray, C.E. and A. Naseem (2003). The Economics of Agricultural Biotechnology Research. *ESA Working Paper No. 03-07.* Rome: The Food and Agriculture Organization of the United Nations. www.fao.org/tempref/docrep/fao/007/ae040e/ae040e00.pdf

Ramankutty, N., A.T. Evan, C. Monfreda and J.A. Foley (2008). Farming the planet: 1. Geographic distribution of global agricultural lands in the year 2000. *Global Biogeochemical Cycles,* 22(1), GB1003. doi.org/10.1029/2007GB002952

Rothaermel, F.T. (2001). Complementary assets, strategic alliances, and the incumbent's advantage: an empirical study of industry and firm effects in the biopharmaceutical industry. *Research Policy,* 30(8), 1235–1251.

Samad, G. and G.D. Graff (2020). The urban concentration of innovation and entrepreneurship in agricultural and natural resource industries. In Iftikhar, M.N., J.B. Justice and D.B. Audretsch (eds), *Urban Studies and Entrepreneurship.* Cham: Springer International Publishing, 91–116. doi.org/10.1007/978-3-030-15164-5_6

Serageldin, I. and G.J. Persley (2000). *Promethean Science: Agricultural Biotechnology, the Environment, and the Poor.* Washington, D.C.: Consultative Group on International Agricultural Research. documents.worldbank.org/curated/en/698501468739325409/Promethean-science-agricultural-biotechnology-the-environment-and-the-poor

Sheldon, I.M. (2004). Europe's regulation of agricultural biotechnology: precaution or trade distortion? *Journal of Agricultural & Food Industrial Organization,* 2(2), 1–28.

Shwartz, M. (2018). CRISPR is a gene-editing tool that's revolutionary, though not without risk. *Stanford Medicine,* Winter. stanmed.stanford.edu/2018winter/CRISPR-for-gene-editing-is-revolutionary-but-it-comes-with-risks.html

Tait, J., J. Chataway and D. Wield (2002). The life science industry sector: evolution of agro-biotechnology in Europe. *Science and Public Policy,* 29(4), 253–258.

Teece, D.J. (1986). Profiting from technological innovation: implications for integration, collaboration, licensing and public policy. *Research Policy,* 15(6), 285–305. doi.org/10.1016/0048-7333(86)90027-2

United States Department of Agriculture (USDA) Foreign Agricultural Service (2018). *EU-28: Agricultural Biotechnology Annual*, GAIN Report No. FR1827. Global Agricultural Information Network. gain. fas.usda.gov/Recent%20GAIN%20 Publications/Agricultural%20 Biotechnology%20Annual_Paris_ EU-28_12-14-2018.pdf

WIPO (2018). *World Intellectual Property Indicators*. Geneva: World Intellectual Property Organization.

Wright, B.D. (2012). Grand missions of agricultural innovation. *Research Policy*, 41(10), 1716–1728. doi. org/10.1016/j.respol.2012.04.021

Zilberman, D., C. Yarkin and A. Heiman (1997). Agricultural Biotechnology: Economic and International Implications. Paper presented at the International Agricultural Economics Association, Sacramento, California, August. are. berkeley.edu/~zilber11/yark.pdf

Innovation is becoming more collaborative as technology becomes more complex. For large multi-skilled teams to thrive, knowledge needs to be able to flow freely across borders.

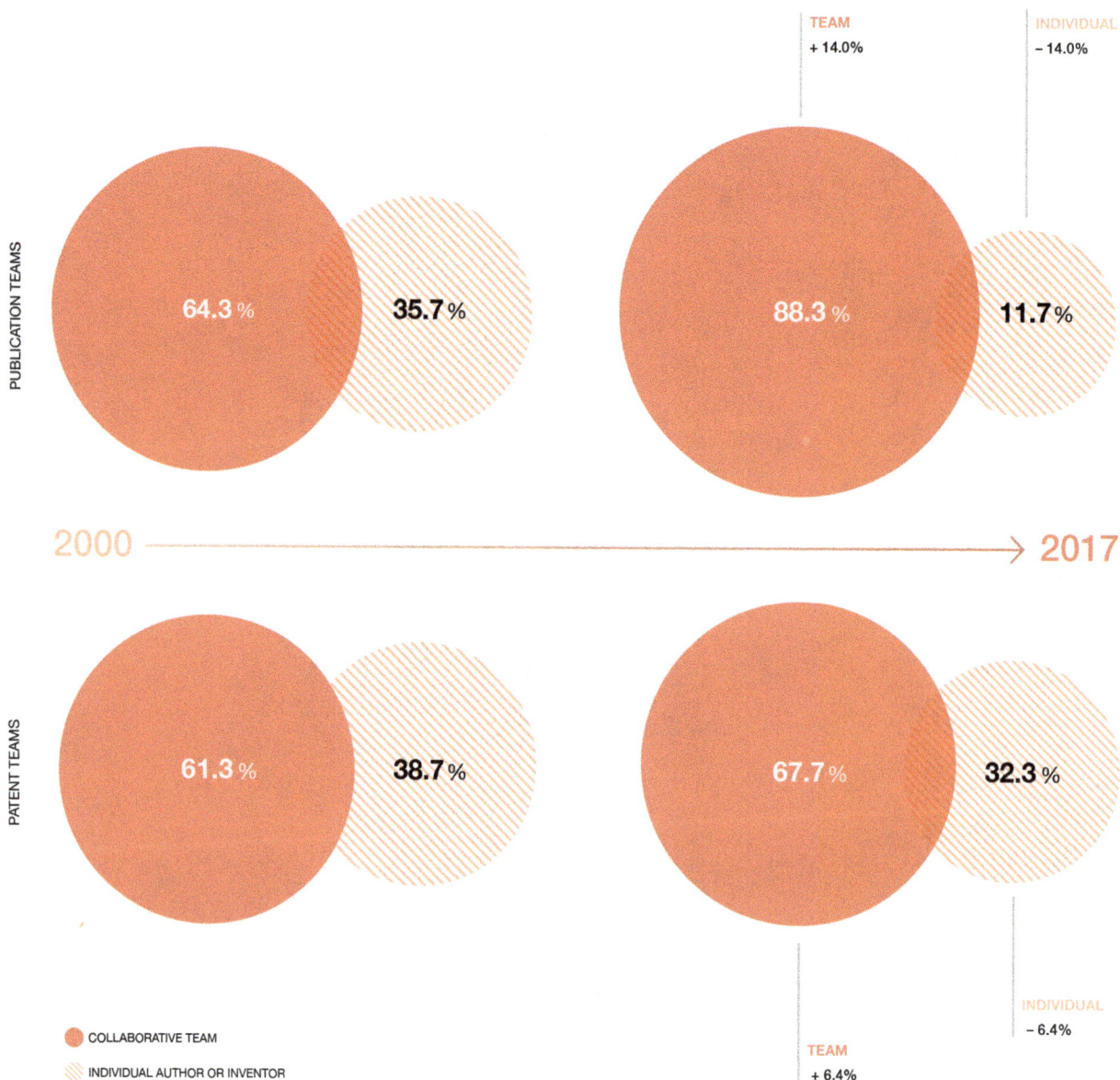

PUBLICATION TEAMS

64.3 %   35.7 %

TEAM
+ 14.0%

INDIVIDUAL
− 14.0%

88.3 %   11.7%

2000 ———————————————→ 2017

PATENT TEAMS

61.3 %   38.7%

67.7 %   32.3 %

TEAM
+ 6.4%

INDIVIDUAL
− 6.4%

● COLLABORATIVE TEAM
▨ INDIVIDUAL AUTHOR OR INVENTOR

Chapter 5

Policy perspectives: the case for openness

Innovation has always spanned countries and continents. At the turn of the 20th century, the Wright brothers in the United States of America (U.S.) and Alberto Santos-Dumont in Brazil invented the first airplanes to fly successfully. Yet, the development of the modern airplane owes much to scientific advances in Europe that explained why heavier-than-air machines could fly.[1] The development and dissemination of the agricultural technologies that unleashed the green revolution after the Second World War relied on partnerships between the Ford and Rockefeller Foundations in the U.S. and a large number of agricultural research institutes in developing economies.[2] Tim Berners-Lee invented the World Wide Web at the European Organization for Nuclear Research (CERN) – a research consortium on the Franco–Swiss border sponsored by 23 (mostly) European countries.[3]

As documented in this report, innovation today is both highly localized and international at the same time. Different agglomeration forces have favored the formation of innovation hotspots that typically fall within large metropolitan regions. A limited set of hotspots lead the way and are at the center of global innovation networks. Various formal and informal links connect the nodes of these networks, with multinational companies playing a key role within them. Evidence from patent and scientific publication records suggests that the cross-border dimension of these links has increased over the past decades.

The growing internationalization of innovation owes much to technology itself. Advances in information and communication technologies (ICTs), in particular, have fueled the flow of knowledge over long distances. Crucially, however, the growth of global innovation networks has relied on policies favoring openness and international cooperation. Such an environment of openness and cooperation should not be taken for granted – especially, as public perceptions have become more skeptical as to the benefits of globalization in general in recent years.

This closing chapter therefore reviews the case for openness in the pursuit of innovation. It does so primarily from an economic perspective. At times, whether and how to partner with foreign innovators involves questions of national security, which go beyond the scope of the chapter's discussion.

5.1 The economics of openness

Openness of national innovation systems entails the free exchange of knowledge between economies. Knowledge may flow across borders when researchers communicate with each other, or when they read scientific journals and patent documents published abroad. It may also occur through international trade, when knowledge is embedded in goods and services; and it may occur through migration, when it is embedded in people.

How do restrictions on the international flow of knowledge affect national economies and the world as a whole? The answer depends crucially on which knowledge flows the restrictions target, the capabilities of national innovation systems, patterns of production and employment, and the nature of the economic growth process. While not offering a definite conclusion, the economic literature offers some guidance on the effects of knowledge flow restrictions, which this section strives to summarize.

Gains from specialization

One simplified way to approach the question is to view knowledge like any other good. Just as the production of cars requires capital and labor inputs, so does the production of new knowledge through innovation.

Restricting international knowledge flows then affects how economies allocate resources toward different production activities. Viewed this way, the traditional predictions of international trade theory apply. Above all, openness leads to production and trade patterns that allow economies to specialize based on their comparative advantage. Trade economists usually consider two forces that give rise to specialization:[4]

- *Differences in factor endowments.* An economy richly endowed with capital will specialize in and export goods that are capital-intensive to produce. Conversely, an economy richly endowed with labor will specialize in and export goods that are labor-intensive to produce.
- *Differentiated varieties and economies of scale.* Where goods come in differentiated varieties – say, different car brands – and production of those varieties entails economies of scale, economies will specialize in and export some varieties and import others.

These predictions can shed light on important facets of the global geography of innovation. Innovation requires highly skilled labor, which explains why most innovative activity takes place in high-income countries where such labor is relatively abundant. At the same time, the decision by multinational companies to locate some research and development (R&D) activities in certain developing economies, such as China and India, reflects the availability of highly skilled labor at lower wages – fully in line with patterns of comparative advantage.[5]

The notion of differentiated varieties, in turn, finds its equivalence in the specialization of different innovation clusters around the world. For example, there are many innovation clusters focusing on medical technology, with each offering specialized knowledge not available elsewhere. This generates bidirectional knowledge flows, even among otherwise similar economies. Global innovation networks act as a broker for such knowledge flows.

Trade theory holds that there are mutual gains from comparative advantage-based trade. These gains take the form of increased economic efficiency and a wider variety of goods available to businesses and end-consumers. Given the highly specialized nature of innovative output, the variety effect seems particularly important to knowledge trade.

Notwithstanding these mutual gains, trade theory also holds that open trade affects the distribution of incomes within economies. Such distributional effects are stronger if differences in capital and labor endowments give rise to international trade. In other words, they are more important for trade between dissimilar economies – notably between economies at different levels of development. As will be further discussed below, these distributional effects matter for policy.

Innovation as a global public good

Viewing knowledge like any other good helps explain important aspects of the global innovation landscape. However, it is a highly simplified view that fails to account for the unique characteristics of knowledge production and knowledge consumption.

Above all, knowledge has attributes of what economists refer to as a public good: many people can use it at the same time, without diminishing the use of the knowledge by those who produce it.[6] For example, the basic science behind artificial intelligence emerged from a limited number of scientific organizations, yet a large number of innovations employ this science for a wide variety of applications around the world.[7]

In practice, there are limits to how widely knowledge can be shared. In fact, a central tenet of economic geography research is that knowledge does not flow freely within and across economies; knowledge flows have distinctive geographical patterns and biases.[8] One reason is that absorbing and applying cutting-edge knowledge often requires highly specialized skills that are in scarce supply.[9] Moreover, for some forms of knowledge to flow, human interaction is required, which is precisely a key reason for innovative activity to agglomerate (see Chapter 1).[10]

Yet, to the extent that knowledge lives up to its public good potential, does this change the case for openness? In fact, it strengthens it. If knowledge outflows generate economic benefits abroad without diminishing the use of knowledge at home, there are bound to be mutual gains from openness.

Innovation and growth

Innovation differs in another important way from other goods produced in the economy. Through innovation, companies can create a competitive edge over their rivals. A successful innovator can gain market share at the expense of a company that fails to be cutting-edge. Competition based on innovation, in turn, drives productivity enhancements and long-term economic growth.

As companies compete on the global stage, commentators have applied the same logic to economies as a whole. Accordingly, those economies that are successful at innovating grow faster at the expense of economies that do not innovate successfully.[11] In such a zero-sum world, restricting knowledge outflows would help economies retain an innovative edge and avoid "falling behind" other successfully innovating economies.

At the outset, the international economics literature would dismiss such "simplistic" zero-sum scenarios. Economies as a whole differ from companies in important ways. For one, economies as a whole cannot go bankrupt. If companies in a particular sector exit the market or lose market share due to foreign competition, they free up labor and capital that can be deployed elsewhere in the economy.

The reverse happens in sectors gaining international market share – they attract labor and capital from elsewhere in the economy. In addition, faster productivity growth in successfully innovating economies enlarges their size and increases demand for foreign products.

Overall, innovation leads to adjustments in prices, wages and exchange rates, which prompt shifts in production and trade patterns. Clearly, economies that are successful at innovating will, in the long term, experience faster overall economic growth than those that fail to do so. However, this does not necessarily mean that one economy's success constrains another economy from being equally successful. In fact, the public good nature of knowledge suggests that innovation can contribute to productivity growth everywhere.

Notwithstanding this general optimism, as national innovation performance shapes patterns of production and trade, it is conceivable for one economy to end up specializing in activities that put it on a permanently faster or slower growth path. Strategically restricting trade and knowledge flows could then tilt production patterns in such a way as to favor faster growth at home. Box 5.1 summarizes theoretical research that identifies the conditions in which such "zero-sum" outcomes can arise.

Whether such conditions prevail in practice is ultimately an empirical question. Rigorously answering it is not easy, given that one does not know how different economies would fare under different trade and knowledge-flow policies. However, one can look at the actual growth experience of economies around the world over the past decades. One important pattern is that today's high-income economies have experienced remarkably similar growth over the past 40 years. Before 1980, per capita incomes of poorer high-income economies saw faster growth than those of richer high-income economies. But this convergence process eventually slowed (Figure 5.1). While differences in per capita incomes persist, the most advanced economies have grown largely at a similar pace since the 1990s (Figure 5.2). This may suggest that new technologies have spread seamlessly across the set of economies already at the technology frontier and they have stimulated growth in comparable magnitudes.

Beyond the group of high-income economies, the growth experience has been mixed. For a long time, incomes across the world diverged.[12] In 1870, the gross domestic product (GDP) per capita of the richest economy was around 10 times that of the poorest one; by 2008 this gap had widened to a factor of 126.[13] For a very long time, poorer economies did not grow any faster than richer ones. More recent data – starting from the 1990s – suggest a reversal of this trend, with incomes converging across economies. In other words, since the 1990s, poorer economies have, on average, grown faster than richer ones.[14]

Box 5.1 Theoretical foundations of strategic trade policy

A branch of trade theory in the 1980s and early 1990s was devoted to analyzing the circumstances in which departures from free-trade policies may be welfare enhancing. Many underlying models focused on imperfectly competitive markets and trade policies that might increase the share of excess economic profits flowing to the domestic economies.[15] Some more complex theories also accounted for the role of innovation in driving long-term growth. The book by Gene Grossman and Elhanan Helpman (1991) provides the most detailed treatment of these latter theories.

In relevant models, firms invest in R&D with the prospect of reaping economic rents in imperfectly competitive product markets. Competitive market forces, in turn, sustain incentives to continuously invest in R&D, thereby generating the productivity gains that sustain growth in the long run. Mindful that companies compete in a global arena, the models then analyze the interdependence of growth processes in different countries.

The predictions stemming from these models confirm, first of all, the general optimism expressed in the text: global interactions generate forces that accelerate growth in every country. But they also point to reasons why this may not always be the case. For example:

- Suppose that an economy has a comparative disadvantage in research due to limited high-skilled labor. Integration with the rest of the world could then lead it to specialize in more stagnant activities, with overall output growing more slowly.
- Suppose that knowledge does not easily flow across borders, because it is difficult to reverse engineer or it requires critical skills not available in recipient countries, as described in the text. Integration may then lead economies that are small in size – or that historically have conducted little research – to specialize in manufacturing activities, preventing the onset of innovative activity. In fact, small differences in initial conditions between economies can lead to perpetual differences in productivity growth.

In the presence of such forces, strategic trade and related policies could well reshape patterns of production and alter an economy's growth path. In practice, successfully implementing such policies is difficult. The choice of policy instruments depends critically on initial conditions, the evolving nature of competition and technological opportunities. Given that the future path of technology and its implications for markets are highly uncertain, choosing the right policy mix in a forward-looking way is a formidable challenge.

Notwithstanding this trend reversal, average convergence does not mean universal or automatic convergence. Some poorer economies have been more successful at catching up to the richer ones than others. Developing countries in East Asia and, more recently, India, have been particularly successful at doing so. Given their central role in the growth process, knowledge flows and innovation must be part of the explanation behind these trends. However, which precise structural forces and economic policies have favored catch-up growth remains the subject of considerable debate.[16] A pessimistic view is that the historical concentration of innovative activities in a limited set of economies and the strong agglomeration forces associated with such activities reinforce a global core–periphery division. Even if policies do not restrict knowledge flows, this division fosters diverging development paths. A more optimistic view is that innovation eventually spreads beyond the core group of innovators; with the right policies, economies in the periphery can absorb foreign knowledge and catch up.

In conclusion, the economic literature offers good reasons why openness is bound to be beneficial in the pursuit of innovation. Theoretically, there may well be circumstances in which strategic restrictions on trade and knowledge flows could alter the growth paths of economies. However, it is difficult to translate this theoretical possibility into concrete policy proposals. As pointed out in Box 5.1, adopting the right policy instruments in a forward-looking way is a formidable challenge. Practically, it may be difficult to prevent knowledge from flowing abroad, without at the same time restricting knowledge circulating within economies. In addition, one economy's policy choices may prompt policy responses from other economies.

High-income economies grow at a similar pace

Figure 5.1 Gini coefficient, real GDP per capita, group of high-income economies

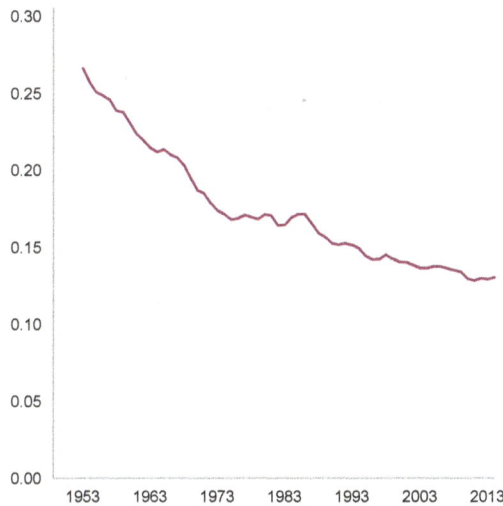

Figure 5.2 Real GDP per hour worked, relative to U.S.

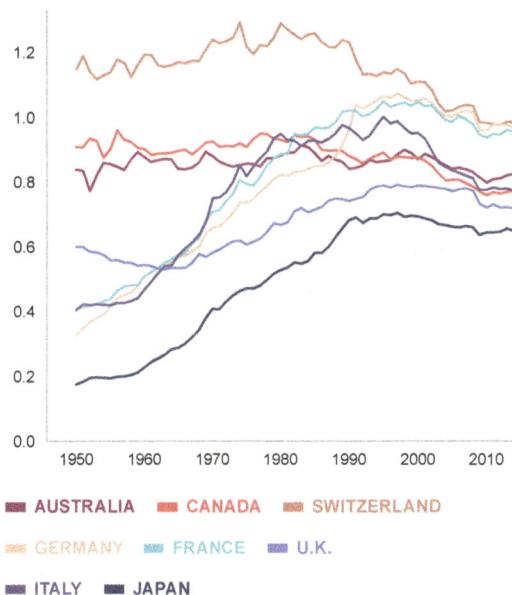

■ AUSTRALIA   ■ CANADA   ■ SWITZERLAND

■ GERMANY   ■ FRANCE   ■ U.K.

■ ITALY   ■ JAPAN

Note: The Gini coefficient measures the distribution of incomes on a scale of 0 to 1; the lower the value, the greater the equality. GDP per capita ratios in figure 5.2 are based on constant 2011 U.S. dollar real GDP figures, with 1.0 representing parity with the U.S. Values greater than 1.0 mean that a country's GDP per hour worked exceeds that of the U.S. The group of high-income countries includes Australia, Austria, Belgium, Canada, Denmark, Finland, France, Germany, Ireland, Israel, Italy, Japan, Netherlands, New Zealand, Norway, Republic of Korea, Spain, Sweden, Switzerland, U.K., U.S.
Source: Penn World Table, version 9.0, available at www.ggdc.net/pwt

Such policy reciprocity may well undermine the case for strategically limiting openness. Finally, the growth experience of high-income economies over the past decades suggests an overall positive-sum impact of new technologies.

5.2   Openness in an age of falling R&D productivity

The case for openness becomes even stronger when considering the context in which innovation takes place today. Continuously pushing the technological frontier is becoming exceedingly difficult. Evidence suggests that achieving the same level of technological progress as in the past requires more and more R&D effort. For example, Gordon Moore – the co-founder of Intel – famously predicted in 1975 that the number of transistors on a computer chip would double every two years. What came to be known as Moore's Law has roughly held up until today. Notably however, to double chip density today requires 18 times more researchers than it did in the early 1970s.[17]

Other fields of technology show similar signs of slowing R&D productivity: it takes multiple times as much medical R&D to achieve similar increases in life expectancy as in the past; investments in agricultural R&D have grown more rapidly than increases in agricultural crop yields.[18] More generally, most high-income economies have seen a gradual decline in the growth of economic productivity over the last half century. Economist Robert Gordon has prominently attributed this decline to innovations of the recent past boosting productivity growth by less than innovations of the more distant past.[19] In particular, he argues that the innovations associated with the second industrial revolution supported fast productivity growth in high-income economies until the 1970s; the innovations associated with the third (digital) industrial revolution have not been able to sustain such fast productivity growth.

Policies cannot alter opportunities for technological progress. However, policies shape to what extent those opportunities are realized. They determine how much resources are invested in R&D, how R&D is performed and how innovations find their way into the economy. Falling R&D productivity calls for constantly increasing investments in innovation – both scientific research and applied R&D. It also calls for collaboration and openness. Finding solutions to increasingly complex technological problems requires larger teams of researchers (see Chapter 2) and greater specialization in research. Openness and international collaboration promote such specialization and can thus help slow declining R&D productivity.

For openness to work, policymakers need to go beyond simply dismantling border barriers. There is an important role for international cooperation to support openness. Equally important, policymakers need to address regional imbalances that openness may partly foster. The final part of this chapter looks at these two critical dimensions.

Fostering international cooperation

International cooperation in relation to innovation has many dimensions. An important one is to promote incentives for innovation investments that reflect the demands and size of the global economy. Setting international rules for the protection of intellectual property (IP) rights serves this purpose. In practice, international treaties on IP typically establish the principle of nondiscrimination, namely that national laws treat domestic and foreign IP owners equally. They also set certain standards for the protection of different types of IP – for example, which inventions should be eligible for patent protection or how long copyright should last. At the same time, these standards do not fully harmonize IP protection across the world and leave room for national policies to tailor IP protection to national needs.

A second important dimension is to promote the ease of doing business internationally. Innovating companies and knowledge workers face a variety of regulatory measures when operating in markets around the world. Promoting the compatibility of national regulatory systems can help reduce the costs of regulatory compliance. For instance, some level of recognition of foreign regulatory standards can reduce the wasteful duplication of product testing and associated paperwork, without necessarily compromising regulatory objectives. Recognition of foreign qualifications in line with domestic standards can help facilitate the international mobility of knowledge workers. Regular dialogues between national regulatory agencies underpin such recognition frameworks. Similarly, setting technical standards at the international level can avoid the costly adaptation of products to different markets. In the area of IP, WIPO's international filing treaties – in particular, the Patent Cooperation Treaty, the Madrid System

and the Hague System – facilitate the acquisition of IP rights in many countries by filing a single international application; the ultimate grant of IP rights remains a national decision.

Finally, governments can pool resources and fund large-scale scientific projects that go beyond the envelopes of national budgets or require technical knowledge available in different countries. CERN – mentioned at the outset of this chapter – is a good example of such cooperation. The International Space Station is another one. It is a joint project between the national space agencies of Canada, Japan, the Russian Federation and the U.S., as well as the European Space Agency. Launched in 1998, it has hosted more than 200 visitors from 18 different countries.[20]

Addressing regional imbalances

As discussed in Chapter 1, one worrying trend of the past few decades is the increasing inter-regional polarization of incomes, innovative activity, high-skilled employment and wages within countries. Up to the 1980s, most high-income economies saw a steady convergence of incomes across regions.[21] Poor regions of countries caught up with rich ones. Since then, inter-regional convergence has slowed and, in some cases, it has even reversed. In the U.S., the convergence process slowed markedly starting in the 1990s.[22] European economies have similarly seen slowing regional convergence and, since the onset of the great recession in 2008, outright divergence. A few "champion" regions within European economies with already high levels of income have seen substantially faster growth than many of the poorer regions.[23]

There are many reasons for the polarization of economic activities within countries. The declining importance of agriculture and mining activities in economic output has long favored a gravitational pull toward big cities. In a knowledge-based and services-dominated economy, businesses have strong incentives to locate within large metropolitan areas. Openness arguably strengthens the gravitational pull toward champion regions. The most vibrant innovation hotspots, which are embedded in global innovation networks, tend to be located in what already are the richest metropolitan agglomerations within countries. Their international success reinforces their domestic lead. As described in Chapter 1, successful innovation agglomerations may also see diverging incomes within them, with fast growth of high-skilled jobs placing pressure on disposable income in low-skilled occupations. Israel offers a good example of how burgeoning innovation activities have raised concerns about a dual track economy (see Box 5.2).

Addressing such rising regional imbalances is one of the most difficult challenges for policymakers. Trying to reverse the gravitational pull of successful regions may be neither feasible nor desirable. Restricting participation in global innovation networks, in particular, would undercut an economy's ability to generate cutting-edge innovations. In any case, openness is but one contributing factor to regional imbalances.[24] The long-term structural transformation of economic activity is arguably the fundamental driving force behind such imbalances. Internal migration from lagging to thriving regions only offers a partial solution to regional divergence. Individuals may not have the capacity or willingness to move. High housing prices in thriving regions alone pose a significant barrier to internal migration.[25]

Policy can play an important role in supporting regions whose fortunes have fallen behind. Development support for weaker regions has, of course, a long history, with mixed success. A full review of historical policy initiatives is beyond the scope of this report. Nonetheless, recent research points to a few considerations that are important when designing regional support policies:[26]

- Ideally, regional development strategies should seek to build on existing capabilities and advantages of regions and aim at amplifying them through investments in infrastructure, education and technology. Existing capabilities and advantages can take the form of relatively cheap land and labor and prevailing industrial capabilities, as well as reputational assets.
- Policy formulation should identify the key barriers toward growing existing capabilities and rely on the input of all relevant local stakeholders.
- Resulting development policies should undergo regular evaluation. The resulting evidence should guide the adaptation of future policies.

While not reversing the gravitational pull of successful regions, such policies can ensure that innovation-driven growth benefits economies as a whole. As such, they critically underpin the openness of national innovation systems.

Box 5.2 Israel's thriving innovation system: startup nation or startup region?

Israel has a thriving innovation economy. Relative to the size of its GDP, no other country spends more on R&D and attracts more venture capital investments. Most of the world's leading technology companies have established R&D centers in Israel to draw on the skills and experience available in the country's dynamic research community. In many fields – notably cybersecurity – Israeli companies set the trend. Its lively startup scene has earned Israel the nickname "Startup Nation."

Israel's vibrant innovation economy has been a key driving force behind the growth of the overall economy. From 2008 to 2018, Israel's economy grew by an average annual rate of 3.5 percent – again, far surpassing most developed economies.[27] Unemployment fell to a record low of 4 percent in 2018.[28]

Yet, the nickname masks the high geographical concentration of innovation activity in Israel. The Tel Aviv metropolitan area stands out as the clear champion region. It accounts for 77 percent of all startups and 60 percent of all high-tech jobs.[29] It hosts more than half of Israel's inventors listed in patent applications (see Figure 5.3).

Wages in the peripheral regions are around 35 percent lower than in Central Israel. Tel Aviv's dominance has even intensified in recent years. The region was responsible for more than two-thirds of the growth in high-tech employees between 2015 and 2017.[30] Tel Aviv is also highly connected to leading innovation hotspots around the world, offering, for example, nonstop flights to San Francisco.

As in other global innovation hotspots, Tel Aviv has seen rising concerns that the expansion of technology companies is driving up housing prices and widening income disparities.[31]

The Government of Israel recognizes that the gravitational pull of the Tel Aviv region reflects relative regional advantages and natural agglomeration forces. Yet it also realizes that this regional imbalance creates economic and social challenges. As a result, Israel's Innovation Authority has adopted a Strategy for an Innovation-Driven Economy in the Periphery.

This strategy has four central pillars:[32]
- Connecting human capital in the periphery to leading high-tech companies;
- Promoting technological innovation in the periphery in the manufacturing, agriculture and food sectors;
- Encouraging entrepreneurship that draws on local academic institutions and other sources of home-grown knowledge and industrial expertise; and
- Strengthening the high-tech ecosystem in those regions – namely, Haifa, Jerusalem and Beersheba – that have the essential foundations for such an ecosystem.

These pillars seek both to reduce a growing shortage of high-skilled workers in the innovation economy and to promote the development of regions that currently are lagging to produce more balanced national growth.

The greater Tel Aviv area hosts most of Israel's inventors

Figure 5.3 Heat map of inventors listed in patent applications, 2008–2018

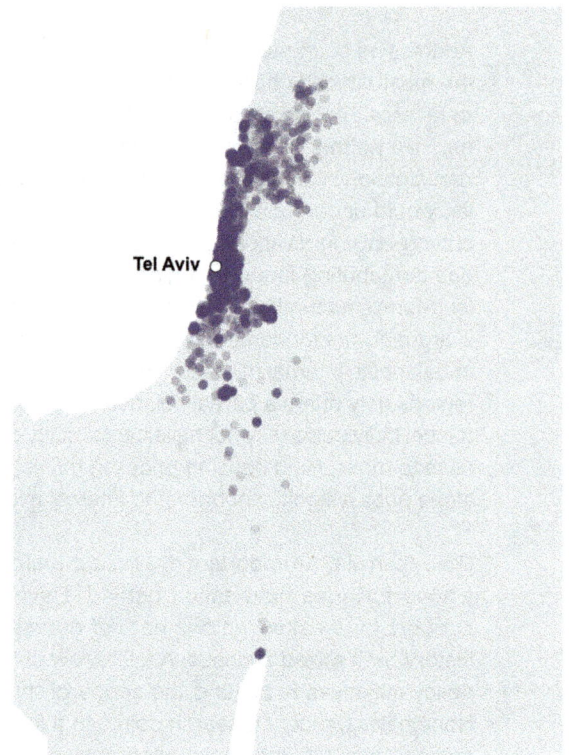

Source: WIPO based on PATSTAT and PCT data (see Technical Notes).
Notes: Patent figures based on international patent families.

Notes

1   See WIPO (2015).

2   See the case study on agricultural biotechnology in Chapter 4.

3   Visit home.cern. Israel is the only CERN member from outside of Europe.

4   See Krugman *et al.* (2018). Differences in productivity levels between countries are a third force driving specialization.

5   Differences in factor endowments can also explain patterns of international migration. Thus, highly skilled workers – say software engineers from India – tend to move to high-income economies where they are paid higher wages (see Krugman *et al.*, 2018). Admittedly, lower wages of R&D personnel are but one motivation for multinational companies to locate R&D activities in developing economies; the growth potential of local markets is often another important factor (see Thursby and Thursby, 2006).

6   Noble prize-winning economist Kenneth Arrow first observed the public good nature of knowledge (Arrow, 1962). In addition to being non-rival in consumption, knowledge producers cannot – without intellectual property (IP) protection – exclude others from using knowledge communicated to the public. See WIPO (2011) for further discussion.

7   See WIPO (2019).

8   See Crescenzi *et al.* (2019).

9   See Cohen and Levinthal (1989) for an early contribution on the importance of absorptive capacity.

10 See von Hippel (1994).

11 Such arguments first became prominent in the 1980s when the rapid growth of East Asian economies was perceived to threaten the technological dominance of Western economies (see, e.g., Tyson, 1984).

12 Pritchett (1997) famously characterized the long-term historical trend as "divergence, big time."

13 See WIPO (2015).

14 See Patel *et al.* (2018).

15 See Brander and Spencer (1985) for a seminal contribution.

16 See WIPO (2015).

17 See Bloom *et al.* (2019).

18 See Bloom *et al.* (2019). The authors also document declining R&D productivity when analyzing firm-level data across the U.S. economy. In addition, they consider and reject the possibility that the emergence of new technologies compensates for declining R&D productivity in existing technologies.

19 See Gordon (2018).

20 Visit en.wikipedia.org/wiki/International_Space_Station.

21 See Crescenzi *et al.* (2019).

22 See Ganong and Shoag (2017).

23 See Alcidi *et al.* (2018).

24 In reviewing two decades of research, Helpman (2018) concludes that globalization is responsible for only a small rise in inequality within nations.

25 See Ganong and Shoag (2017).

26 See Foray (2015) and Rodríguez-Pose (2018).

27 Based on constant 2010 U.S. dollar GDP values, as reported by the World Bank.

28 As per International Labour Organization country profile for Israel.

29 See Israel Innovation Authority (2019).

30 See Israel Innovation Authority (2019).

31 See Srivastava (2018).

32 See Israel Innovation Authority (2019).

References

Alcidi, C., J.N. Ferrer, M. Di Salvo, R. Musmeci and M. Pilati (2018). Income Convergence in the EU: A Tale of Two Speeds. *Commentary*, January 9. Brussels: Centre for European Policy Studies.

Arrow, K. (1962). Economic welfare and the allocation of resources for invention. In Nelson, R.R. (ed.), *The Rate and Direction of Inventive Activity: Economic and Social Factors*. Princeton, NJ: Princeton University Press, 609–626.

Bloom, N., C.I. Jones, J. Van Reenen and M. Webb (2019). Are Ideas Getting Harder to Find? *NBER Working Paper Series, No. 23782*. Cambridge, MA: National Bureau of Economic Research.

Brander, J.A. and B.J. Spencer (1985). Export subsidies and international market share rivalry. *Journal of International Economics*, 18(2), 83–100.

Cohen, W.M. and D.A. Levinthal (1989). Innovation and learning: two faces of R&D. *Economic Journal*, 99, 569–596.

Crescenzi, R., S. Iammarino, C. Ioramashvili, A. Rodríguez-Pose and M. Storper (2019). The Geography of Innovation: Local Hotspots and Global Innovation Networks. *WIPO Economic Research Working Paper No. 57*. Geneva: WIPO.

Foray, D. (2015). *Smart Specialisation: Opportunities and Challenges for Regional Innovation Policy*. Abingdon: Routledge.

Ganong, P. and D. Shoag (2017). Why has regional income convergence in the U.S. declined? *Journal of Urban Economics*, 102, 76–90.

Gordon, R.J. (2018). Declining American economic growth despite ongoing innovation. *Explorations in Economic History*, 69, 1–12.

Grossman, G.M. and E. Helpman (1991). *Innovation and Growth in the Global Economy*. Cambridge, MA: MIT Press.

Helpman, E. (2018). *Globalization and Inequality*. Cambridge, MA: Harvard University Press.

Israel Innovation Authority (2019). *State of Innovation in Israel 2018*. www.innovationisrael.org.il

Krugman, P.R., M. Obstfeld and M. Melitz (2018). *International Economics: Theory and Policy* (11th edition). Boston, MA: Pearson Education.

Patel, D., J. Sandefur and A. Subramanian (2018). Everything you know about cross-country convergence is (now) wrong. *Realtime Economic Issues Watch*, October 15. Peterson Institute for International Economics. www.piie.com/blogs/realtime-economic-issues-watch/everything-you-know-about-cross-country-convergence-now-wrong

Pritchett, L. (1997). Divergence, big time. *Journal of Economic Perspectives*, 11(3), 3–17.

Rodríguez-Pose, A. (2018). The revenge of the places that don't matter. *VOX*, February 6. voxeu.org/article/revenge-places-dont-matter

Srivastava, M. (2018). Israel's tech expansion stokes glaring inequality in Tel Aviv. *Financial Times*, December 10.

Thursby, J. and M. Thursby (2006). *Here or There? A Survey of Factors in Multinational R&D Location*. Washington, D.C.: The National Academies Press.

Tyson, L.D. (1984). *Who's Bashing Whom: Trade Conflict in High-technology Industries*. Washington, D.C.: Institute for International Economics.

von Hippel, E. (1994). 'Sticky information' and the locus of problem solving: implications for innovation. *Management Science*, 40, 429–439.

WIPO (2011). *World Intellectual Property Report 2011: The Changing Face of Innovation*. Geneva: WIPO.

WIPO (2015). *World Intellectual Property Report 2015: Breakthrough Innovation and Economic Growth*. Geneva: WIPO.

WIPO (2019). *Technology Trends 2019: Artificial Intelligence*. Geneva: WIPO.

Technical notes

Country income groups

This report uses the World Bank income classification to refer to particular country groups. The classification is based on gross national income per capita in 2018 and establishes the following four groups: low-income economies (USD 1,025 or less); lower middle-income economies (USD 1,026 to USD 3,995); upper middle-income economies (USD 3,996 to USD 12,375); and high-income economies (USD 12,376 or more).

More information on this classification is available at data.worldbank.org/about/country-classifications

Country region groups

The country regions used in this report are closely based on the geographic regions from the Standard Country or Area Codes for Statistics Use, 1999 (Revision 4) known as M49 and published by the Statistics Division (UNDS) of the Department of Economic and Social Affairs, United Nations (UN). The full methodology can be found at unstats.un.org.

To simplify the analysis, some changes are introduced to this methodology. These are the following: *Western Europe* includes Andorra, Austria, Belgium, Denmark, Finland, France, Germany, Greece, Iceland, Ireland, Italy, Liechtenstein, Luxembourg, Malta, Monaco, Netherlands, Norway, Portugal, San Marino, Spain, Sweden, Switzerland, and United Kingdom. *Central and Eastern Europe* includes all countries in the M49's *Northern* and *Southern Europe* regions not included in *Western Europe*. The geographical subregions *Southern Asia*, *Central Asia* and *South-eastern Asia* are grouped in one category, which also includes Mongolia.

Scientific publication data

The scientific publication data used in this report comes from 27,726,805 records published from 1998 to 2017 in the Science Citation Index Expanded (SCIE) of the Web of Science (WOS), the citation database operated by the Clarivate Analytics company. The analysis focuses on 23,789,354 observations referring only to scientific articles, conference proceedings, scientific abstracts and data papers. Scientific articles constitute the bulk of the resulting dataset.

Patent data

The patent data used in this report are from the European Patent Office's (EPO) Worldwide Patent Statistical Database (PATSTAT, April 2019) and WIPO's Patent Cooperation Treaty (PCT) collections. In the analyzed period (1970–2017), these sources account for 49,286,675 first patent filings and 26,626,660 subsequent patent filings, totaling 75,913,335 patent applications from 168 different patent offices.

The main unit of analysis is the first filing for a set of patent applications filed in one or more countries and claiming the same invention. Each set containing one first and, potentially, several subsequent filings is defined as a patent family. The analysis also distinguishes foreign-oriented patent families – also referred to as international patent families – from domestic-only ones. Foreign-oriented patent families concern those inventions for which the applicant has sought patent protection beyond its home patent office. This definition includes also patent applications by applicants filing only abroad, filing only through the PCT system or filing only at the EPO. Reciprocally, domestic-only patent families refer to those patent applications filed only at the applicant's home office – regardless of how many filings in the home office there are within the same family – without any subsequent foreign filing though the Paris or PCT routes. Likewise, patent applications with applicants of more than one origin are by definition foreign-oriented patent families. In addition, about 30 percent of the patent families relate only to utility model protection, which are mostly domestic only.

Unless otherwise stated, the report makes use of international patent families only as the unit of analysis for all patent statistics reported. This relates mostly to the incomplete coverage of the domestic-only patents (and utility models) of many national collections in PATSTAT. While the top national and international offices are usually well covered – namely U.S. Patent and Trademark Office (USPTO), Japan Patent Office (JPO), Korean Intellectual Property Office (KIPO), National Intellectual Property Administration of the People's Republic of China (CNIPA), EPO and WIPO – some other offices have limited coverage in PATSTAT. For instance, the coverage in PATSTAT of national collection data from some top 20 patent offices – such as India, Indonesia, Iran (Islamic Republic of), Mexico and Turkey – is limited. As a result, the report makes use of the information of 8,955,990 international patent families containing 35,582,650 different patent applications.

Geocoding

The geocoding – i.e., attributing the latitude and longitude to a given location – of the scientific publication and patent data was performed using all available information on addresses and already existing geocoding exercises for these data.

In the case of scientific publications, the report assumes that research conducted for any publication takes place at the institutions and organizations to which the authors declare their affiliation. Ninety-seven percent of all the available affiliation addresses were geocoded at the postal code or sub-city level. In the case of authors with more than one affiliation in the same publication, all different addresses were considered.

In the case of patents, 87 percent of the international patent families filed from 1976 to 2015 were geocoded. Most of the non-geocoded cases had no usable address information. As far as possible, the geocoding was applied to the inventors' addresses by using the most complete and reliable data source available within each patent family. In addition, the data were enriched with exiting geocoded patent data (see Yin and Motohashi, 2018; Ikeuchi et al., 2017; Li et al., 2014; de Rassenfosse et al., 2019; Morrison et al., 2017). All these sources and WIPO's geocoding were analyzed and consolidated to get the best possible geocoded data for each patent family. When there was more than one source for a given patent family, the following order of priority was given: (1) sources having information from the inventor (inventor principle); (2) sources having more inventors' addresses covered (coverage principle); (3) sources with the best geocoding resolution (resolution principle); (4) sources closest to the address country – e.g., entrusting Chinese addresses to CNIPA data, Japanese addresses to Japan Patent Office (JPO) data, etc. (local principle); and (5) manual check and ad hoc selection when two or more sources were still available. As a result, many inventor's addresses were geocoded at a precise level – i.e., street or block – but others only at the postal code or other sub-city level. Patent families containing more offices are more likely to be geocoded and at higher quality. This is another reason why the report relies only on international patent families. For more information, please refer to Miguelez et al. (2019).

Measuring innovation agglomeration

In order to handle the modifiable areal unit problem (MAUP) and its resulting statistical distortions, this report created two sets of ad hoc comparable areas to be used in place of administrative ones (see Ester et al., 1996). A first set – named global innovation hotspots (GIHs) – captures the most innovation-dense geographical areas of the world in terms of scientific articles or patent families per square kilometer (km). By definition, these areas are internationally comparable and geographically distinct. The same scientific publication or patent density determines the same hotspot anywhere in the world, although the threshold is different for scientific publication and patent data. No patent or scientific publication address can be in two hotspots at the same time.

A second set, named specialized niche clusters (SNCs), was created to avoid biases arising from some scientific or technological fields being overrepresented in the scientific publication and patent data, respectively. The SNCs capture areas with high innovation density in one or more specific scientific publication or patenting fields, and that otherwise have not met the criteria to be a global innovation hotspot (GIH). The resulting clusters are also distinct geographical areas, as the overlapping clusters for different fields are consolidated into one cluster. But they are only internationally comparable within their specific scientific or technological field (or fields).

As a result, the report identifies 174 GIHs and 313 SNCs worldwide. The detailed identification method is described as follows:

First, the points within GIHs are identified using the Density-based spatial clustering of applications with noise (DBSCAN) clustering algorithm applied separately to the geocoded patent and scientific publication data. The DBSCAN method requires two parameters – minimum radius and points – to establish the minimum acceptable density to form a candidate area. These two parameters were set differently for patents and scientific publications. The radius for scientific publication data was set to 23 km, which is the average commuting distance to work in OECD countries. Given the more precise geocoding of patent data, and based on visual inspection, the radius was set to the smaller value of 13 km. The minimum points parameter was set to the median patent and scientific publication density of all possible circumferences given the radius of each dataset. As a result, the minimum patent density of GIHs was set to 1,453 patents per 10 km^2 and the minimum scientific publication density is 3,328 scientific publications per 10 km^2.

Second, the resulting groups of points from DBSCAN are used to determine the candidate geographical areas – i.e., boundaries – of the GIHs. The borders of each scientific publication and patent agglomeration are determined using the k-nearest neighbors concave hull approach for each patent and scientific publication group of points (see Moreira and Santos, 2007). In order to avoid abnormal polygon shapes, the concave algorithm was set to have at least 75 percent of the convex area covered by all the outer points of a given group. In the handful of cases where the group had less than three coordinates, the polygon was set to a circumference of 13 km radius. The overlapping polygons are merged, keeping only the outer borders of all concerned agglomerations. However, if the overlap was less than 5 percent of either polygon, these were manually inspected and corrected. All patents and scientific articles within the resulting polygons are considered in the analysis, regardless whether they were or were not part of the DBSCAN results.

Third, the above method is repeated for 25 sub-samples of the same publication and patent data, which refer to 12 scientific fields and 13 technological ones, respectively. The radius parameters are again set as 13 km for patents and 25 km for scientific publications. The minimum points are set to the median patent density of each of the 13 technological fields and the median scientific publication density of each of the 12 scientific fields of all possible circumferences given the radius of each dataset. From the resulting groups of each of these 25 iterations, only the points not contained within a GIH hotspot are kept to compute the concave polygon areas. From the resulting polygons, the overlapping ones are merged in the same way as mentioned above.

Mapping strategies

The patent mapping strategy for each of the two sectors – autonomous vehicles in Chapter 3 and plant biotechnologies in Chapter 4 – is based on prior studies and experts' suggestions. Whenever possible, each strategy relied on and was compared to existing equivalent scientific publication and patent mapping exercises. For more details please see Graff and Hamdan-Livramento (2019) and Zehtabchi (2019).

Autonomous vehicles (AV)

The AV mapping is based on a combination of patents in PATSTAT data and scientific articles in WoS SCIE data sampled based on patent classifications, scientific subjects and keywords. These are detailed as follows.

The following IPC and CPC symbols were used to determine the AV-related patents and are based on prior patent landscapes of the UKIPO, EPO and JPO. Some of the CPC and IPC symbols were used in combination only with some keywords.

Standalone symbols: G05D 1/0088; G05D2201/0207; G05D2201/0212; G08G 1/22; B60L2260/40%; B60L2230%; B60K31/0008; B60K31/0008; B60K2031/0091; B60K31/0058; B60K31/0066; B60W2550/40; B60W2600%; G01S15/88; G06K9/00791; G06T2207/30252; G08G1/096791; G08G1/16; G08G1/22; H04L67/12; Y02P90/285.

Symbols in combination with keywords: B60L%; B60W%; B60W2030/%; B60W2040/%; B60W2050/%; B60W30/%; B60W40/%; B60W50/%; B60Y%; B60Y2200/11; B62D%; G01S13/93; G01S13/931; G01S15/93; G01S15/931/%; G01S17/88; G01S17/93; G01S17/936; G01S7/022; G01S7/4806; G05D1/02; G05D1/021/%; G08G1/16; Y02T10/%; Y02T90/%.

Keywords: (ground | car | cars | lorri | lorry | road | street | highway | convoy | platoon | fleet), (autonomous | unmanned | driver[.]{0,}less | agv), and NOT (air | aer | drone | flight | flies | fly).

In the case of scientific publication data, an iterative process was applied. First, a keyword-based strategy was made on the abstracts of the WoS SCIE data by combining the following two lists of terms: (1) automated, autonomous, self-driving, driverless, unmanned, robotic, pilotless and unpiloted; and (2) vehicle, car, truck, taxi, shuttle, lorry, driving, transport(ation) and automobile.

Second, the tags declared by the authors of the resulting scientific articles were then manually inspected to build a new list of the following 40 terms: adaptive cruise control; advanced driver assistance system; automated driving system; automated lane change maneuver; automatic vehicle control; automatic vehicle following; automotive radar; automotive sensors; autonomous mobile robots; autonomous navigation; autonomous valet parking; autonomous vehicular networks; autonomous-vehicle lane; collision avoidance; crash avoidance; DARPA; DARPA urban challenge; Defense Advanced Research Projects Agency (DARPA) urban challenge; drivable-region detection; intelligent cruise control vehicles; intelligent unmanned autonomous system; LADAR; laser imaging detection and ranging; LIDAR; LIDAR object detection; light detection and ranging (LIDAR); look-ahead sensing; moving vehicle detection; obstacle avoidance; obstacle detection; pedestrian detection; pedestrian-crossing detection; platoon; predictive cruise control; unmanned ground vehicle; unmanned surface vehicles; vehicle automation; vehicle detection; vision-based guidance; wheeled robotic vehicle.

Third, the 40 terms were used in the abstracts and titles of articles to extract a new set. To avoid false positives, articles published in journals tagged in the following WoS subjects were excluded: Anatomy/ Morphology; Art; Astronomy/Astrophysics; Audiology/ Speech-Language Pathology; Behavioral Sciences; Biochemistry/Molecular Biology; Biodiversity/ Conservation; Biophysics; Biotechnology/Applied Microbiology; Cardiovascular System/Cardiology; Cell Biology; Chemistry; Crystallography; Developmental Biology; Education/Educational Research; Emergency Medicine; Endocrinology/Metabolism; Entomology; Environmental Sciences/Ecology; Evolutionary Biology; Fisheries; Food Science/Technology; Forestry; Gastroenterology/Hepatology; General/ Internal Medicine; Geochemistry/Geophysics; Geography; Geology; Geriatrics/Gerontology; Health Care Sciences/Services; Immunology; Infectious Diseases; Information Science/Library Science; Life Sciences/Biomedicine – other topics; Linguistics; Marine/Freshwater Biology; Medical Informatics; Medical Laboratory Technology; Meteorology/ Atmospheric Sciences; Microbiology; Mineralogy; Mining/Mineral Processing; Neurosciences/Neurology; Nuclear Science/Technology; Nursing; Nutrition/ Dietetics; Obstetrics/Gynecology; Oceanography; Ophthalmology; Orthopedics; Otorhinolaryngology; Pathology; Pediatrics; Pharmacology/Pharmacy; Physiology; Plant Sciences; Psychiatry; Psychology; Public Environmental/Occupational Health; Radiology Nuclear Medicine/Medical Imaging; Rehabilitation; Research/Experimental Medicine; Respiratory System; Rheumatology; Social Sciences – other topics; Sport Sciences; Surgery; Toxicology; Transplantation; Tropical Medicine; Urology/Nephrology; Veterinary Sciences; Water Resources; Zoology.

Crop biotechnologies

The crop biotechnology mapping is based on a combination of patents in PATSTAT data and scientific articles in WoS SCIE data sampled based on patent classifications, scientific journals and keywords. These are detailed as follows.

The following IPC and CPC symbols were used to determine the patents on each crop biotech category and the union of these constitute the total of crop biotech patents:

Crop genetic improvement: A01H1%; A01H3%; A01H4%; A01H5%; A01H6%; A01H7%; A01H17%; C12N5/04%; C12N5/14%; C12N15/05%; C12N15/29%; C12N15/79%; C12N15/82%; C12N15/83%; C12N15/84%; (C07K14/415% but not A61K%).

Pest control in crops: A01N63%; A01N65%; C12N15/31%; C12N/32%; (C07K14/325% but not A61K%).

Soil fertility: C05F%.

Climate change: Y02A40/146; Y02A40/162; Y0240/164.

The scientific publications were extracted from top plant biotechnology scientific journals and from the conjunction of top scientific journals for agriculture biotechnology and keywords. These are:

(1) All articles from the following top plant biotechnology journals: *Agri Gene*; *Crop Science*; *Euphytica*; *Genetics, Selection, and Evolution*; *Journal of Experimental Botany*; *Journal of Plant Physiology*; *New Phytologist*; *Physiologia Plantarum*; *Plant and Cell Physiology*; *Plant Cell*; *Plant Cell and Environment*; *Plant Cell Reports*; *Plant Journal*; *Plant Molecular Biology*; *Plant Physiology*; *Plant Physiology and Biochemistry*; *Plant Science*; *Planta*.

(2) Top agriculture biotechnology scientific journals and keywords:

Top agriculture biotechnology scientific journals: *Biochemical and Biophysical Research Communications*; *Cell*; *Journal of Biological Chemistry*; *Journal of Biology*; *Journal of Cell Biology*; *Journal of Molecular Biology*; *Journal of the American Medical Association*; *Molecular and Cellular Biology*; *Nature*; *Nature Biotechnology*; *New England Journal of Medicine*; *PlosBio*; *Proceedings of the National Academy of Sciences of the USA*; *Science*; *The EMBO Journal*; *Theoretical and Applied Genetics*.

Keywords: abscisic acid; ACC oxidase; ACC synthase; aerenchyma; *agrobacterium rhizogenes*; *agrobacterium tumefaciens*; *agrobacterium*; alfalfa; ammonium; anther culture; anthocyanins; apoplast; arabidopsis;

arbuscular mycorrhiza*; auxin; bacterial blight; banana; barley; *beta vulgaris*; *rachypodium distachyon*; brassica; bread wheat; breeding; breeding value; C-4 photosynthesis; canola; *capsicum annuum*; carrot; cassava; chickpea; chinese cabbage; chlorophyll a fluorescence; chloroplast DNA; citrus; *coffea arabica*; cold tolerance; common bean; conifer*; cotton; crossbreeding; *cucumis melo*; *cucumis sativus*; cytokinins; cytoplasmic male sterility; *daucus carota*; defoliation; distillers grains; doubled; downy mildew; drought resistance; ectomycorrhizal; eucalyptus; flaxseed; forage; fructan; fruit development; fruit quality; fruit ripening; fusarium; *fusarium graminearum*; *fusarium* head blight; garlic; genome; genotype x environment interaction; genotype; germplasm; gibberellins; glycine max; *gossypium hirsutum*; grain; grain filling; grain yield; grapevine; hairy root; haploid; *hevea brasiliensis*; high; *hordeum vulgare*; hypersensitive response; kiwifruit; leaf anatomy; leaf growth; leaf rust; legume; linseed; *lolium perenne*; *lycopersicon esculentum*; maize; male sterility; marker; *medicago truncatula*; methyl jasmonate; micropropagation; mycorrhiza*;

nicotiana tabacum; nitrogen fixation; orchid; *oryza*; *oryza sativa*; osmotic adjustment; osmotic potential; pea; peach; pectin; pepper; perennial ryegrass; *phaseolus vulgaris*; phenotyping; phloem transport; *physcomitrella patens*; phytic acid; phytotoxicity; *picea abies*; *pinus*; *pinus pinaster*; *pinus taeda*; *pisum*; plant breeding; plant defence; plant regeneration; plant transformation; pollen development; pollen germination; pollen tube; potato; *prunus persica*; QTL*; QTL analysis; QTL mapping; QTLs; quantitative trait loc*; rapeseed; resveratrol; RFLP; rice; root elongation; root exudates; *rubisco activase*; rye; sap flow; seed; self-incompatibility; shoot regeneration; *solanum lycopersicum*; *solanum tuberosum*; somaclonal variation; somatic embryogenesis; sorghum; soybean; *spinacia oleracea*; stomatal conductance; strawberry; sucrose synthase; sugar beet; sugarcane; sunflower; suppression subtractive hybridization; tall fescue; *thlaspi caerulescens*; tomato; transgenic plant*; transgenic rice; transgenic tobacco; tritic*; *triticum aestivum*; *vicia faba*; *vitis vinifera*; water potential; water use efficiency; wheat; winter wheat; xylem sap; zea may*.

References

de Rassenfosse, G., J. Kozak and F. Seliger (2019). Geocoding of worldwide patent data. papers.ssrn.com/sol3/papers.cfm?abstract_id=3425764

Ester, M., H.-P Kriegel, J., Sander and X. Xu (1996). A density-based algorithm for discovering clusters in large spatial databases with noise. *Proceedings of the 2nd International Conference on Knowledge Discovery and Data Mining* (KDD-96), Portland, Oregon, August 2–4, Menlo Park, CA: AAAI Press, 226–231.

Graff, G. and I. Hamdan-Livramento (2019). The Global Innovation Network of Plant Biotechnology. *WIPO Economic Research Working Paper No. 59*. Geneva: WIPO.

Ikeuchi, K., K. Motohashi, R. Tamura and N. Tsukada (2017). Measuring Science Intensity of

Industry using Linked Dataset of Science, Technology and Industry. *RIETI Discussion Paper Series*, 17-E-056. www.rieti.go.jp/en/publications/summary/17030073.html

Li, G.-C., R. Lai, A. D'Amour, D.M. Doolin, Y. Sun, V.I. Torvik, A.Z. Yu and L. Fleming (2014). Disambiguation and co-authorship networks of the U.S. patent inventor database (1975–2010). *Research Policy*, 43, 941–955.

Miguelez, E., J. Raffo, C. Chacua, M. Coda-Zabetta, D. Yin, F. Lissoni and G. Tarasconi (2019). Tied In: The Global Network of Local Innovation. *WIPO Working Paper No. 58*, November. Geneva: WIPO.

Moreira, A. and M.Y. Santos (2007). Concave hull: A k-nearest neighbours approach for the computation of the region occupied by a set of points. In *Proceedings of the*

Second International Conference on Computer Graphics Theory and Applications (GRAPP 2007), Barcelona, March 8–11. INSTICC Press. ISBN 978-972-8865-71-9, pp. 61–68.

Morrison, G., M. Riccaboni and F. Pammolli (2017). Disambiguation of patent inventors and assignees using high-resolution geolocation data. *Scientific Data*, 4. doi.org/10.1038/sdata.2017.64

Yin, D. and K. Motohashi (2018). Inventor Name Disambiguation with Gradient Boosting Decision Tree and Inventor Mobility in China (1985–2016), *RIETI Discussion Paper Series*, 18-E-018.

Zehtabchi, M. (2019). Measuring Innovation in the Autonomous Vehicle Technology. *WIPO Economic Research Working Paper No. 60*. Geneva: WIPO.

Acronyms

ADAS	advanced driver assistance systems	GIH	global innovation hotspot
ADS	automated driving systems	GIN	global innovation network
AHS	automated highway systems	GIO	genetically improved organism
AI	artificial intelligence	GM	General Motors
AV	autonomous vehicle	GMO	genetically modified organism
BIO	Biotechnology Innovation Organization	IARC	International Agriculture Research Center
Bt	Bacillus thuringiensis	ICT	information and communication technology
CAAS	China Academy of Agricultural Sciences	IP	intellectual property
CBD	Convention on Biodiversity	IPC	International Patent Classification
CEO	chief executive officer	IRRI	International Rice Research Institute
CERN	European Organization for Nuclear Research	IT	information technologies
		MaaS	Mobility-as-a-Service
CGIAR	Consultative Group for International Agricultural Research	MAUP	modifiable areal unit problem
		MIT	Massachusetts Institute of Technology
CIMMYT	International Maize and Wheat Improvement Center	MNC	multinational company
CIP	International Potato Center	NARS	national agriculture research systems
CMU	Carnegie Mellon University	NOAA	National Oceanic and Atmospheric Administration
CNRS	Conseil National de Recherche Scientifique		
		OECD	Organisation for Economic Co-operation and Development
Commission	European Commission		
CPC	Cooperative Patent Classification	OEM	original equipment manufacturer
CRISPR-Cas9	clustered regularly interspaced short palindromic repeats-CRISPR associated protein 9	PCT	Patent Cooperation Treaty
		R&D	research and development
		rDNA	recombinant DNA
CSAIL	MIT's Computer Science and Artificial Intelligence Laboratory	S&T	Science and Technology
		SCIE	Science Citation Index Expanded
CTO	chief technology officer	SNC	specialized niche cluster
C-V2X	cellular vehicle-to-everything	TRI	Toyota Research Institute
DARPA	Defense Advanced Research Projects Agency	U.K.	United Kingdom
		U.S.	United States of America
DNA	deoxyribonucleic acid	UN	United Nations
ECJ	European Court of Justice	UPOV	Union for the Protection of New Varieties of Plants
EMBRAPA	Brazilian Agricultural Research Corporation		
		USDA	U.S. Department of Agriculture
EPA	U.S. Environmental Protection Agency	USPTO	U.S. Patent and Trademark Office
		V2I	vehicle-to-infrastructure
EU	European Union	V2V	vehicle-to-vehicle
FAO	Food and Agriculture Organization of the United Nations	VW	Volkswagen
		WatCAR	Waterloo Centre for Automotive Research
FCA	Fiat Chrysler Automobiles		
FDA	U.S. Food and Drug Administration	WIPO	World Intellectual Property Organization
FDI	foreign direct investment		
GDP	gross domestic product	WTO	World Trade Organization
GEO	genetically engineered organisms		

www.ingramcontent.com/pod-product-compliance
Lightning Source LLC
Chambersburg PA
CBHW082311210326
41599CB00030B/5764